THE JUDAISM BEHIND THE TEXTS

SOUTH FLORIDA STUDIES IN THE HISTORY OF JUDAISM

Edited by
Jacob Neusner
William Scott Green, James Strange
Darrell J. Fasching, Sara Mandell

Number 98
THE JUDAISM BEHIND THE TEXTS
The Generative Premises of Rabbinic Literature
II. Tosefta, Tractate Abot,
and Earlier Midrash Compilations:
Sifra, Sifré to Numbers, and **Sifré to Deuteronomy**
by
Jacob Neusner

THE JUDAISM BEHIND THE TEXTS

The Generative Premises of
Rabbinic Literature

II. Tosefta, Tractate Abot,
and Earlier Midrash Compilations:
Sifra, Sifré to Numbers, and Sifré to Deuteronomy

by

Jacob Neusner

Scholars Press
Atlanta, Georgia

THE JUDAISM BEHIND THE TEXTS
The Generative Premises of Rabbinic Literature
II. Tosefta, Tractate Abot,
and Earlier Midrash Compilations:
Sifra, Sifré to Numbers, and Sifré to Deuteronomy

©1994
University of South Florida

Publication of this book was made possible by a grant from the Tisch Family Foundation, New York City. The University of South Florida acknowledges with thanks this important support for its scholarly projects.

Library of Congress Cataloging in Publication Data
Neusner, Jacob, 1932-
    The Judaism behind the texts : the generative premises of rabbinic
literature. II. Tosefta, Tractate Abot, and earlier midrash
compilations: Sifra, Sifré to Numbers, and Sifré to Deuteronomy / by
Jacob Neusner.
        p.   cm. — (South Florida studies in the history of Judaism ;
no. 98)
    Includes index.
    ISBN 1-55540-935-0
    1. Tosefta. Tohorot (Order)—Sources. 2. Mishnah. Avot—
Sources. 3. Sifra—Sources. 4. Sifrei—Sources. 5. Bible. O. T.
Pentateuch—Criticism, interpretation, etc. 6. Judaism—Essence,
genius, nature. I. Title. II. Series.
BM508.5.T73N48   1994
296.1'206—dc20   93-39348
                                             CIP

Printed in the United States of America
on acid-free paper

Table of Contents

Part Four
SIFRÉ TO NUMBERS

Part Five
SIFRÉ TO DEUTERONOMY

Preface

...One must press behind the contents of the Mishnah and attempt to discover what the contents of the Mishnah presuppose....

E.P. Sanders[1]

This protracted exercise asks a deceptively simple question, if I know this, what else do I know? If an author tells me something, what else does he thereby tell me about what he is thinking or how? Can I press behind the contents of a Rabbinic document and attempt to discover what the contents presuppose? Can I ask about the author's premises: what he knows and how he thinks he knows it? Can I move back from the text to the intellectual context the text presupposes? The only way to find the answers to these questions is to reread documents, line by line, and see what lies behind what is there. This I do in a multi-volume exercise on selected, critical documents of Rabbinic Judaism. I now proceed to the first two principal exegetical works of the Judaism of the Dual Torah, Tosefta to the Oral Torah comprised by the Mishnah, Sifra to the Written Torah.

Both are exegetical composites, and it goes without saying, identifying premises and presuppositions in documents that are built as amplifications and clarifications of prior writings is not so simple. We have to eliminate from consideration what these documents have learned from the ones on which they depend, since what is secondary and derivative tells us not premises of later authors but lessons imparted by earlier ones. Hence our interest lies in what is fresh to the compilations under study: What do these writers bring to their work? That question forms the complement to the one we addressed to the Mishnah: What do these writers know before they start their work?

It follows that in the case of Tosefta we shall ignore those passages that amplify the Mishnah's statements and concentrate on the ones that

---

[1]E.P. Sanders, "Puzzling Out Rabbinism," in William Scott Green, ed., *Approaches to Ancient Judaism* (Chicago, 1980: Scholars Press for Brown Judaic Studies), p. 73.

stand on their own. The counterpart definition of the work on Sifra will be given in due course. Because Tosefta yields only a modest volume of free-standing and independent statements, I choose to deal only with the largest of its six divisions, its counterpart to the Mishnah's Division of Purities. Given the character of Tosefta, we cannot expect to find a large corpus of pertinent entries for an analysis of premises and presuppositions autonomous of those of the Mishnah; I was surprised by how little I could discern; others, who will surely replicate these experiments, may do better in that regard. In any event, the paucity of results in this volume explains why I chose not to survey the first five. But readers who wish to replicate my results for the other divisions can readily do so, since my translation clearly marks the Mishnah dependent, from the independent, Tosefta compositions and composites.

The same decision affects the analysis of Sifra's premises and presuppositions, though in a slightly different way. Sifra inherits the Mishnah and also Scripture, organizing its materials around the latter, finding its generative problematic in the question of the relationship of the former to the latter. Where Sifra's composition or composite simply paraphrases Scripture or amplifies in some fairly routine way, on the one side, or undertakes to demonstrate the scriptural origin or authority of the Mishnah's or the Tosefta's rule, cited verbatim, there I bypass the passage. My assumption is that we have in hand only what the writers of Sifra have learned from the received documents. Where I find a fresh idea or proposition, I ask whether I can identify a premise on which the idea rests, or a presupposition that generates said proposition.

As the work unfolds, we shift in the focus of interest in yet another, more fundamental way, than that just noted. For there is a much more profound question to be studied than the one that Sanders has phrased for us in the citation at the head of this statement. Along with Sanders and others, I have wanted to know what documents presuppose. But unlike others, I have an interest not in some other religion, but in a very particular Judaism, and that interest is what defines my work. In the case of this Judaism, with its sizable canon of authoritative and holy books – Scripture, the Mishnah, Tosefta, two Talmuds, score of Midrash compilations – we want to know how the various writings hold together. Can we identify a set of premises that animate all writers, presuppositions that guide every compilation's compositions' authors and compositors' framers? If we can, then we shall have found what makes that Judaism into a single coherent religious system. If we cannot, then we shall have to ask a fresh set of descriptive questions concerning the theology of that religious system – a different set from those that guide the present work. When at the end of this exercise I reach the conclusion, in *Judaism from before 70 to 600: The Judaism That is Taken for*

Granted, I shall exploit the facts that will turn up in the present book and its companions: Is there a Judaism behind the texts at all? And if not, what explains the coherence of the Judaism of the Dual Torah – for, by all reckoning, it is a remarkably cogent and stable religious system, with a body of ideas that for centuries have formed a single statement and today, with numerous variations and nuances, continues to say some one thing in many ways. Let me state with heavy emphasis what I want to find out:

At stake is not only the Mishnah and its premises (presumably bringing us back into circles of first-century thinkers) but the presuppositions of numerous representative documents of Rabbinic Judaism throughout its formative period.

The second question vastly outweighs the one that animates interest in premises and presuppositions: Is there a Judaism that infuses all texts and forms of each part of a coherent whole? At issue in the quest for presuppositions is not the Judaism that lies beyond the texts (which the texts by definition cannot tell us and indeed do not pretend to tell us), but the Judaism that holds together all of the texts and forms the substrate of conviction and conscience in each one.

That body of writings is continuous, formed as it is as commentaries on the Written Torah or the Mishnah, and the period in which they took shape for formal and substantive reasons also is continuous and of course not to be truncated at its very starting point, with the Mishnah, as Sanders's formulation proposes. For the Mishnah presents only the first among a long sequence of problems for analysis, and cutting that writing off from its continuators and successors, in both Midrash compilations and Talmuds, represents a gross error, one commonplace, to be sure, among Christian scholars of Judaism, for whom, as in Sanders's case, Judaism ends in the first century or early second and ceases beyond that point to require study at all. But the Judaism of the Dual Torah, viewed in its formative canon, is single and whole, and the premises and presuppositions of any of its writings, treated in isolation from those of all the others, contain nothing of interest for the analysis of that massive and complex Judaic system, only for the Judaism of a given piece of writing.

The plan of the work as a whole is to examine important and representative writings – not every canonical document but only those that strike me as systemically generative, on the one side, or exemplary, on the other. My sense is that, if there really are premises of systemic consequence, they should turn up nearly everywhere, so that a sample of the documents must suffice. If that should not be the case, then the very notion of a single Judaism behind the Rabbinic texts will prove parlous, beyond all examination, testing, and demonstration, and probably untenable. But for now, I retain as my given the notion that the canonical writings of Rabbinic Judaism do come together and cohere, on which account a sample will suffice; others may pursue the same questions in the analysis of omitted documents. The following indicates how I plan to proceed with this project in particular:

The Judaism behind the Texts. The Generative Premises of Rabbinic Literature. I. *The Mishnah.* A. *The Division of Agriculture* (Atlanta, 1993: Scholars Press for South Florida Studies in the History of Judaism).

The Judaism behind the Texts. The Generative Premises of Rabbinic Literature. I. *The Mishnah.* B. *The Divisions of Appointed Times, Women, and Damages (through Sanhedrin* (Atlanta, 1993: Scholars Press for South Florida Studies in the History of Judaism).

The Judaism behind the Texts. The Generative Premises of Rabbinic Literature. I. *The Mishnah.* C. *The Divisions of Damages (from Makkot), Holy Things and Purities* (Atlanta, 1993: Scholars Press for South Florida Studies in the History of Judaism).

The Judaism behind the Texts. The Generative Premises of Rabbinic Literature. II. *The Tosefta and Earlier Midrash Compilations: Sifra and Sifré to Deuteronomy.* A. *The Tosefta to the Division of Purities and Sifra* (Atlanta, 1993: Scholars Press for South Florida Studies in the History of Judaism).

The Judaism behind the Texts. The Generative Premises of Rabbinic Literature. II. *The Tosefta and Earlier Midrash Compilations: Sifra and Sifré to Deuteronomy.* B. *Sifré to Deuteronomy* (Atlanta, 1993: Scholars Press for South Florida Studies in the History of Judaism).

The Judaism behind the Texts. The Generative Premises of Rabbinic Literature. III. *The Talmud of the Land of Israel. Selected Chapters* (Atlanta, 1993: Scholars Press for South Florida Studies in the History of Judaism).

The Judaism behind the Texts. The Generative Premises of Rabbinic Literature. IV. *The Intermediate Midrash Compilations: Genesis Rabbah, Leviticus Rabbah, and Pesiqta deRab Kahana* (Atlanta, 1993: Scholars Press for South Florida Studies in the History of Judaism).

The Judaism behind the Texts. The Generative Premises of Rabbinic Literature. V. *The Talmud of Babylonia* (Atlanta, 1994: Scholars Press for South Florida Studies in the History of Judaism).

The Judaism behind the Texts. The Generative Premises of Rabbinic Literature. VI. *The Later Midrash Compilations: Song of Songs Rabbah and Lamentations Rabbati* (Atlanta, 1994: Scholars Press for South Florida Studies in the History of Judaism).

Judaism from before 70 to 600: The Judaism That Is Taken for Granted.

How the documents will break up beyond Volume II I cannot now predict, but the groupings seem to me justified. If there are results that will sustain the final title on this list, the *Vorstudien* contemplated here will yield them, if not, not.

The final work should yield a sustained book, not just a research report, and that will survey the main premises that are identified in the documentary analysis and will ask how the various premises and presuppositions hold together: the intellectual foundations of Judaism. That will present my first effort at defining the unity of the Oral Torah, identifying the main principles that transcend various documents but animate them all.

No work of mine can omit reference to the exceptionally favorable circumstances in which I conduct my research as Distinguished Research Professor in the Florida State University System at the University of South Florida. I wrote this book as part of my labor of research scholarship, expressed through both publication and teaching at the University of South Florida, which has afforded me an ideal situation in which to conduct a scholarly life. I express my thanks for not only the advantage of a Distinguished Research Professorship in the Florida State University System, which for a scholar must be the best job in the world, but also of a substantial research expense fund, ample research time, and some stimulating and cordial colleagues. In the prior chapters of my career, I never knew a university that prized professors' scholarship and publication and treated with respect those professors who actively and methodically pursue research.

The University of South Florida, among all ten universities that comprise the Florida State University System as a whole, exemplifies the high standards of professionalism that prevail in publicly sponsored higher education in the United States and provides the model that privately sponsored universities would do well to emulate. Here there are rules, achievement counts, and presidents, provosts, and deans honor and respect the University's principal mission: scholarship, scholarship alone – both in the class room and in publication. Here at last I find integrity, governing in the lives of people true to their vocation and their mission.

I defined the work at hand in conversation with Professor William Scott Green, who gave me substantial help in clearly formulating my problem in its own terms. As ever, I acknowledge my real debt to him for his scholarly acumen and perspicacity.

JACOB NEUSNER

Distinguished Research Professor of Religious Studies
UNIVERSITY OF SOUTH FLORIDA
Tampa, FL 33620-5550 USA

Introduction

At stake in any study of a religion is the definition of that religion and of religion in general, and what I am trying to do here is to find the correct way to define Judaism in its formative age, which is to say, describe, analyze, and interpret the earliest stage in the formation of the Judaism of the Dual Torah. To that project, which has occupied me for thirty years, the question of premise and presupposition is critical. No one can imagine that the explicit statements of a generative text, such as the Mishnah or the Talmud of Babylonia, for example, exhaust all that that text conveys – or means to convey – about God's truth. With what Sanders correctly emphasizes no one can argue, and with that obvious premise, none has argued. To the contrary, even in the founding generation of the field that used to be called "Talmudic history," the true founder and greatest mind in the field, Y.I. Halevi, *Dorot harishonim* (Vienna-Berlin, 1923 et seq.), insisted that a statement rested on a prior history of thought, which can and should be investigated, and that premises of available facts yield a pre-history that we can describe. Everybody understands that the definitive documents of a religion expose something, but contain everything. Sanders is in good company.

But it is not enough to posit such premises; we have in detail to identify just what they were. So it is the task of learning to explore the premises, presuppositions, and processes of imagination and of critical thought, that yield in the end the statements that we find on the surface of the writings. But the work has to be done systematically and not episodically, in a thorough way and not through episode, anecdote, and example. We address an entire canon with the question: Precisely what are the premises demonstrably present throughout, the generative presuppositions not in general but in all their rich specificity? Here I take up this analytical problem, having completed my descriptive work.

This book therefore continues a protracted, systematic and detailed answer to two questions, first, the question set forth in Professor Sanders's quite reasonable proposal to "press behind the contents...to

1

discover what the contents...presuppose." While Sanders speaks of the Mishnah, in fact the commanding question – if I know this, what else do I know about the intellect of the writers of a document or a whole canon? – pertains to the entirety of the oral part of the Torah. And the second question, as I have explained, is a still more urgent one: Are there premises and presuppositions that engage thought throughout the documents? Or are the documents discrete episodes in a sustained procession of thought that requires description upon some basis other than a documentary one?

The project thus presents an exercise in the further definition of the Judaism of the Dual Torah that encompasses not only what its principal documents make articulate but also what they mean to imply, on the one end, and how what they presuppose coheres (if it does), on the other. Since many of the answers to those questions are either obvious or trivial or beg the question, we have to refine matters with a further critical consideration. It is this: Among the presuppositions, the critical one is, which ones matter? And how can we account for the emergence of the system as a whole out of the presuppositions demonstrably present at the foundations of systemic documents? The program of this project, in three volumes for the Mishnah and further volumes for selected documents thereafter, aims at uncovering the foundations of the Judaism of the Dual Torah.

When I ask the general question about "the Judaism behind the texts," I refer to a variety of specific matters. All of them concern the premises or presuppositions of a document and of important statements within said document. I want to know what someone must take for granted as fact in order to make an allegation of some consequence within a legal or theological writing. Taking as our given what is alleged in a document, we ask, in order to take that position, what do I have to have known as fact? What must I have taken for granted as a principle? What set of issues or large-scale questions – fundamental issues that seem to me to pop up everywhere – has to have preoccupied me, so as to lead me to identify a given problem for solution, a given possibility awaiting testing?

These statements left unsaid but ubiquitously assumed may be of three kinds, from [1] the obvious, conventional, unsurprising, unexceptional, uninteresting, [2] routine and systemically inert to [3] the highly suggestive, provocative and systemically generative.

First, a statement in a text may presuppose a religious norm of belief or behavior (*halakhah* or *aggadah*, in the native categories). For one example, if a rule concerns itself with when the Shema is to be recited, the rule presupposes a prayer, the Shema – and so throughout. Such a presupposition clearly is to be acknowledged, but ordinarily, the fact that is taken for granted will not stand behind an exegetical initiative or intellectual problem to which a document pays substantial attention.

Second, a statement in a text may presuppose knowledge of a prior, authoritative text. For instance, rules in the Mishnah take for granted uncited texts of Scripture, nearly the whole of Tractate Yoma providing a particularly fine instance, since the very order and structure of that tractate prove incomprehensible without a verse-by-verse review of Leviticus Chapter Sixteen. Knowing that the framers of a document had access to a prior holy book by itself does not help us to understand what the framers of that document learned from the earlier one; they will have selected what they found relevant or important, ignoring what they found routine; we cannot simply assign to the later authorship complete acquiescence in all that a prior set of writers handed on, merely because the later authorship took cognizance of what the earlier one had to say. It is one thing to acknowledge, it is another to make use of, to respond to, a received truth.

Third, a concrete statement in a text may rest upon a prior conception of a more abstract character, much as applied mathematics rests upon theoretical mathematics, or technology upon principles of engineering and physics. And this set of premises and presuppositions does lead us deep into the foundations of thought of a given, important and systematic writing. In the main, what I want to know here concerns the active and generative premises of Rabbinic documents: the things the writers had to know in order to define the problems they wished to solve. I seek the key to the exegesis of the law that the framers of the Mishnah put forth, the exegesis of Scripture that they systematically provided. When we can say not only what they said but also what they took for granted, if we can explain their principles of organization and the bases for their identification of the problems they wished to solve, then, but only then, do we enter into that vast Judaic system and structure that their various writings put forth in bits and pieces and only adumbrated in its entirety.

Accordingly, this project, covering the principal documents of Rabbinic Judaism in its formative age, while paying attention to data of the first two classes, focuses upon the third category of presuppositions, stipulating that the first two require no more than routine inquiry. That is to say, we all know that the sages of the Rabbinic writings deemed the Scriptures of ancient Israel, which they knew as the written part of the Torah, to be authoritative; they took for granted the facticity and authority of every line of that writing, to be sure picking and choosing, among available truths, those that required emphasis and even development. That simple fact permits us to take for granted, without laboring to prove the obvious, that the Judaism not articulated in the

Rabbinic literature encompassed the way of life and world view and conception of Israel that, in broad outlines, Scripture set forth. But that fact standing on its own is trivial. It allows for everything but the main thing: what characterized the specific, distinctive character of the Judaic system set forth in Rabbinic writings, and, it goes without saying, how the particular point of view of those writings dictated the ways in which Scripture's teachings and rules gained entry into, and a place for themselves in, the structure and system of the Judaism of the Dual Torah.

Prior to a vast number of rulings, generating the problems that require those rulings, a few fundamental conceptions or principles, never articulated, await identification. And, once identified, these several conceptions or principles demand a labor of composition: How does the generative problematic that precipitates the issues of one tractate, or forms the datum of that tractate's inquiry, fit together with the generative problematic of some other tractate and its sustained exegesis of the law? Once we know what stands behind the law, we have to ask, what holds together the several fundamental principles, all of them of enormous weight and vast capacity for specification in numerous detailed cases? Before we know how to define this Judaism, we have to show that a coherent metaphysics underpins the detailed physics, a cogent principle the concrete cases, a proportioned, balanced, harmonious statement the many, derivative and distinct cases of which the law and theology of Judaism are comprised.

What Rabbinic documents tell us that bears consequence for the definition of their Judaism in particular – not merely what was likely to be common to all Judaism, for example, a sacred calendar, a record of generations' encounter with God and the like – then requires specification, and the third of the three types of presuppositions or premises points toward the definition of what is at stake and under study here. That is, specifically, the deeper, implicit affirmations of documents: what they know that stands behind what they say, the metaphysics behind the physics (to resort to the metaphor just now introduced). For a close reading of both law and lore, *halakhah* and *aggadah,* yields a glimpse at a vast structure of implicit conceptions, those to which Sanders makes reference in his correct prescription of what is to be done: "...one must press behind the contents of the Mishnah and attempt to discover what the contents of the Mishnah presuppose."

Some of these implicit conceptions pertain to law, some to questions of philosophy and metaphysics, some to theology. Once we have examined important constitutive documents, we shall see that all of them circulate hither and yon through the law and the theology of the various documents; and only when we identify the various notions that are presupposed and implicit and show how they coalesce shall we

understand the details of the Judaic system – law and theology alike –
that comes to concrete expression in the Rabbinic writings. I have
already set forth a systematic account, treating the Mishnah as a whole,
of the document's premises in regard to philosophy, politics, and
economics, and these results are summarized in the first three chapters.
These are large-scale exercises in answering the question, "if I know this,
what else do I know?" My answer is, if I know the specific rulings of the
Mishnah on topics relevant to economics and politics, I know that the
Mishnah sets forth a philosophical politics and a philosophical
economics. If I know how the Mishnah formulates and solves a problem,
I know that the framers of the Mishnah thought philosophically – but
mostly, though not entirely, about questions of a very different order
from those that philosophers pursued.

This detailed work follows a simple and consistent program. Let me
undertake to spell out the procedures of this and its companion volumes.
What is needed is a patient sifting of details. Therefore I review the
entire document under study here, and in each of its divisions and
subdivisions examine data by the following criteria:

1. UNARTICULATED PREMISES. THE GIVENS OF CORRECT
   PUBLIC CONDUCT: I want to know what generative
   practices the halakhah at hand takes for granted, which
   customs or rites or social rules and laws are refined and
   improved, applied and analyzed, being simply givens. Very
   frequently, the law will provide detailed exegeses, in terms
   of a number of distinct cases and problems, of a single
   principle. The law therefore shows how in concrete and
   practical ways a principle operates. That is what is critical in
   this category.

2. UNARTICULATED PREMISES. THE GIVENS OF RELIGIOUS
   CONVICTION: At issue here are the givens of generative
   conviction: this category is identical to the foregoing, now
   with attention to matters within the native category of
   aggadah and the academic category of theology and
   exegesis. Where many texts presuppose the same premise
   but none articulates it, or the premise is never made explicit
   in such a way as to extend to a variety of cases, I classify the
   matter as an unarticulated premise. But, I readily concede,
   the difference between this category and the next is not
   always obvious to me.

3. MATTERS OF PHILOSOPHY, NATURAL SCIENCE AND
   METAPHYSICS: This category covers general principles that
   concern not theological but philosophical questions.

"Natural science" and "philosophy" for our documents coincide, being two ways of referring to the same corpus of knowledge. The questions that fall into the present category are not theological but concern issues of natural philosophy, science, and metaphysics, for example, sorting out matters of doubt, discovering the rules of classification, working out problems of applied logic and practical reason, and the like. Now as a matter of fact, many rulings presuppose answers to philosophical questions of a broad and abstract character. Here we identify the premises of the documents that operate widely but do not concern questions particular to the situation of Israel.[1]

In *Judaism behind the Texts* Volume I. Part A, readers will recall, I asked also about two other matters: articulated premises, points of stress, and traits of self-differentiation. But these produced nothing of sustained interest, only some casual and episodic entries at which I thought a tractate or a major component of a tractate struck me as laying heavy emphasis on a given proposition, on the one side, or point of difference between the document's "Israel" and the rest of the Jews, on the other. I found the categories too subjective for further use, since I could not always identify the objective and indicative traits that would lead me to categorize an item's premise as either a point of stress or a point of differentiation. Accordingly, I omit these categories from further use.

What I want to undertake in due course is a cogent account of all of the premises that appear to me to play a role in the specific rulings of the law, on the one side, and in the concrete propositions of theology and exegesis, on the other. But that ultimate goal concerning the unity and coherence of the Judaism of these writings – the unity of the oral part of the Torah – is not going to be easily attained. Once we have assembled the data of all sixty-two tractates of the Mishnah (excluding Tractate

---

[1]In some measure, also, I recapitulate the findings of *The Philosophical Mishnah. Volume I. The Initial Probe* (Atlanta, 1989: Scholars Press for Brown Judaic Studies); *The Philosophical Mishnah. Volume II. The Tractates' Agenda. From Abodah Zarah to Moed Qatan* (Atlanta, 1989: Scholars Press for Brown Judaic Studies); *The Philosophical Mishnah.* Volume III. *The Tractates' Agenda. From Nazir to Zebahim* (Atlanta, 1989: Scholars Press for Brown Judaic Studies); *The Philosophical Mishnah.* Volume IV. *The Repertoire* (Atlanta, 1989: Scholars Press for Brown Judaic Studies). But the work done here is not focused so narrowly as the survey accomplished in those volumes; I am more interested in finding as broad a range of premises and presuppositions as I can. In *The Philosophical Mishnah*, my program was carefully framed to identify clearly-philosophical matters.

Abot), we shall see how they relate to one another and even coalesce into a metaphysical structure and system.

It remains to explain that, when I refer to "generative premises," I mean to exclude a variety of other givens that strike me as demonstrably present but systemically inert. There are many facts our documents know and acknowledge but leave in the background; there are others, that is, premises and presuppositions, that generate numerous specific problems, indeed that turn out, upon close examination of the details of documents, to stand behind numerous concrete inquiries. The former are systemically inert, the latter, systemically provocative and formative. Such premises as the sanctity of Israel and the Land of Israel, the election of Israel, the authority of the Torah (however defined), and the like in these writings prove systemic givens, assumed but rarely made the focus of exegetical thought.

Not only so: a very long list of platitudes and banalities can readily be constructed and every item on the list shown to be present throughout the documents under study here; but those platitudes and banalities make no contribution to the shaping of our documents and the formulation of their system. Therefore, having proven that the sun rises in the east, from those systemically inert givens, we should know no more about matters than we did beforehand. True, to those in search of "Judaism," as distinct from the diverse Judaic systems to which our evidence attests, that finding – God is one, God gave the Torah, Israel is God's chosen people, and the like – bears enormous consequence. But that God is one in no way accounts for the system's specific qualities and concerns, any more than does the fact that the laws of gravity operate.

What makes a Judaic system important is what marks that system as entire and imparts to that system its integrity: what makes it different from other systems, what holds that system together. Defining that single, encompassing "Judaism" into which genus all species, all Judaisms, fit helps us understand nothing at all about the various Judaisms. But all we really have in hand are the artifacts of Judaisms. As the prologue has already argued, efforts to find that one Judaism that holds together all Judaisms yields suffocating banalities and useless platitudes: we do not understand anything in particular any better than we did before we had thought up such generalities. So by "generative premises," I mean, the premises that counted: those that provoked the framers of a document's ideas to do their work, that made urgent the questions they address, that imparted self-evidence to the answers they set forth.

In the earliest Midrash compilations, not to mention the Tosefta, premises and presuppositions – "the Judaism behind the texts" – prove rare and episodic. The reason is that the character of the documents under study imposes limitations upon the free exercise of speculation. They undertake the systematic exposition of a prior document. Consequently, most of the task finds its definition in the statements that have been received and now require paraphrase, clarification, extension, and augmentation. The way in which this work is done – the hermeneutics that govern the exegesis of Scripture – yields no premises or presuppositions susceptible of generalization. And the result of the exegesis itself proves from our perspective sparse and anecdotal. Let me commence with a single example of how a sublime text is treated in a manner that, while not trivial, still in no way yields the kind of theological or moral or legal principles that at various points in the Mishnah show the document to rest upon deep foundations of thought. Our example is the exposition of the priestly benediction, and it shows us what to expect in the Midrash compilations that are treated here, therefore explaining, also, why the results of the survey prove frustrating:

Sifré to Numbers XXXIX

I.1   A.   "The Lord said to Moses, Say to Aaron and his sons: Thus shall you bless the people of Israel. [You shall say to them: 'The Lord bless you and keep you, the Lord make his face to shine upon you and be gracious to you, the Lord lift up his countenance upon you and give you peace.' So shall they put my name upon the people of Israel, and I will bless them]" (Num. 6:22-27):

         B.   Since the deed required in the present passage is to be carried out by Aaron and his sons, the statement that is made is not only to Moses but also to Aaron and his sons.

         C.   For this is the encompassing rule:

         D.   Whenever the statement is made to the priests, then the deed is required only of the priests.

         E.   When the statement is made to Israel, then the entirety of what is required is incumbent on Israel.

         F.   When the statement is made to Israel but the deed is to be done by everyone, then one has to encompass proselytes as well.

II.1   A.   "The Lord said to Moses, Say to Aaron and his sons: Thus shall you bless the people of Israel":

         B.   The blessing is to be said in the Holy Language [Hebrew].

         C.   For any passage in which reference is made to "responding" or "saying" or "thus," the statement is to be made in Hebrew.

III.1   A.   "The Lord said to Moses, Say to Aaron and his sons: Thus shall you bless the people of Israel":

         B.   [This must be done when the priests are] standing.

         C.   You maintain that this must be done when the priests are standing.

         D.   But perhaps it may be done either standing or not standing?

         E.   Scripture states, "And these shall *stand* to bless the people" (Deut. 27:42).

         F.   The word "blessing" occurs here and the word "blessing" occurs there. Just as the word "blessing" when it occurs at the later passage involves the priests' standing, so, here, too, the word blessing indicates that the priests must be standing.

G. R. Nathan says, "It is not necessary to invoke that analogy. For it is said, 'And the Levitical priests shall draw near, for the Lord has chosen them to serve him and to bestow a blessing in the name of the Lord' (Deut. 21:5). The act of bestowing a blessing is compared to the act of service. Just as service is performed only when standing, so bestowing a blessing is bestowed when standing."

IV.1 A. "The Lord said to Moses, Say to Aaron and his sons: Thus shall you bless the people of Israel":

B. It must be done by raising the hands.

C. You say it must be done by raising the hands.

D. But perhaps it may be done either by raising the hands or not by raising the hands?

E. Scripture says, "And Aaron raised his hands toward the people and blessed them" (Lev. 9:22).

F. Just as Aaron bestowed the blessing by raising his hands, so his sons will bestow the blessing by raising their hands.

G. R. Jonathan says, "But may one then say that just as that passage occurs in the setting of a blessing bestowed at the new moon, on the occasion of a public offering, and through the medium only of the high priest, so, here, too, the blessing may be bestowed only at the new moon, on the occasion of a public offering, and through the medium only of the high priest!

H. "Scripture states, 'For the Lord your God has chosen him above all your tribes' (Deut. 18:5). The Scripture compares his sons to him: just as he bestowed the blessing by raising his hands, so his sons will bestow the blessing by raising their hands."

V.1 A. "The Lord said to Moses, Say to Aaron and his sons: Thus shall you bless the people of Israel":

B. It is to be done by expressing the fully spelled out Name of God.

C. You maintain that it is to be done by expressing the fully spelled out Name of God. But perhaps it may be done with a euphemism for the Name of God?

D. Scripture says, "So shall they put my name upon the people of Israel" (Num. 6:27).

V.2 A. "In the sanctuary it is to be done by expressing the fully spelled out Name of God. And in the provinces it is to be done by a euphemism," the words of R. Josiah.

B. R. Jonathan says, "Lo, Scripture states, 'In every place in which I shall cause my name to be remembered' (Ex. 20:20). This verse of Scripture is out of order, and how should it be read? 'In every place in which I appear before you, there should my Name be mentioned.' And where is it that I appear before you? It is in the chosen house [the Temple]. So you should mention my name [as fully spelled out] only in the chosen house.

C. "On this basis sages have ruled: 'As to the fully spelled out Name of God, it is forbidden to express it in the provinces [but only in the sanctuary].'"

VI.1 A. "The Lord said to Moses, Say to Aaron and his sons: Thus shall you bless the people of Israel":

B.   On this basis I know only that the blessing is directed to Israel.

C.   How do I know that it is directed to women, proselytes, and bondsmen?

D.   Scripture states, "...and I will bless *them*" (Num. 6:27), [encompassing not only Israel, but also women, proselytes, and bondsmen].

VI.2 A.   How do we know that a blessing is bestowed on the priests?

B.   Scripture states, "...and I will bless them" (Num. 6:27).

VII.1 A.   "The Lord said to Moses, Say to Aaron and his sons: Thus shall you bless the people of Israel":

B.   It must be done face to face [with the priests facing the people and the people facing the priests].

C.   You say that it must be done face to face [with the priests facing the people and the people facing the priests]. But may it be back to face?

D.   Scripture says, "You shall say *to* them" (Num. 6:23), [which can only be face to face].

VIII.1 A.   "The Lord said to Moses, Say to Aaron and his sons: Thus shall you bless the people of Israel":

B.   The sense is that the entire congregation should hear what is said.

C.   Or may it be that the priests say the blessing to themselves [and not in audible tones]?

D.   Scripture says, "*Say* to them...," (Num. 6:23), meaning that the entire congregation should hear the blessing.

E.   And how do we know that the leader of the prayers has to say to the priests, "Say..."?

F.   Scripture says, "*You* shall say to them" (Num. 6:23).

Whatever the hermeneutics that is taken for granted, the unarticulated layer of law and theology is scarcely to be discerned; the givens are Scripture and its facts and formulations, on the one side, and a set of principles of exegesis deriving from a transparent hermeneutics, on the other. For our survey, I find nothing in the treatment of a passage of surpassing interest to enrich our grasp of the law or theology behind the text. What we see is what there is – that alone. When I observe that most of the documents surveyed here generate little of interest to an inquiry into the Judaism behind the texts, this passage speaks for me. What we derive is refinement and clarification, but the passage scarcely suggests that taken for granted is a deep layer of theological or moral speculation. What we see is what we get, which is, a text with some minor points of refinement.

Even though these results prove paltry, the issues remain vital, and a negative result itself bears formidable implications. Let me spell out what I conceive to be at stake in this protracted study. In fact, the issue of premises, the question, if I know this, what else do I know? – these form the entry point. But my goal is other. For the task of history of religions always is that of definition of religions: what can we possibly mean by those encompassing categories, "Judaism" or "Buddhism" or

"Islam" or "Christianity" that descriptively conform to data? In the case of "Judaism," I want to know whether the construct refers to documents that cohere, or whether the fabricated category is imposed thereon. So I aim at finding out whether, and how, the various documents valued by the Judaism of the Dual Torah relate, not in imputed but in substantive ways. Do I find that the various writings that the Judaism of the Dual Torah produced in late antiquity rest upon shared and common fundamental convictions, that is, this "Judaism behind the texts," or does each piece of writing stand essentially on its own? It is clear that as a matter of theory documents that are held by those who deem them authoritative to cohere relate in three ways. First, they stand each on its own, that is, each is autonomous. Second, in some ways they may intersect, for example, citations or long quotations of one writing appear in some other. They are therefore connected in some specific ways. But, third, do these writings also form a continuous whole? That is what I want to find out in this exercise. Let me spell out these three dimensions of relationship: autonomy, connection, and continuity.

Documents – cogent compositions made up of a number of complete units of thought – by definition exist on their own. That is to say, by invoking as part of our definition the trait of cogency of individual units as well as of the entire composite, we complete a definition of what a document is and is not. A document is a cogent composite of cogent statements. But, also by definition, none of these statements is read all by itself. A document forms an artifact of a social culture, and that in diverse dimensions. Cogency depends on shared rhetoric, logic of intelligible discourse, topic and program – all of these traits of mind, of culture. Someone writes a document, someone buys it, an entire society sustains the labor of literature. But people value more than a single document, so we want to know how several documents may stand in connection with one another.

Each document therefore exists in both a textual and literary context, and also a social dimension of culture and even of politics. As to the former, documents may form a community whose limits are delineated by shared conventions of thought and expression. Those exhibiting distinctive, even definitive traits, fall within the community, those that do not, remain without. These direct the author to one mode of topic, logic, and rhetoric, and not to some other. So much for intrinsic traits. As to the extrinsic ones, readers bring to documents diverse instruments of intelligibility, knowledge of the grammar of not only language but also thought. That is why they can read one document and not some other. So one relationship derives from a literary culture, which forms the authorship of a document, and the other from a social culture. The literary bond links document to document, and the essentially social bond links reader to document – and also document (through the authorship, individual or collective) to reader. The one relationship is exhibited through intrinsic traits of language and style, logic, rhetoric, and topic, and the other through extrinsic traits of curiosity, acceptance and authority. While documents find their place in their own literary world and also in a larger social one, the two aspects have to remain distinct, the one textual, the other contextual.

It follows that relationships between and among documents also matter for two distinct reasons. The intrinsic relationships, which are formal, guide us to traits of intelligibility, teaching us through our encounter with one document how to read some other of its type or class. If we know how to read a document of one type, we may venture to read another of the same type, but not – without instruction – one of some other type altogether. The extrinsic relationships, which derive from context and are relative to community, direct us to how to understand a document as an artifact of culture and society. Traits not of documents but of doctrines affecting a broad range of documents come into play. The document, whatever its contents, therefore becomes an instrument of social culture, for example, theology and politics, a community's public policy. A community then expresses itself through its choice of documents, the community's canon forming a principal mode of such self-definition. So, as I said, through intrinsic traits a document places itself within a larger community of texts. Extrinsic traits, imputed to a document by not its authorship but its audience, select the document as canonical and make of the document a mode of social definition. The community through its mode of defining itself by its canonical choices forms a textual community – a community expressed through the books it reads and values.

So to summarize: the relationships among the documents produced by the sages of Judaism may take three forms: complete dependence, complete autonomy, intersection in diverse manner and measure. That second dimension provokes considerable debate and presents a remarkably unclear perspective. For while the dimensions of autonomy and continuity take the measure of acknowledged traits – books on their own, books standing in imputed, therefore socially verified, relationships – the matter of connection hardly enjoys the same clear definition. On the one side, intrinsic traits permit us to assess theories of connection. On the other, confusing theological and social judgments of continuities and literary and heuristic ones of connection, people present quite remarkable claims as to the relationships between and among documents, alleging, in fact, that the documents all have to be read as a single continuous document: the Torah. As we shall now see, some maintain that the connections between and among documents are such that each has to be read in the light of all others. So the documents assuredly do form a canon, and that is a position adopted not in some distant past or alien society but among contemporary participants to the cultural debate.

While I take up a community of texts and explore those intrinsic traits that link book to book, my inquiry rests on the premise that the books at issue derive from a textual community, one which, without reference to the intrinsic traits of the writings, deems the set of books as a group to constitute a canon. My question is simple but critical:

If in advance I did not know that the community of Judaism treats the writings before us (among others) as a canon, would the traits of the documents have told me that the writings at hand are related?

In this study, these "traits of documents" are the most profound and pervasive: premises and presuppositions. I cannot think of a more penetrating test of the proposition that the documents form a unity and are continuous with one another. The inquiry is inductive, concerns intrinsic traits of not form or proposition but premise, and therefore pursues at the deepest layers of intellect, conviction, attitude, and even emotion the matter of connection between document and document.

What makes the work plausible and necessary? It is a simple fact. All of the writings of Judaism in late antiquity copiously cite Scripture. Some of them serve (or are presented and organized) as commentaries on the former, others as amplifications of the latter. Since Judaism treats all of these writings as a single, seamless Torah, the one whole Torah revealed by God to Moses, our rabbi, at Mount Sinai, the received hermeneutic naturally does the same. All of the writings are read in light of all others, and words and phrases are treated as autonomous units of tradition, rather than as components of particular writings, for example, paragraphs – units of discourse – and books – composite units of sustained and cogent thought. The issue of connection therefore is legitimate to the data. But the issue of continuity is a still more profound and urgent one, and it is that issue that the present project is formulated to address.

With reference to the determinate canon of the Judaism of the Dual Torah, therefore, I ask about what is unstated and presupposed. I want to know the large-scale premises that form the foundations for the detailed statements of those writings. I turn to what is beneath the surface because I have completed my account of what lies right on the surface: the canon's articulated, explicit statements. It is time to look beneath the surface. In my tripartite program for the study of the Judaism of the Dual Torah in its formative age, an enterprise of systematic description, analysis, and interpretation, I have now completed the first stage and proceed to the second. Now that I know what the canonical writings say and have described the whole in the correct, historical manner and setting, I proceed to ask about what they do not say but take for granted. That defines the question here.

These questions bear a more profound implication than has been suggested. What I really want to find out here is not the answer to the question, if I know this, what else do I know? It is, rather, what are the things that all of the documents that make up the writings accorded the status of the Oral Torah know and share? When I ask about the Judaism behind the texts, I mean to find out what convictions unite diverse writings and form of them all a single statement, a cogent religious system? As I have explained, every document stands on its own; each is autonomous. Many documents furthermore establish points of contact or intersection; they are connected. But, as a matter of fact, the Judaism of the Dual Torah maintains that every writing is continuous with all other writings, forming a whole, a statement of comprehensive integrity. If that is so, then at the premises or presuppositions of writings I ought to be able to identify what is continuous, from one writing to another, and what unites them all at their deepest layers of conviction, attitude, or sentiment. That is what is at stake in this study.

Accordingly, the experimental work of an analytical character that is undertaken here and in the companion volumes forms a natural next step, on the path from description through analysis to interpretation. From my beginning work on the Mishnah, in 1972, I have undertaken a sustained and systematic description of that Judaism. In 1992, twenty years later, that sustained and uninterrupted work reached its conclusion in the two volumes that state the final results of the two programs that I pursued simultaneously: description of the literature, description of the history of the religious ideas set forth in that literature. The results are now fully in print in a variety of books and have now been systematically summarized, for a broad academic audience, in my *Introduction to Rabbinic Literature* and *Rabbinic Judaism: A Historical Introduction* (New York, 1994 and 1995, respectively: Doubleday Anchor Reference Library). These two books state my final results for the description of the literature and the history of Rabbinic Judaism; at this time, I have nothing to add to the descriptive process, and not much to change in the results set forth over this long span of time.

In finding the way into the deeper layers of conviction and consciousness of the Rabbinic documents, I propose to move inward from my description of Rabbinic Judaism, its writings and its historical development, document by document, to the analysis of the inner structure of that Judaism; and this search, in due course, should open the way to an interpretation of the system of that same Judaism. Here I offer the first results of the analytical work, consequent upon completed description, that I have considered for some time.

It remains to explain the appendix to this book. There I lay out the several approaches presently worked out for the description of the history of Judaism in late antiquity, which I call Nominalist, Harmonistic, Theological, and Historical. The first two define the setting in which the project of investigating the premises and presuppositions of documents finds its place, since, as is clear, I am responding to an absolutely correct and critical question Professor Sanders, discussed in the Appendix, has asked. The rather laborious response to his question represented by this multi-volumed project can be grasped only when the context in which he asks his question is grasped. For he has asked the right question for all the wrong reasons, as the Appendix explains.

Part One

TOSEFTA TO THE DIVISION OF PURITIES

1

The Character of Tosefta and Tosefta to Mishnah-Tractate Kelim

I. The Character of Tosefta

A huge supplement to the Mishnah, four times larger than the document it amplifies, the Tosefta, ca. 300, exhibits none of the documentary traits that mark as autonomous the other Rabbinic writings. Wholly depending upon the Mishnah for its rhetoric, topical program, and logic of coherent discourse, the Tosefta is like a vine on a trellis. It has no structure of its own but most commonly cites and glosses a passage of the Mishnah, not differentiating its forms and wording of sentences from those of the cited passage. Only seldom – for somewhat under a sixth of the whole of its volume – does the Tosefta present a statement that may be interpreted entirely independent of the Mishnah's counterpart (if any). The Tosefta covers nearly the whole of the Mishnah's program but has none of its own.

What marks the document as dependent, further, is that its sentences by themselves do not hold together at all. Their order consistently refers to that of the Mishnah's statements. The logic of coherent discourse, affecting more than two or three sentences at a time, is wholly fixed associative. The dependent status of the Tosefta derives from the simple fact that, for most of the document, we simply cannot understand a line without first consulting the Mishnah's counterpart statement. Once a text derives from some other document not only its coherence, but even the first level of meaning of its sentences one by one, we no longer can maintain that we have a free-standing statement, let alone a systemic one. The document contains three kinds of writings:

1. The first consists of verbatim citations and glosses of sentences of the Mishnah. In this study we shall ignore compositions and composites of this first classification.

19

2.   The second is made up of free-standing statements that
      complement the sense of the Mishnah but do not cite a
      Mishnah paragraph verbatim. These statements can be fully
      understood only in dialogue with the Mishnah's counterpart.
      We shall pay some attention to compositions and composites
      of this classification, though I do not anticipate that they will
      yield premises or presuppositions independent of those of
      the Mishnah.

3.   The third comprises free-standing, autonomous statements,
      formulated in the manner of the Mishnah but fully
      comprehensible on their own. These are the items that will
      present whatever interesting data the document will give us.

The editors or compilers of the Tosefta arranged their materials in
accord with two principles, and these govern the order of the Tosefta's
statements in correspondence to the Mishnah's.   First will come
statements that cite what the Mishnah's sentences say, and this ordinarily
will occur in the order of the Mishnah's statements. Second, in general,
Mishnah citation and gloss will be succeeded by Mishnah amplification,
which is to say, sentences that do not cite the Mishnah's corresponding
ones, but that cannot be understood without reference to the Mishnah's
rule or sense. The first two kinds of statements are the ones that cannot
be fully understood without knowledge of the Mishnah, which defines
their context. Third in sequence, commonly, will be the small number of
free-standing statements, which can be wholly understood on their own
and without appeal to the sense or principle of the corresponding
Mishnah passage; and in some few cases, these compositions and even
composites will have no parallel in the Mishnah at all.

Autonomous statements require attention in their own right. These
comprise paragraphs that make their own point and can be fully
understood in their own terms. These free-standing materials are of two
kinds. First, some autonomous materials work on topics important to a
passage in the Mishnah and are placed by Tosefta's framers in a position
corresponding to the thematic parallel in the Mishnah. What marks
these materials as autonomous is that, while they intersect with the
Mishnah's topic, their interest in that topic bears no point in common
with the Mishnah's treatment of the same topic. A second criterion,
which is complementary, is that we can understand what follows
without referring to the Mishnah for any purpose. The second type of
autonomous materials addresses topics omitted in the Mishnah, and that
type is included only because, in the Mishnah, there may be a tangential
reference to the topic treated by Tosefta's composition. The criterion of
classification, then, is even simpler than that governing the first type.

The Tosefta's authorship has collected this kind of material we know not where. It can have been composed in the same period as the writing of the Mishnah.

While these free-standing statements that could as well have stood in the Mishnah as in the Tosefta itself may have reached final formulation prior to the closure of the Mishnah, most of the document either cites the Mishnah verbatim and comments upon it, or can be understood only in light of the Mishnah even though the Mishnah is not cited verbatim, and that is sound reason for assigning the formulation of most of the document and the compilation of the whole to the time after the Mishnah was concluded. The first two types of materials certainly were written after the closure of the Mishnah. The Tosefta as a whole, covering all three types, was compiled sometime after the conclusion of the Mishnah in ca. 200 but before the formation of the Talmud of the Land of Israel, ca. 400, which frequently cites materials found in the Tosefta and interprets the Mishnah in light of the Tosefta's complements. The compilation therefore is a work of the third century, 200-300.

But in substance the document's claim proves still stronger. The Tosefta's materials, incoherent and cogent not among themselves but only in relationship to the Mishnah, serve as the Mishnah's first commentary, first amplification, and first extension. If by "a talmud," we mean a sustained, systematic commentary to the Mishnah, following a program of exegesis and analysis, then the Tosefta must be called the first talmud, prior to the ones done in the Land of Israel by ca. 400 or completed in Babylonia by ca. 600. Since both Talmuds read Mishnah passages through Tosefta complements to the Mishnah, the Tosefta forms the bridge between the Talmuds and much of the Mishnah.

But that does not mean the Tosefta is a very accessible document. The opposite is the case. And the reason derives from the Tosefta's very character as a document of mediation, expansion, and extension of another piece of writing. The Tosefta as is now clear makes sense only in relationship to the Mishnah. That is so not only for its program and order, which are defined by the Mishnah, but also for its individual compositions. Each completed unit of thought of the Tosefta is to be understood, to begin with, in relationship with the Mishnah: Is it a citation of and commentary to the Mishnah passage that forms its counterpart? Is the passage fully to be comprehended on its own or only in relationship to a counterpart passage of the Mishnah? Or is the passage free-standing? The answers to these three questions define the first step in making any sense at all of a passage of the Tosefta.

I remind readers that, as noted in the Preface, we focus solely upon those compositions or composites of the Tosefta independent of the Mishnah and bypass the ones that cite and gloss the Mishnah, since these latter items, which form a huge portion of the whole, cannot tell us about premises but only about received principles. Items that are formulated as autonomous statements but in fact rely for full meaning and consequence upon the Mishnah's rules will be noted where of special interest. That methodological decision limits the range of this survey. Let me give a single, transparent example that shows how Tosefta's compilers have simply amplified a point in the Mishnah and present no independent opinion of their own:

Mishnah-Tractate Ohalot

11:1 A. The house which split –
      B. uncleanness is on the outer side –
      C. utensils which are on the inner side are clean.
      D. Uncleanness is on the inner side –
      E. utensils which are on the outer side –
      F. the House of Shammai say, "Until there is in the split four handbreadths."
      G. The House of Hillel say, "Any amount."
      H. R. Yosé says in the name of the House of Hillel, "A square handbreadth."

Tosefta Ahilot to Mishnah-Tractate Oholot

12:1 A. And how much should this crack be?
      B. The House of Hillel say, "Any amount:
      C. "The breadth of the plumbline."
      D. And R. Yosé says in the name of the House of Hillel, "A square handbreadth."

Tosefta at A-B cites and augments the Mishnah's statement at 11:1B, and then C glosses the foregoing. Clearly, we cannot understand a word in the Tosefta composition without the Mishnah statement before us, and, further, Tosefta yields no premise or presupposition independent of the Mishnah. To uncover the substrate of thought in the Tosefta passage at hand, we have to turn to the Mishnah statement.

II. Unarticulated Premises: The Givens of Religious Conduct

I find nothing relevant.

III. Unarticulated Premises: The Givens of Religious Conviction

There are no statements that clearly express principles of a philosophical interest, other than those already identified in the Mishnah tractate itself.

IV. Matters of Philosophy, Natural Science and Metaphysics

1. One point strikes me as new, namely, the status of an object is determined by the character of its functionally effective component(s):

Tosefta Kelim Baba Mesia

1:3   E.   A spade which one made from the unclean [utensil], [with] (and) its adze [made] from the clean [utensil], is clean. [If] he made it from clean [material] and its adze from unclean, it is unclean.

       F.   Everything follows after [the status of the part of the object which actually] does the work.

       G.   [If] one made it from clean [material], even though it is covered [with metal] from the unclean, it is clean.

Tosefta Kelim Baba Mesia

1:13   A.   All ornaments of a beast, such as the chains and the nose-rings and the hooklets and the rings, are clean. Unclean is only the clapper which makes a sound for the man to hear.

       B.   One who makes bells for the mortar and for a cradle and for mantels for scrolls or for children's mantels – [lo,] they are clean. [If] one made for them a clapper, they are unclean. [If] their clapper is removed, they are clean.

       C.   The bell of the door is clean, and of the beast is unclean.

       D.   The bell of a door which one made for a beast is unclean, and of a bell which one made for a door, even if one affixed it to the ground and even if one nailed it with a nail, is unclean.

But the case can be made that this presupposed principle operates in some Mishnah rules as well.

2

Tosefta to Mishnah-Tractate Ohalot

This tractate yields no independent premises that I can identify.

3

Tosefta to Mishnah-Tractate Negaim

I. Unarticulated Premises: The Givens of Religious Conduct

1. One who is subject to uncleanness stands at a higher level of
    sanctification than one who does not. Gentiles, who are not subject
    to uncleanness, do not afford protection against uncleanness;
    Israelites, who are subject to uncleanness, also afford protection
    against uncleanness:

    #### 7:9

    A. [If] one was standing inside and stretched his hand outside, and his
        fellow gave him his sandals and his rings in the palm of his hand,
        he and they are unclean forthwith.
    B. But if he had been dressed in them, he would have been clean until
        he had remained long enough to eat a piece of bread.
    C. [If] he was standing outside, with his sandals on his feet,
    D. and he stretched [his hand] inside,
    E. with his ring on his finger,
    F. and he stretched them [it] inside –
    G. R. Judah declares unclean forthwith.
    H. And sages say, "Until he will remain there [for an interval]
        sufficient for eating a piece of bread."
    I. They said to R. Judah, "When his entire body is unclean, he does
        not render what is on him unclean until he remains for a sufficient
        time to eat a piece of bread. So when his entire body is not unclean,
        should he (not) render unclean what is on him before he remains for
        a time sufficient to eat a piece of bread?"
    J. Said to them R. Judah, "The reason is that the power of that which
        is capable of becoming unclean is stronger to afford protection than
        is the power of the clean to afford protection.
    K. "Israelites receive uncleanness and afford protection for clothing in
        the house afflicted with plague. But the gentile and the beast do not

receive uncleanness and do not afford protection for clothing in the house afflicted with plague."

II. Unarticulated Premises: The Givens of Religious Conviction

1. There are laws of the Torah that are of purely theoretical interest, bearing no practical consequence; but one receives a reward for studying those laws, as much as practical ones:

6:1

A. A diseased house has never come into existence and is never going to come into existence. And why was it written? To tell you, Expound and receive a reward.
B. And R. Leazar b. R. Simeon says, "A place was on the border of Gaza, and they called it, 'A Quarantined Ruin.'"
C. R. Simeon b. Judah of Kefar 'Akkum said, "A place was in Galilee which they marked off, for they said, 'Diseased stones were in it.'"

2. Jerusalem is in a class by itself:

6:1D-E

D. And Jerusalem is not made unclean through plagues.
E. Said R. Judah, "I heard only the Sanctuary alone."

6:2

A. They do not measure from it [Jerusalem] toward the corpse;
B. they do not bring [on its account] the calf whose neck is broken [Deut. 21:18].
C. And it [Jerusalem] is not made a "destroyed city."
D. R. Nathan says, "Also the law concerning the rebellious son does not apply to it, as it is said, 'And they shall bring him to the elders of his town and to the gate of his place' (Deut. 21:19) – excluding Jerusalem, which belongs to [all] Israel."
E. They do not keep the corpse in it overnight.
F. And they do not carry the bones of a man through it.
G. And they do not rent houses in it.
H. And in it they do not provide a place for a resident alien.
I. And they do not set up graves in it, except for the graves of the house of David and the grave of Huldah the prophetess, which were there from the days of the former prophets.
J. And it is not planted, and it is not sown, and it is not ploughed, and they do not raise trees in it, except for rose gardens, which were there from the times of the former prophets.
K. And they do not raise dung-heaps in it, because of the uncleanness.
L. And they do not build from [houses in] it projections and balconies to the public domain, because of thereby making a tent for the transmission of uncleanness.

3. Uncleanness is a heavenly penalty for certain moral sins:

6:7D-J

D. He would come to the priest, and the priest says to him, "My son, Go and examine yourself and return [from your evil ways].

E. "For plagues come only because of gossip, and leprosy comes only to those who are arrogant.

F. "And the Omnipresent judges man only in mercy."

G. Lo, they [plagues] come on his house: [if] he repents, it requires dismantling; and if not, it requires demolishing.

H. Lo, they appear on his clothing: [if] he repents, it requires tearing; and if not, it requires burning.

I. Lo, they appear on his body: [if] he repents, he repents; and if not, "Solitary shall he dwell; outside of the camp is his dwelling" (Lev. 13:46).

J. R. Simeon b. Leazar says in the name of R. Meir, "Even on the arrogant do plagues come, for so we find concerning Uzziah [2 Chron. 26:1-6]."

III. Matters of Philosophy, Natural Science and Metaphysics

There are no statements that clearly express principles of a philosophical interest, other than those already identified in the Mishnah tractate itself.

4

Tosefta to Mishnah-Tractate Parah

I. Unarticulated Premises: The Givens of Religious Conduct

1. Once one has formed an improper intention, that intention takes over and invalidates the consequence rite, however briefly it was in effect:

4:14

    A.   An *'am haares* who said, "These utensils have I brought for my purification, and I changed my mind concerning them and decided to use them for my heave-offering" – since they were designated [for a baser purpose] in the possession of the *'am haares* [even] for one moment, lo, these are unclean.

II. Unarticulated Premises: The Givens of Religious Conviction

I find nothing of interest.

III. Matters of Philosophy, Natural Science and Metaphysics

1. Matters of doubt about topics subject to stringent rules of cleanness are resolved negatively. Matters of doubt concerning what is already subject to doubt are resolved negatively:

11:1B-D

    B.   Any matter of doubt which is clean for heave-offering is clean for the purification rite

    C.   except for the hands, since they are a matter of doubt which pertains to the body.

    D.   A matter of doubt concerning QWPSYN [?] is clean for heave-offering [and] unclean for the purification rite, since it is a matter of doubt about that which is unfit.

5

Tosefta to Mishnah-Tractate Tohorot

I. Unarticulated Premises: The Givens of Religious Conduct

1. Intentionality has no bearing upon substances the classification of which is determined by their physical characteristics. It can classify only when there is a choice:

2:5

A. Honey which oozes from the hive of bees receives uncleanness as liquid.

B. [If] one gave thought to it as food, it receives uncleanness as food.

C. Oil is neither food nor liquid.

D. [If] one gave thought to it to make use of it as food and not as liquid his intention is of no effect.

E. Blood which congealed is neither food nor liquid.

F. [If] one gave thought to it to make use of it as food, it receives uncleanness as food. And [if one gave thought to use it as] liquid his intention is null.

G. The honey of palms is neither food nor liquid.

H. [If] one gave thought to it to make use of it for food, it receives uncleanness as food.

I. And [if one gave thought to it to use it] for liquid, his intention is null.

J. And as to all other fruit juice, [it is] neither food nor liquid.

K. [If] one gave thought to it, whether for liquid or for food, his intention is null.

L. [Sens:] Snow is neither food nor liquid. If one gave thought to it for food, his intention is null. For liquid – it receives uncleanness as liquid.

M. [If] part of it is made unclean, the liquid is made unclean.

N. [If] part of it is made unclean, the whole of it is not made unclean.

O. [If] part of it is clean, the whole of it is clean.

A corollary is, what is available for food and intended for food is subject to uncleanness as food:

2:7

A.   He who gives thought to the milk which is in the udder – it is clean.

B.   And [he who gives thought to the milk] which is in the maw – it is unclean .

C.   The hide and the placenta do not receive uncleanness as food.

D.   The hide which one boiled and the placenta to which one gave thought [for use as food] receive uncleanness as food.

II. Unarticulated Premises: The Givens of Religious Conviction

I discern nothing pertinent.

III. Matters of Philosophy, Natural Science and Metaphysics

1.   In cases of doubt, we resolve matters by assessing possibilities; where something is impossible, that resolves the doubt:

4:1

A.   [If a person] was wrapped in his cloak,

B.   with unclean things and clean things at his side,

C.   and unclean things and clean things above –

D.   there is doubt whether he touched or did not touch –

E.   his matter of doubt is deemed clean.

F.   And if it is not possible for him [not to come] into [contact] –

G.   his matter of doubt is deemed unclean.

6

Tosefta to Mishnah-Tractate Miqvaot

I. Unarticulated Premises: The Givens of Religious Conduct

There is nothing that pertains.

II. Unarticulated Premises: The Givens of Religious Conviction

I find no candidates for inclusion here.

III. Matters of Philosophy, Natural Science and Metaphysics

1. When we have a case of doubt, we have to discover the governing analogy, and then resolve the doubt by appeal to the rule yielded by that analogy. In the following, the governing analogy is decided by the parallel in the source of invalidation, and that solves the problem:

1:16

A. An immersion pool which was measured and found lacking – all the acts requiring cleanness which were carried out depending upon it,

B. whether this immersion pool is in the private domain, or whether this immersion pool is in the public domain – [Supply: are unclean.]

C. R. Simeon says, "In the private domain, it is unclean. In the public domain, it is clean."

1:17

A. Said R. Simeon, "There was the following precedent: the water reservoir of Disqus in Yavneh was measured and found lacking.

B. "And R. Tarfon did declare clean, and R. Aqiva unclean.

C. "Said R. Tarfon, 'Since this immersion pool is in the assumption of being clean, it remains perpetually in this presumption of cleanness until it will be known for sure that it is made unclean.'

D. "Said R. Aqiva, 'Since this immersion pool is in the assumption of being unclean, it perpetually remains in the presumption of uncleanness until it will be known for sure that it is clean.'

1:18

A. "Said R. Tarfon, 'To what is the matter to be likened? To one who was standing and offering [a sacrifice] at the altar, and it became known that he is a son of a divorcée or the son of a *halusah* – for his service is valid.'

B. "Said R. Aqiva, 'To what is the matter to be likened? To one who was standing and offering [a sacrifice] at the altar, and it became known that he is disqualified by reason of a blemish – for his service is invalid.'

1:19

A. "Said R. Tarfon to him, 'You draw an analogy to one who is blemished. I draw an analogy to the son of a divorcée or to the son of a *halusah*.

B. "'Let us now see to what the matter is appropriately likened.

C. "'If it is analogous to a blemished priest, let us learn the law from the case of the blemished priest. If it is analogous to the son of a divorcée or to the son of a *halusah*, let us learn the law from the case of the son of the divorcée or the son of a *halusah*.'

1:20

A. "R. Aqiva says, 'The unfitness affecting an immersion pool affects the immersion pool itself, and the unfit aspect of the blemished priest affects the blemished priest himself.

B. "'But let not the case of the son of a divorcée or the son of a *halusah* prove the matter, for his matter of unfitness depends upon others.

C. "'A ritual pool's unfitness [depends] on one only, and the unfitness of a blemished priest [depends] on an individual only, but let not the son of a divorcée or the son of a *halusah* prove the matter, for the unfitness of this one depends upon ancestry.'

D. "They took a vote concerning the case and declared it unclean.

E. "Said R. Tarfon to R. Aqiva, 'He who departs from you is like one who perishes.'"

7

Tosefta to Mishnah-Tractate Niddah

I find nothing pertinent to our inquiry.

8

Tosefta to Mishnah-Tractate Makhshirin

Tosefta to this tractate yields not a single fresh idea for consideration here.

9

Tosefta to Mishnah-Tractate Zabim

The question raised in this monograph does not pertain to the tractate at hand.

10

Tosefta to Mishnah-Tractate Tebul Yom

The tractate contains nothing to which our question is relevant.

11

Tosefta to Mishnah-Tractate Yadayim

I. Unarticulated Premises: The Givens of Religious Conduct

I find nothing relevant.

II. Unarticulated Premises: The Givens of Religious Conviction

1. Uncleanness is a mark of sanctification. Books that were said through the Holy Spirit impart uncleanness to hands; those not, do not:

2:14

A. R. Simeon b. Menassia says, "The Song of Songs imparts uncleanness to hands, because it was said by the Holy Spirit.

B. "Qohelet does not impart uncleanness of hands, because it is [merely] the wisdom of Solomon."

C. They said to him, "And did he write only this alone? Lo, it says, 'And Solomon uttered three thousand proverbs and his songs were a thousand and five' (1 Kgs. 5:12).

D. "And it says, 'Do not add to his words lest he rebuke you and you be found a liar' (Prov. 30:6)."

2:19

A. Said to them Rabban Yohanan b. Zakkai, "The preciousness of Holy Scriptures accounts for their uncleanness,

B. "so that a man should not make them into bedding for his cattle."

III. Matters of Philosophy, Natural Science and Metaphysics

I do not see anything of broad, philosophical interest.

12

Tosefta to Mishnah-Tractate Uqsin

We do not ask a productive question to this tractate.

Part Two

TRACTATE ABOT

13

The Character of Tractate Abot
and its Premises

I. Tractate Abot and the Mishnah

Tractate Abot is made up of five chapters of wisdom sayings, neither legal nor exegetical in character, but mainly a handbook of wise sayings for disciples of sages, especially those involved in administration of the law. These sayings, miscellaneous in character, are assigned to named authorities. The rhetoric of The Fathers is dictated by aphoristic style, producing wise sayings presented as a list. The topic, overall, derives from the realm of wisdom: right conduct with God, society, self. The logic of cogent discourse derives from the notion that a list of sages constitutes a principle of coherent composition, and the diverse sayings fit together within the sustaining logic of a list of authorities of a given classification. The list holds together because everything on it is part of a chain of formulation and transmission – tradition – beginning at Moses on Sinai. So one sentence joins the next because all the sentences enjoy the same status, that imparted by the Torah. That logic deriving from authority makes it possible for the audience of the document to see relationships of order, proportion, and sustained discourse, where we see merely a sequence of essentially discrete sayings. The rhetorical device rests upon the same principle of cogent discourse: listing authorities suffices as a principle of rhetorical composition – and persuasion. The topical program – with its recurrent emphasis on Torah study and the social and intellectual and personal virtues required for Torah study – is equally cogent with the logical and rhetorical decisions made by the authorship of the whole.

Always published along with the Mishnah but autonomous of that document in all differentiating formal and programmatic attributes, the compilation cites authorities of the generation generally assumed to have flourished after the closure of the Mishnah and hence may be situated at ca. 250 C.E. – a mere guess. The Mishnah's rhetorical program exercised no influence whatsoever on the formulation of Tractate Abot. The mnemonic patterns characteristic of the Mishnah are not to be found. The topical division and organization of the Mishnah tractates one by one and as a set play no role in this tractate, which is not topically structured at all. Tractate Abot therefore bears no formal, or substantive, relationship to the Mishnah. Its rhetoric, logic of coherent discourse, and topic mark the document as utterly anomalous in Rabbinic literature; it has no parallel.

But its proposition and message form the keystone and centerpiece of that literature, which explains the inclusion, in this chapter, of the entire text of the tractate. The document serves as the Mishnah's first and most important documentary apologetic, stating in abstract and general terms the ideals for the virtuous life that are set forth by the Mishnah's sages and animate its laws. Its presentation of sayings of sages extending from Sinai to figures named in the Mishnah itself links the Mishnah to Sinai. The link consists of the chain of tradition handed on through the chain of sages itself. It follows that, because of the authorities cited in its pages, the Mishnah constitutes part of the Torah of Sinai, for by the evidence of the chain of tradition, the Mishnah, too, forms a statement of revelation, that is, "Torah revealed to Moses at Sinai." This is expressed in the opening sentence, given below.

II. Unarticulated Premises: The Givens of Religious Conduct

The character of the tractate is such that we cannot expect to find norms of conduct framed as concrete rules of behavior.

III. Unarticulated Premises: The Givens of Religious Conviction

I find the following basic theological propositions paramount in this tractate:

1. The theological proposition that validates the Mishnah is that the Torah is a matter of tradition. The tradition goes from master to disciple, Moses to Joshua. And, further, those listed further on include authorities of the Mishnah itself. That fact forms an implicit claim that (1) part of the Torah was, and is, orally formulated and orally transmitted, and (2) the Mishnah's authorities stand in the tradition of Sinai, so that (3) the Mishnah, too, forms part of the Torah of Sinai.

1:1

Moses received the Torah at Sinai and handed it on to Joshua, Joshua to elders, and elders to prophets. And prophets handed it on to the men of the great assembly. They said three things: Be prudent in judgment. Raise up many disciples. Make a fence for the Torah.

The verbs, receive...hand on..., in Hebrew yield the words *qabbalah*, tradition, and *masoret*, also tradition.

This position is different from that taken by pseudepigraphic writers, who imitate the style of Scripture, or who claim to speak within that same gift of revelation as Moses. It is one thing to say one's holy book is Scripture because it is like Scripture, or to claim that the author of the holy book has a revelation independent of that of Moses. These two positions concede to the Torah of Moses priority over their own holy books. The Mishnah's first apologists make no such concession, when they allege that the Mishnah is part of the Torah of Moses. They appeal to the highest possible authority to the Israelite framework, claiming the most one can claim in behalf of the book which, in fact, bears the names of men who lived fifty years before the apologists themselves. The sages' apologia for the Mishnah, therefore, rests upon the persons of the sages themselves: incarnations of the Torah of Sinai in the here-and-now.

2.   Torah forms one of the foundations of the world, along with the Temple and acts of supererogatory kindness:

1:2

Simeon the Righteous was one of the last survivors of the great assembly. He would say: "On three things does the world stand: On the Torah, and on the Temple service, and on deeds of loving kindness."

Study of the Torah is the primary moral obligation:

1:13

B.   And who does not learn is liable to death. And the one who uses the crown, passes away.

Study of the Torah must not be exploitative and must be done in a spirit of humility:

4:5

B.   R. Sadoq says, "Do not make [Torah teachings] a crown in which to glorify yourself or a spade with which to dig. So did Hillel say, 'He who uses the crown perishes.' Thus have you learned: Whoever derives worldly benefit from teachings of the Torah takes his life out of this world."

4:6

R. Yosé says, "Whoever honors the Torah himself is honored by people. And whoever disgraces the Torah himself is disgraced by people."

5:16

[In] any loving relationship which depends upon something, [when] that thing is gone, the love is gone. But any which does not depend upon something will never come to an end. What is a loving relationship which depends upon something? That is the love of Amnon and Tamar [2 Sam. 13:15]. And one which does not depend upon something: That is the love of David and Jonathan.

5:17

Any dispute which is for the sake of Heaven will in the end yield results, and any which is not for the sake of Heaven will in the end not yield results. What is a dispute for the sake of Heaven? This is the sort of dispute between Hillel and Shammai. And what is one which is not for the sake of Heaven? It is the dispute of Korach and all his party.

This must be done on a regular and permanent basis:

1:15

Shammai says: Make your learning of the Torah a fixed obligation. Say little and do much. Greet everybody cheerfully.

Humanity was created to study the Torah and must do so with humility:

2:8

A.   Rabban Yohanan ben Zakkai received [the Torah] from Hillel and Shammai. He would say: If you have learned much Torah, do not puff yourself up on that account, for it was for that purpose that you were created.

When people study the Torah, God is present with them:

3:2

B.   R. Hananiah b. Teradion says, "[If] two sit together and between them do not pass teachings of the Torah, lo, this is a seat of the scornful, as it is said, 'Nor sits in the seat of the scornful' (Ps. 1:1). But two who are sitting, and words of the Torah do pass between them – the Presence is with them, as it is said, 'Then they that feared the Lord spoke with one another, and the Lord hearkened and heard, and a book of remembrance was written before him, for them that feared the Lord and gave thought to his name' (Mal. 3:16)." I know that this applies to two. How do I know that even if a single person sits and works on the Torah, the Holy One, blessed

be He, set aside a reward for him? As it is said, "Let him sit alone
and keep silent, because he has laid it upon him" (Lam. 3:28).

3:3

R. Simeon says, "Three who ate at a single table and did not talk
about teachings of the Torah while at that table are as though they
ate from dead sacrifices, as it is said, 'For all tables are full of vomit
and filthiness [if they are] without God' (Ps. 106:28). But three who
ate at a single table and did talk about teachings of the Torah while
at that table are as if they ate at the table of the Omnipresent,
blessed is He, as it is said, 'And he said to me, This is the table that
is before the Lord' (Ezek. 41:22)."

3:6

R. Halafta of Kefar Hananiah says, "Among ten who sit and work
hard on the Torah the Presence comes to rest, as it is said, 'God
stands in the congregation of God' (Ps. 82:1). And how do we now
that the same is so even of five? For it is said, 'And he has founded
his group upon the earth' (Am. 9:6). And how do we know that this
is so even of three? Since it is said, 'And he judges among the
judges' (Ps. 82:1). And how do we know that this is so even of two?
Because it is said, 'Then they that feared the Lord spoke with one
another, and the Lord hearkened and heard' (Mal. 3:16). And how
do we know that this is so even of one? Since it is said, 'In every
place where I record my name I will come to you and I will bless
you' (Ex. 20:24)."

The stakes in Torah study are therefore very high, and one must
make every effort not to forget what he knows:

3:7

B.   R. Simeon says, "He who is going along the way and repeating [his
         Torah tradition] but interrupts his repetition and says, 'How
         beautiful is that tree! How beautiful is that ploughed field!' –
         Scripture reckons it to him as if he has become liable for his life."

3:8

R. Dosetai b. R. Yannai in the name of R. Meir says, "Whoever
forgets a single thing from what he has learned – Scripture reckons
it to him as if he has become liable for his life, as it is said, 'Only
take heed to yourself and keep your soul diligently, lest you forget
the words which your eyes saw' (Deut. 4:9). Is it possible that this is
so even if his learning became too much for him? Scripture says,
Lest they depart from your heart all the days of your life. Thus he
becomes liable for his life only when he will sit down and actually
remove [his learning] from his own heart."

4:1

A.   R. Judah says, "Be meticulous about learning, for error in learning leads to deliberate [violation of the Torah]."

3.   The correct attitude for the service of God is to do so unconditionally and without expectation of reward; selflessly; one should make what God wants into what he wants:

1:3

Antigonus of Sokho received [the Torah] from Simeon the Righteous. He would say: "Do not be like servants who serve the master on condition of receiving a reward, but [be] like servants who serve the master not on condition of receiving a reward. And let the fear of Heaven be upon you."

2:4

He would say: "Make His wishes into your own wishes, so that He will make your wishes into His wishes. Put aside your wishes on account of His wishes, so that He will put aside the wishes of other people in favor of your wishes."

4.   Reward for righteous deeds and punishment for wicked ones is guaranteed in the world to come:

1:7

Nittai the Arbelite says: "Keep away from a bad neighbor. And don't get involved with a bad person. And don't give up hope of retribution."

2:1

Rabbi says: "What is the straight path which a person should choose for himself? Whatever is an ornament to the one who follows it, and an ornament in the view of others. Be meticulous in a small religious duty as in a large one, for you do not know what sort of reward is coming for any of the various religious duties. And reckon with the loss [required] in carrying out a religious duty against the reward for doing it; and the reward for committing a transgression against the loss for doing it. And keep your eye on three things, so you will not come into the clutches of transgression. Know what is above you. An eye which sees, and an ear which hears, and all your actions are written down in a book."

2:6

Also, he saw a skull floating on the water and said to it [in Aramaic]: "Because you drowned others, they drowned you, and in the end those who drowned you will be drowned."

2:15

Rabbi Tarfon says: "The day is short, the work formidable, the workers lazy, the wages high, the employer impatient."

2:16

He would say: "It's not your job to finish the work, but you are not free to walk away from it. If you have learned much Torah, they will give you a good reward. And your employer can be depended upon to pay your wages for what you do. And know what sort of reward is going to be given to the righteous in the coming time."

3:1

A.   Aqabiah b. Mehallalel says, "Reflect upon three things and you will not fall into the clutches of transgression: Know (1) from whence you come, (2) whither you are going, and (3) before whom you are going to have to give a full account of yourself.

B.   "From whence do you come? From a putrid drop. Whither are you going? To a place of dust, worms, and maggots.

C.   "And before whom are you are going to give a full account of yourself? Before the King of kings of kings, the Holy One, blessed be He."

3:15

"Everything is foreseen, and free choice is given. In goodness the world is judged. And all is in accord with the abundance of deed[s]."

3:16

A.   He would say, "(1) All is handed over as a pledge, (2) and a net is cast over all the living. (3) The store is open, (4) the storekeeper gives credit, (5) the account book is open, and (6) the hand is writing.

B.   "(1) Whoever wants to borrow may come and borrow. (2) The charity collectors go around every day and collect from man whether he knows it or not. (3) And they have grounds for what they do. (4) And the judgment is a true judgment. (5) And everything is ready for the meal."

4:4

A.   R. Levitas of Yavneh says, "Be exceedingly humble, for the future of humanity is the worm."

B.   R. Yohanan b. Beroqa says, "Whoever secretly treats the Name of Heaven as profane publicly pays the price. All the same are the one who does so inadvertently and the one who does so deliberately, when it comes to treating the name of Heaven as profane."

4:9

R. Jonathan says, "Whoever keeps the Torah when poor will in the end keep it in wealth. And whoever treats the Torah as nothing when he is wealthy in the end will treat it as nothing in poverty."

4:10

R. Meir says, "Keep your business to a minimum and make your business the Torah. And be humble before everybody. And if you treat the Torah as nothing, you will have many treating you as nothing. And if you have labored in the Torah, [the Torah] has a great reward to give you."

4:11

A.   R. Eleazar b. Jacob says, "He who does even a single religious duty gets himself a good advocate. He who does even a single transgression gets himself a powerful prosecutor. Penitence and good deeds are like a shield against punishment."

4:15

A.   R. Yannai says, "We do not have in hand [an explanation] either for the prosperity of the wicked or for the suffering of the righteous."

4:16

R. Jacob says, "This world is like an antechamber before the world to come. Get ready in the antechamber, so you can go into the great hall."

4:17

He would say, "Better is a single moment spent in penitence and good deeds in this world than the whole of the world to come. And better is a single moment of inner peace in the world to come than the whole of a lifetime spent in this world."

4:22

A.   R. Eleazar Haqqappar would say, "Those who are born are [destined] to die, and those who die are [destined] for resurrection. And the living are [destined] to be judged – so as to know, to make known, and to confirm that (1) He is God, (2) He is the one who forms, (3) He is the one who creates, (4) He is the one who understands, (5) He is the one who judges, (6) He is the one who gives evidence, (7) He is the one who brings suit, (8) and He is the one who is going to make the ultimate judgment.

C.   "Blessed be He, for before Him are no (1) guile, (2) forgetfulness, (3) respect for persons, or (4) bribe-taking, for everything is His. And know that everything is subject to reckoning. And do not let your evil impulse persuade you that Sheol is a place of refuge for you. For (1) despite your wishes were you formed, (2) despite your wishes were you born, (3) despite your wishes do you live, (4) despite your wishes do you die, and (5) despite your wishes are you going to give a full accounting before the King of kings of kings, the Holy One, blessed be He."

5:8

There are seven forms of punishment which come upon the world for seven kinds of transgression. (1) [If] some people give tithes and some people do not give tithes, there is a famine from drought. So some people are hungry and some have enough. (2) [If] everyone decided not to tithe, there is famine of unrest and drought. (3) [If all decided] not to remove dough-offering, there is a famine of totality. (4) Pestilence comes to the world on account of the death penalties which are listed in the Torah but which are not in the hands of the court [to inflict]; and because of the produce of the Seventh Year [which people buy and sell]. (5) A sword comes into the world because of the delaying of justice and perversion of justice, and because of those who teach the Torah not in accord with the law.

5:9

A.   (6) A plague of wild animals comes into the world because of vain oaths and desecration of the Divine Name. (7) Exile comes into the world because of those who worship idols, because of fornication, and because of bloodshed, and because of the neglect of the release of the Land [in the year of release].

B.   At four turnings in the year pestilence increases: in the fourth year, in the seventh year, in the year after the seventh year, and at the end of the Festival [of Tabernacles] every year: (1) in the fourth year, because of the poorman's tithe of the third year [which people have neglected to hand over to the poor]; (2) in the seventh year, because of the poorman's tithe of the sixth year; (3) in the year after the Seventh Year, because of the dealing in produce of the Seventh Year; and (4) at the end of the Festival every year, because of the thievery of the dues [gleanings and the like] owing to the poor [nor left for them in the antecedent harvest].

5.   One should fear sin and carry out the required deeds of the Torah, its being more important to act properly even than to attain wisdom:

3:9

A.   R. Haninah b. Dosa says, "For anyone whose fear of sin takes precedence over his wisdom, his wisdom will endure. And for anyone whose wisdom takes precedence over his fear of sin, wisdom will not endure."

B.   He would say, "Anyone whose deeds are more than his wisdom – his wisdom will endure. And anyone whose wisdom is more than his deeds – his wisdom will not endure."

3:17

A.   R. Eleazar b. Azariah says, "If there is no learning of the Torah, there is no proper conduct. If there is no proper conduct, there is no learning in the Torah. If there is no wisdom, there is no reverence. If there is no reverence, there is no wisdom. If there is no understanding, there is no knowledge. If there is no knowledge, there is no understanding. If there is no sustenance, there is no Torah learning. If there is no Torah learning, there is no sustenance."

B.   He would say, "Anyone whose wisdom is greater than his deeds – to that is he to be likened? To a tree with abundant foliage, but few roots. When the winds come, they will uproot it and blow it down. as it is said, 'He shall be like a tamarisk in the desert and shall not see when good comes, but shall inhabit the parched places in the wilderness' (Jer. 17:6). But anyone whose deeds are greater than his wisdom – to what is he to be likened? To a tree with little foliage but abundant roots. For even if all the winds in the world were to come and blast at it, they will not move it from its place, as it is said, 'He shall be as a tree planted by the waters, and that spreads out its roots by the river, and shall not fear when heat comes, and his leaf shall be green, and shall not be careful in the year of drought, neither shall cease from yielding fruit' (Jer. 17:8)."

6.   Prayer should be recited in an attitude of beseeching and not in a routine manner:

2:13

Rabbi Simeon says: "Be meticulous about the recitation of the Shema and the Prayer. And when you pray, don't treat your praying as a matter of routine; but let it be a [plea for] mercy and supplication before the Omnipresent, the blessed, as it is said, 'For He is gracious and full of compassion, slow to anger and full of mercy, and repents of the evil' (Joel 2:13). And never be evil in your own eyes."

7.   Humanity is made in the image of God, and the Torah is an act of divine grace, since it informs humanity that it is made in the image of God; so, too, with regard to Israel:

3:14

A.   R. Aqiba would say, "Precious is the human being, who was created in the image [of God]. It was an act of still greater love that it was made known to him that he was created in the image [of God], as it is said, 'For in the image of God he made man' (Gen. 9:6).

B.   "Precious are Israelites, who are called children to the Omnipresent. It was an act of still greater love that it was made known to them that they were called children to the Omnipresent, as it is said, 'You are the children of the Lord your God' (Deut. 14:1).

C.   "Precious are Israelites, to whom was given the precious thing. It
        was an act of still greater love that it was made known to them that
        to them was given that precious thing with which the world was
        made, as it is said, 'For I give you a good doctrine. Do not forsake
        my Torah' (Prov. 4:2)."

8. The world was made by God through an act of speech; God is long-
    suffering; God especially loved Abraham; God did wonders for our
    ancestors; God did miracles in the Temple:

5:1

By ten acts of speech was the world made. And what does
Scripture mean [by having God say say ten times]? But it is to exact
punishment from the wicked, who destroy a world which was
created through ten acts of speech, and to secure a good reward for
the righteous, who sustain a world which was created through ten
acts of speech.

5:2

There are ten generations from Adam to Noah, to show you how
long-suffering is [God]. For all those generations went along spiting
him until he brought the water of the flood upon them. There are
ten generations from Noah to Abraham, to show you how long-
suffering is [God]. For all those generations went along spiting him,
until Abraham came along and took the reward which had been
meant for all of them.

5:3

Ten trials were inflicted upon Abraham, our father, may he rest in
peace, and he withstood all of them, to show you how great is His
love for Abraham, our father, may he rest in peace.

5:4

Ten wonders were done for our fathers in Egypt, and ten at the Sea.
Ten blows did the Holy One, blessed be He, bring upon the
Egyptians in Egypt, and ten at the Sea. Ten trials did our fathers
inflict upon the Omnipresent, blessed be He, in the Wilderness, as it
is said, "Yet they have tempted me these ten times and have not
listened to my voice" (Num. 14:22).

5:5

Ten wonders were done for our fathers in the Temple: (1) A woman
never miscarried on account of the stench of the meat of Holy
Things. (2) And the meat of the Holy Things ever turned rotten. (3)
A fly never made an appearance in the slaughterhouse. (4) A high
priest never suffered a nocturnal emission on the eve of the Day of
Atonement. (5) The rain never quenched the fire on the altar. (6) No
wind ever blew away the pillar of smoke. (7) An invalidating factor
never affected the 'omer, the Two Loaves, or the showbread. (8)

When the people are standing, they are jammed together. When they go down and prostrate themselves, they have plenty of room. (9) A snake and a scorpion never bit anybody in Jerusalem. (10) And no one ever said to his fellow, "The place is too crowded for me [Isa. 49:20] to stay in Jerusalem."

IV. Matters of Philosophy, Natural Science and Metaphysics

While one may maintain that some of the moral and ethical maxims bear affinities with those of philosophers, the kind of philosophical premises concerning matters of nature that we have found elsewhere do not appear to me to occur in this tractate.

Part Three

SIFRA

14

Identifying the Premises of Sifra (to Leviticus).
Sifra Section Vayyiqra Debura Denedabah

I. Sifra and the Mishnah

Sifra, a compilation of Midrash exegeses on the book of Leviticus, forms a massive and systematic statement concerning the definition of the Mishnah in relationship to Scripture. Unlike the other exegetical (nonpropositional) Midrash compilations that concern the Pentateuch, the two Sifrés and Mekhilta attributed to R. Ishmael, the document is programmatically cogent, beginning to end, in its sustained treatment of the issues defined by the Mishnah. For the heirs of the Mishnah, the relationship of the Mishnah to Scripture, in mythic language, of the oral to the written part of the Torah, required definition. The authorship of Sifra composed the one document to accomplish the union of the two Torahs, Scripture, or the Written Torah, and the Mishnah, or the Oral Torah. This was achieved not merely formally, by provision of prooftexts from Scripture for statements of the Mishnah – as in the two Talmuds. It rather was accomplished through a profound analysis of the interior structure of thought of the Mishnah, criticized in light of the Torah as here defined. It was by means of the critique of practical logic and the rehabilitation of the probative logic of hierarchical classification (accomplished through the form of *Listenwissenschaft*) in particular that the authorship of Sifra accomplished this remarkable feat of intellect. That authorship achieved the (re-)union of the two Torahs into a single cogent statement within the framework of the Written Torah by penetrating into the deep composition of logic that underlay the creation of the world in its correct components, rightly classified, and in its right order, as portrayed by the Torah.

This was done in two ways. Specifically, it involved, first of all, systematically demolishing the logic that sustains an autonomous Mishnah, which appeals to the intrinsic traits of things to accomplish classification and hierarchization. Secondly, it was done by demonstrating the dependency, for the identification of the correct classification of things, not upon the traits of things viewed in the abstract, but upon the classification of things by Scripture in particular. The framers of Sifra recast the two parts of the Torah into a single coherent statement through unitary and cogent discourse. So in choosing, as to structure, a book of the Pentateuch, and, as to form, the exegetical form involving paraphrase and amplification of a phrase of a base text of Scripture, the authorship of Sifra made its entire statement *in nuce.* Then by composing a document that for very long stretches simply cannot have been put together without the Mishnah and at the same time subjecting the generative logical principles of the Mishnah to devastating critique, that same authorship took up its position. The destruction of the Mishnah as an autonomous and free-standing statement, based upon its own logic, is followed by the reconstruction of (large tracts of the Mishnah) as a statement wholly within, and in accord with, the logic and program of the Written Torah in Leviticus. That is what defines Sifra, the one genuinely cogent and sustained statement among the four Midrash compilations that sustain exegetical discourse on the Pentateuch.

The dominant approach to uniting the two Torahs, oral and written, into a single cogent statement involved reading the Written Torah into the oral. In form, as we noted in the two Talmuds, this was done through inserting into the Mishnah (that is, the Oral Torah) a long sequence of prooftexts. The other solution required reading the Oral Torah into the written one, by inserting into the Written Torah citations and allusions to the oral one, and, as a matter of fact, also by demonstrating, on both philosophical and theological grounds, the utter subordination and dependency of the Oral Torah, the Mishnah, to the Written Torah – while at the same time defending and vindicating that same Oral Torah. Sifra, followed unsystematically to be sure by the two Sifrés, did just that. Sifra's authorship attempted to set forth the Dual Torah as a single, cogent statement, doing so by reading the Mishnah into Scripture not merely for proposition but for expression of proposition. On the surface that decision represented a literary, not merely a theological, judgment. But within the deep structure of thought, it was far more than a mere matter of how to select and organize propositions.

That judgment upon the Mishnah forms part of the polemic of Sifra's authorship – but only part of it. Sifra's authorship conducts a sustained polemic against the failure of the Mishnah to cite Scripture very much or systematically to link its ideas to Scripture through the medium of formal demonstration by exegesis. Sifra's rhetorical exegesis follows a standard redactional form. Scripture will be cited. Then a statement will be made about its meaning, or a statement of law correlative to that Scripture will be given. That statement sometimes cites the Mishnah, often verbatim. Finally, the author of Sifra invariably states, "Now is that not (merely) logical?" And the point of that statement will be, Can this position not be gained through the working of mere logic, based upon facts supplied (to be sure) by Scripture?

The polemical power of Sifra lies in its repetitive demonstration that the stated position, citation of a Mishnah pericope, is not only not the product of logic, but is, and only can be, the product of exegesis of Scripture. That is only part of the matter, as I shall explain, but that component of the larger judgment of Sifra's authorship does make the point that the Mishnah is subordinated to Scripture and validated only through Scripture. In that regard, the authorship of Sifra stands at one with the position of the authorships of the other successor writings, even though Sifra's writers carried to a much more profound level of thought the critique of the Mishnah. They did so by rethinking the logical foundations of the entire Torah.

The framers of the Mishnah effect their taxonomy through the traits of things. The authorship of Sifra insists that the source of classification is Scripture. Sifra's authorship time and again demonstrates that classification without Scripture's data cannot be carried out without Scripture's data, and, it must follow, hierarchical arguments based on extrascriptural taxa always fail. In the Mishnah we seek connection between fact and fact, sentence and sentence, by comparing and contrasting two things that are like and not alike. At the logical level the Mishnah falls into the category of familiar philosophical thought. Once we seek regularities, we propose rules. What is like another thing falls under its rule, and what is not like the other falls under the opposite rule. Accordingly, as to the species of the genus, so far as they are alike, they share the same rule. So far as they are not alike, each follows a rule contrary to that governing the other.

So the work of analysis is what produces connection, and therefore the drawing of conclusions derives from comparison and contrast: the *and*, the *equal*. The proposition then that forms the conclusion concerns the essential likeness of the two offices, except where they are different, but the subterranean premise is that we can explain both likeness and difference by appeal to a principle of fundamental order and unity. To make these observations concrete, we turn to the case at hand. The important contrast comes at the outset. The high priest and king fall into a single genus, but speciation, based on traits particular to the king, then distinguishes the one from the other. All of this exercise is conducted essentially independently of Scripture; the classifications derive from the system, are viewed as autonomous constructs; traits of things define classifications and dictate what is like and what is unlike.

Let us now examine one sustained example of how Sifra's authorship rejects the principles of the logic of hierarchical classification *as these are worked out by the framers of the Mishnah*. It is a critique of designating classifications of things without scriptural warrant. The critique applies to the way in which a shared logic is worked out by the other authorship. For it is not the principle that like things follow the same rule, unlike things, the opposite rule, that is at stake. Nor is the principle of hierarchical classification embodied in the argument a fortiori at issue. What our authorship disputes is that we can classify things on our own by appeal to the traits or indicative characteristics, that is, utterly without reference to Scripture. The argument is simple. On our own, we cannot classify species into genera. Everything is different from everything else in some way. But Scripture tells us what things are like what other things for what purposes, hence Scripture imposes on things the definitive classifications, that and not traits we discern in the things themselves. When we see the nature of the critique, we shall have a clear picture of what is at stake when we examine, in some detail, precisely how the Mishnah's logic does its work. That is why at the outset I present a complete composition in which Sifra's authorship tests the modes of classification characteristic of the Mishnah, resting as they do on the traits of things viewed out of the context of Scripture's categories of things.

Parashat Vayyiqra Dibura Denedabah Parashah 3

I.1   A.   "[If his offering is] a burnt-offering [from the herd, he shall offer a male without blemish; he shall offer it at the door of the tent of meeting, that he may be accepted before the Lord; he shall lay his hand upon the head of the burnt-offering, and it shall be accepted for him to make atonement for him]" (Lev. 1:2):

       B.   Why does Scripture refer to a burnt-offering in particular?

       C.   For one might have taken the view that all of the specified grounds for the invalidation of an offering should apply only to the burnt-offering that is brought as a freewill-offering.

       D.   But how should we know that the same grounds for invalidation apply also to a burnt-offering that is brought in fulfillment of an obligation [for instance, the burnt-offering that is brought for a leper who is going through a rite of purification, or the bird brought by a woman who has given birth as part of her purification rite, Lev. 14, 12, respectively]?

E.   It is a matter of logic.

F.   Bringing a burnt-offering as a freewill-offering and bringing a burnt-offering in fulfillment of an obligation [are parallel to one another and fall into the same classification].

G.   Just as a burnt-offering that is brought as a freewill-offering is subject to all of the specified grounds for invalidation, so to a burnt-offering brought in fulfillment of an obligation, all the same grounds for invalidation should apply.

H.   No, [that reasoning is not compelling. For the two species of the genus, burnt-offering, are not wholly identical and can be distinguished, on which basis we may also maintain that the grounds for invalidation that pertain to the one do not necessarily apply to the other. Specifically:] if you have taken that position with respect to the burnt-offering brought as a freewill-offering, for which there is no equivalent, will you take the same position with regard to the burnt-offering brought in fulfillment of an obligation, for which there is an equivalent? [For if one is obligated to bring a burnt-offering by reason of obligation and cannot afford a beast, one may bring birds, as at Lev. 14:22, but if one is bringing a freewill-offering, a less expensive form of the offering may not serve.]

I.   Accordingly, since there is the possibility in the case of the burnt-offering brought in fulfillment of an obligation, in which case there is an acceptable equivalent [to the more expensive beast, through the less expensive birds], all of the specified grounds for invalidation [which apply to the, in any case, more expensive burnt-offering brought as a freewill-offering] should not apply at all.

J.   That is why in the present passage, Scripture refers simply to "burnt-offering," [and without further specification, the meaning is then simple:] all the same are the burnt-offering brought in fulfillment of an obligation and a burnt-offering brought as a freewill-offering in that all of the same grounds for invalidation of the beast that pertain to the one pertain also to the other.

I.2   A.   And how do we know that the same rules of invalidation of a blemished beast apply also in the case of a beast that is designated in substitution of a beast sanctified for an offering [in line with Lev. 27:10, so that, if one states that a given, unconsecrated beast is to take the place of a beast that has already been consecrated, the already consecrated beast remains in its holy status, and the beast to which reference is made also becomes consecrated]?

B.   The matter of bringing a burnt-offering and the matter of bringing a substituted beast fall into the same classification [since both are offerings that in the present instance will be consumed upon the altar, and, consequently, they fall under the same rule as to invalidating blemishes].

C.   Just as the entire protocol of blemishes applies to the one, so in the case of the beast that is designated as a substitute, the same invalidating blemishes pertain.

D. No, if you have invoked that rule in the case of the burnt-offering, in which case no status of sanctification applies should the beast that is designated as a burnt-offering be blemished in some permanent way, will you make the same statement in the case of a beast that is designated as a substitute? For in the case of a substituted beast, the status of sanctification applies even though the beast bears a permanent blemish! [So the two do not fall into the same classification after all, since, to begin with, one cannot sanctify a permanently blemished beast, which beast can never enter the status of sanctification, but through an act of substitution, a permanently blemished beast can be placed into the status of sanctification.]

E. Since the status of sanctification applies [to a substituted beast] even though the beast bears a permanent blemish, all of the specified grounds for invalidation as a matter of logic should not apply to it.

F. That is why in the present passage, Scripture refers simply to "burnt-offering," [and without further specification, the meaning is then simple:] all the same are the burnt-offering brought in fulfillment of an obligation and a burnt-offering brought as a substitute for an animal designated as holy, in that all of the same grounds for invalidation of the beast that pertain to the one pertain also to the other.

I.3 A. And how do we know [that the protocol of blemishes that applies to the burnt-offering brought as a freewill-offering applies also to] animals that are subject to the rule of a sacrifice as a peace-offering?

B. It is a matter of logic. The matter of bringing a burnt-offering and the matter of bringing animals that are subject to the rule of a sacrifice as a peace-offering fall into the same classification [since both are offerings and consequently under the same rule as to invalidating blemishes].

C. Just as the entire protocol of blemishes applies to the one, so in the case of animals that are subject to the rule of a sacrifice as a peace-offering, the same invalidating blemishes pertain.

D. And it is furthermore a matter of an argument a fortiori, as follows:

E. If to a burnt-offering which is valid when in the form of a bird, [which is inexpensive], the protocol of invalidating blemishes applies, to peace-offerings, which are not valid when brought in the form of a bird, surely the same protocol of invalidating blemishes should also apply!

F. No, if you have applied that rule to a burnt-offering, in which case females are not valid for the offering as male beasts are, will you say the same of peace-offerings? For female beasts as much as male beasts may be brought for sacrifice in the status of the peace-offering. [The two species may be distinguished from one another].

G. Since it is the case that female beasts as much as male beasts may be brought for sacrifice in the status of the peace-offering, the protocol of invalidating blemishes should not apply to a beast designated for use as peace-offerings.

H. That is why in the present passage, Scripture refers simply to "burnt-offering," [and without further specification, the meaning is then simple:] all the same are the burnt-offering brought in fulfillment of an obligation and an animal designated under the rule of peace-offerings, in that all of the same grounds for invalidation of the beast that pertain to the one pertain also to the other.

The systematic exercise proves for beasts that serve in three classifications of offerings, burnt-offerings, substitutes, and peace-offerings, that the same rules of invalidation apply throughout. The comparison of the two kinds of burnt-offerings, voluntary and obligatory, shows that they are sufficiently different from one another so that as a matter of logic, what pertains to the one need not apply to the other. Then come the differences between an animal that is consecrated and one that is designated as a substitute for one that is consecrated. Finally we distinguish between the applicable rules of the sacrifice; a burnt-offering yields no meat for the person in behalf of whom the offering is made, while one sacrificed under the rule of peace-offerings does. We run the changes on three fundamental differences and show that in each case, the differences between like things are greater than the similarities

In Sifra no one denies the principle of hierarchical classification. That is an established fact, a self-evident trait of mind. The argument of Sifra's authorship is that, by themselves, things do not possess traits that permit us finally to classify species into a common genus. There always are traits distinctive to a classification. Accordingly, it is the argument of Sifra's authorship that without the revelation of the Torah, we are not able to effect any classification at all, are left, that is to say, only with species, no genus, only with cases, no rules. The thrust of Sifra's authorship's attack on the Mishnah's taxonomic logic is readily discerned. Time and again, we can easily demonstrate, things have so many and such diverse and contradictory indicative traits that, comparing one thing to something else, we can always distinguish one species from another. Even though we find something in common, we also can discern some other trait characteristic of one thing but not the other. Consequently, we also can show that the hierarchical logic on which we rely, the argument a fortiori or *qol vehomer*, will not serve. For if on the basis of one set of traits which yield a given classification, we place into hierarchical order two or more items, on the basis of a different set of traits, we have either a different classification altogether, or, much more commonly, simply a different hierarchy. So the attack on the way in which the Mishnah's authorship has done its work appeals to not merely the limitations of classification solely on the basis of traits of things. The more telling argument addresses what is, to *Listenwissenschaft*, the source of power and compelling proof: hierarchization. That is why, throughout, we must designate the

Mishnah's mode of *Listenwissenschaft* a logic of hierarchical classification. Things are not merely like or unlike, therefore following one rule or its opposite. Things also are weightier or less weighty, and that particular point of likeness of difference generates the logical force of *Listenwissenschaft*.

Sifra's authorship repeatedly demonstrates that the formation of classifications based on monothetic taxonomy, that is to say, traits that are not only common to both items but that are shared throughout both items subject to comparison and contrast, simply will not serve. For at every point at which someone alleges uniform, that is to say, monothetic likeness, Sifra's authorship will demonstrate difference. Then how to proceed? Appeal to some shared traits as a basis for classification: this is not like that, and that is not like this, but the indicative trait that both exhibit is such and so, that is to say, polythetic taxonomy. The self-evident problem in accepting differences among things and insisting, nonetheless, on their monomorphic character for purposes of comparison and contrast, cannot be set aside: who says? That is, if I can adduce in evidence for a shared classification of things only a few traits among many characteristic of each thing, then what stops me from treating all things alike? Polythetic taxonomy opens the way to an unlimited exercise in finding what diverse things have in common and imposing, for that reason, one rule on everything. Then the very working of *Listenwissenschaft* as a tool of analysis, differentiation, comparison, contrast, and the descriptive determination of rules yields the opposite of what is desired. Chaos, not order, a mass of exceptions, no rules, a world of examples, each subject to its own regulation, instead of a world of order and proportion, composition and stability, will result.

Sifra's authorship affirms taxonomic logic when applied to the right categories. It systematically demonstrates the affirmative case, that *Listenwissenschaft* is a self-evidently valid mode of demonstrating the truth of propositions. But *the* source of the correct classification of things is Scripture and only Scripture. Without Scripture's intervention into the taxonomy of the world, we should have no knowledge at all of which things fall into which classifications and therefore are governed by which rules. How then do we appeal to Scripture to designate the operative classifications? Here is a simple example of the alternative mode of classification, one that does not appeal to the traits of things but to the utilization of names by Scripture. What we see is how by naming things in one way, rather than in another, Scripture orders all things, classifying and, in the nature of things, also hierarchizing them. Here is one example among many of how our authorship conceives the right way of logical thought to proceed:

Parashat Vayyiqra Dibura Denedabah Parashah 4

V.1   A.   "...and Aaron's sons the priests shall present the blood and throw the blood [round about against the altar that is at the door of the tent of meeting]":

      B.   Why does Scripture make use of the word "blood" twice [instead of using a pronoun]?

      C.   [It is for the following purpose:] How on the basis of Scripture do you know that if blood deriving from one burnt-offering was confused with blood deriving from another burnt-offering, blood deriving from one burnt-offering with blood deriving from a beast that has been substituted therefor, blood deriving from a burnt-offering with blood deriving from an unconsecrated beast, the mixture should nonetheless be presented?

      D.   It is because Scripture makes use of the word "blood" twice [instead of using a pronoun].

V.2   A.   Is it possible to suppose that while if blood deriving from beasts in the specified classifications, it is to be presented, for the simple reason that if the several beasts while alive had been confused with one another, they might be offered up?

      B.   But how do we know that even if the blood of a burnt-offering were confused with that of a beast killed as a guilt-offering, [it is to be offered up]?

      C.   I shall concede that in the case of the mixture of the blood of a burnt-offering confused with that of a beast killed as a guilt-offering, it is to be presented, for both this one and that one fall into the classification of Most Holy Things.

      D.   But how do I know that if the blood of a burnt-offering were confused with the blood of a beast slaughtered in the classification of peace-offerings or of a thanksgiving-offering, [it is to be presented]?

      E.   I shall concede that in the case of the mixture of the blood of a burnt-offering confused with that of a beast slaughtered in the classification of peace-offerings or of a thanksgiving-offering, [it is to be presented], because the beasts in both classifications produce blood that has to be sprinkled four times.

      F.   But how do I know that if the blood of a burnt-offering were confused with the blood of a beast slaughtered in the classification of a firstling or a beast that was counted as tenth or of a beast designated as a Passover-offering, [it is to be presented]?

      G.   I shall concede that in the case of the mixture of the blood of a burnt-offering confused with that of a beast slaughtered in the classification of firstling or a beast that was counted as tenth or of a beast designated as a Passover-offering, [it is to be presented], because Scripture uses the word "blood" two times.

      H.   Then while I may make that concession, might I also suppose that if the blood of a burnt-offering was confused with the blood of beasts that had suffered an invalidation, it also may be offered up?

      I.   Scripture says, "...its blood," [thus excluding such a case].

J.   Then I shall concede the case of a mixture of the blood of a valid burnt-offering with the blood of beasts that had suffered an invalidation, which blood is not valid to be presented at all.

K.   But how do I know that if such blood were mixed with the blood deriving from beasts set aside as sin-offerings to be offered on the inner altar, [it is not to be offered up]?

L.   I can concede that the blood of a burnt-offering that has been mixed with the blood deriving from beasts set aside as sin-offerings to be offered on the inner altar is not to be offered up, for the one is offered on the inner altar, and the other on the outer altar [the burnt-offering brought as a freewill-offering, under discussion here, is slaughtered at the altar "...that is at the door of the tent of meeting," not at the inner altar].

M.   But how do I know that even if the blood of a burnt-offering was confused with the blood of sin-offerings that are to be slaughtered at the outer altar, it is not to be offered up?

N.   Scripture says, "...its blood," [thus excluding such a case].

In place of the rejection of arguments resting on classifying species into a common genus, we now demonstrate how classification really is to be carried on. It is through the imposition upon data of the categories dictated by Scripture: Scripture's use of language. That is the force of this powerful exercise. No. 1 sets the stage, simply pointing out that the use of the word "blood" twice encompasses a case in which blood in two distinct classifications is somehow confused in the process of the conduct of the cult. In such a case it is quite proper to pour out the mixture of blood deriving from distinct sources, for example, beasts that have served different, but comparable purposes. We then systemically work out the limits of that rule, showing how comparability works, then pointing to cases in which comparability is set aside. Throughout the exposition, at the crucial point we invoke the formulation of Scripture, subordinating logic or in our instance the process of classification of like species to the dictation of Scripture. I cannot imagine a more successful demonstration of what the framers wish to say.

The reason for Scripture's unique power of classification is the possibility of polythetic classification that only Scripture makes possible. Because of Scripture's provision of taxa, we are able to undertake the science of *Listenwissenschaft*, including hierarchical classification, in the right way. What can we do because we appeal to Scripture, which we cannot do if we do not rely on Scripture? It is to establish the possibility of polythetic classification. We can appeal to shared traits of otherwise distinct taxa and so transform species into a common genus for a given purpose. Only Scripture makes that initiative feasible, so our authorship maintains. What is at stake? It is the possibility of doing precisely what the framers of the Mishnah wish to do. That is to join together masses of diverse data into a single, encompassing statement, to show the rule that inheres in diverse cases. In what follows, we shall see an enormous, coherent, and beautifully articulated exercise in the comparison and contrast of many things of a single genus. The whole holds together, because Scripture makes possible the statement of all things within a single rule. That is, as we have noted, precisely what the framers of the Mishnah proposed to accomplish. Our authorship maintains that only by appeal to The Torah is this fete of learning possible. If, then, we wish to understand all things all together and all at once under a single encompassing rule, we had best revert to The Torah, with its account of the rightful names, positions, and order, imputed to all things.

Parashat Vayyiqra Dibura Denedabah Parashah 11

I.1   A.   [With reference to M. Men. 5:5:] There are those [offerings which require bringing near but do not require waving, waving but not bringing near, waving and bringing near, neither waving nor bringing near: These are offerings which require bringing near but do not require waving: the meal-offering of fine flour and the meal-offering prepared in the baking pan and the meal-offering prepared in the frying pan, and the meal-offering of cakes and the meal-offering of wafers, and the meal-offering of priests, and the meal-offering of an anointed priest, and the meal-offering of gentiles, and the meal-offering of women, and the meal-offering of a sinner. R. Simeon says, "The meal-offering of priests and of the anointed priest – bringing near does not apply to them, because the taking of a handful does not apply to them. And whatever is not subject to the taking of a handful is not subject to bringing near."] [Scripture] says, "When you present to the Lord a meal-offering that is made in any of these ways, it shall be brought [to the priest who shall take it up to the altar]":

       B.   What requires bringing near is only the handful alone. How do I know that I should encompass under the rule of bringing near the meal-offering?

       C.   Scripture says explicitly, "meal-offering."

       D.   How do I know that I should encompass all meal-offerings?

       E.   Scripture says, using the accusative particle, "the meal-offering."

I.2   A.   I might propose that what requires bringing near is solely the meal-offering brought as a freewill-offering.

       B.   How do I know that the rule encompasses an obligatory meal-offering?

       C.   It is a matter of logic.

       D.   Bringing a meal-offering as a freewill-offering and bringing a meal-offering as a matter of obligation form a single classification. Just as a meal-offering presented as a freewill-offering requires bringing near, so the same rule applies to a meal-offering of a sinner [brought as a matter of obligation], which should likewise require bringing near.

       E.   No, if you have stated that rule governing bringing near in the case of a freewill-offering, on which oil and frankincense have to be added, will you say the same of the meal-offering of a sinner [Lev. 5:11], which does not require oil and frankincense?

F. The meal-offering brought by a wife accused of adultery will prove to the contrary, for it does not require oil and frankincense, but it does require bringing near [as is stated explicitly at Num. 5:15].

G. No, if you have applied the requirement of bringing near to the meal-offering brought by a wife accused of adultery, which also requires waving, will you say the same of the meal-offering of a sinner, which does not have to be waved?

H. Lo, you must therefore reason by appeal to a polythetic analogy [in which not all traits pertain to all components of the category, but some traits apply to them all in common]:

I. The meal-offering brought as a freewill-offering, which requires oil and frankincense, does not in all respects conform to the traits of the meal-offering of a wife accused of adultery, which does not require oil and frankincense, and the meal-offering of the wife accused of adultery, which requires waving, does not in all respects conform to the traits of a meal-offering brought as a freewill-offering, which does not require waving.

J. But what they have in common is that they are alike in requiring the taking up of a handful and they are also alike in that they require bringing near.

K. I shall then introduce into the same classification the meal-offering of a sinner, which is equivalent to them as to the matter of the taking up of a handful, and also should be equivalent to them as to the requirement of being drawn near.

L. But might one not argue that the trait that all have in common is that all of them may be brought equally by a rich and a poor person and require drawing near, which then excludes from the common classification the meal-offering of a sinner, which does not conform to the rule that it may be brought equally by a rich and a poor person, [but may be brought only by a poor person,] and such an offering also should not require being brought near!

M. [The fact that the polythetic classification yields indeterminate results means failure once more, and, accordingly,] Scripture states, "meal-offering,"

N. with this meaning: all the same are the meal-offering brought as a freewill-offering and the meal-offering of a sinner, both this and that require being brought near.

The elegant exercise draws together the various types of meal-offerings and shows that they cannot form a classification of either a monothetic or a polythetic character. Consequently, Scripture must be invoked to supply the proof for the classification of the discrete items. The important language is at H-J: these differ from those, and those from these, but what they have in common is.... Then we demonstrate, with our appeal to Scripture, the sole valid source of polythetic classification, M. And this is constant throughout Sifra.

While setting forth its critique of the Mishnah's utilization of the logic of comparison and contrast in hierarchical classification, the authorship of Sifra is careful not to criticize the Mishnah. Its position favors restating the Mishnah within the context of Scripture, not rejecting the conclusions of the Mishnah, let alone its authority. Consequently, when we find a critique of applied reason divorced from Scripture, we rarely uncover an explicit critique of the Mishnah, and when we find a citation of the Mishnah, we rarely uncover linkage to the ubiquitous principle that Scripture forms the source of all classification and hierarchy. When the Mishnah is cited by our authorship, it will be presented as part of the factual substrate of the Torah. When the logic operative throughout the Mishnah is subjected to criticism, the language of the Mishnah will rarely, if ever, be cited in context. The operative language in dealing with the critique of the applied logic of *Listenwissenschaft* as represented by the framers of the Mishnah ordinarily is, "is it not a matter of logic?" Then the sorts of arguments against taxonomy pursued outside of the framework of Scripture's classifications will follow. When, by contrast, the authorship of Sifra wishes to introduce into the context it has already established a verbatim passage of the Mishnah, it will ordinarily, though not always, use *mikan amru*, which, in context, means, "in this connection [sages} have said." It is a simple fact that when the intent is to demolish improper reasoning, the Mishnah's rules in the Mishnah's language rarely, if ever, occur. When the authorship of Sifra wishes to incorporate paragraphs of the Mishnah into their re-presentation of The Torah, they will do so either without fanfare, as in the passage at hand, or by the neutral joining language "in this connection [sages] have said."

The authorship of Sifra never called into question the self-evident validity of taxonomic logic. Its critique is addressed only to how the Mishnah's framers identify the origins of, and delineate, taxa. But that critique proves fundamental to the case that that authorship proposed to make. For, intending to demonstrate that "The Torah" was a proper noun, and that everything that was valid came to expression in the single, cogent statement of The Torah, the authorship at hand identified the fundamental issue. It is the debate over the way we know things. In insisting, in agreement with the framers of the Mishnah, that there are not only cases but also rules, not only species but also genera, the authorship of Sifra also made its case in behalf of the case for The Torah as a proper noun. This carries us to the theological foundation for Sifra's authorship's sustained critique of applied reason.

At stake is the character of The Torah and what it is, in The Torah, the thing that we wish to discern. And the answer to that question requires theological, not merely literary and philosophical, reflection on our part. For in their delineation of correct hierarchical logic, our authorship uncovered, within The Torah (hence by definition, written and oral components of The Torah alike) an adumbration of the working of the mind of God. That is because the premise of all discourse is that The Torah was written by God and dictated by God to Moses at Sinai. And that will in the end explain why our authorship for its part has entered into The Torah long passages of not merely clarification but active intrusion, making itself a component of the interlocutorial process. To what end we know: it was to unite the Dual Torah. The authorship of Sifra proposed to regain access to the modes of thought that guided the formation of the Torah, Oral and Written alike: comparison and contrast in this way, not in that, identification of categories in one manner, not in another. Since those were the modes of thought that, in our authorship's conception, dictated the structure of intellect upon which the Torah, the united Torah, rested, a simple conclusion is the sole possible one.

In their analysis of the deepest structures of intellect of the Torah, the authorship of Sifra supposed to enter into the mind of God, showing how God's mind worked when God formed the Torah, written and oral alike. And there, in the intellect of God, in their judgment humanity gained access to the only means of uniting the Torah, because that is where the Torah originated. But in discerning how God's mind worked, the intellectuals who created Sifra claimed for themselves a place in that very process of thought that had given birth to The Torah. Our authorship could rewrite the Torah because, knowing how The Torah originally was written, they, too, could write (though not reveal) The Torah.

Rhetoric

Three forms dictate the entire rhetorical repertoire of this document. The first, the dialectical, is the demonstration that if we wish to classify things, we must follow the taxa dictated by Scripture rather than relying solely upon the traits of the things we wish to classify. The second, the citation form, invokes the citation of passages of the Mishnah or the Tosefta in the setting of Scripture. The third is commentary form, in which a phrase of Scripture is followed by an amplificatory clause of some sort. The forms of the document admirably expressed the polemical purpose of the authorship at hand. What they wished to prove was that a taxonomy resting on the traits of things without reference to Scripture's classifications cannot serve. They further wished to restate the Oral Torah in the setting of the Written Torah. And, finally, they wished to accomplish the whole by rewriting the Written Torah. The dialectical form accomplishes the first purpose, the citation form the second, and the commentary form the third.

The simple commentary form is one in which a verse, or an element of a verse, is cited, and then a very few words explain the meaning of that verse. Second come the complex forms, in which a simple exegesis is augmented in some important way, commonly by questions and answers, so that we have more than simply a verse and a brief exposition of its elements or of its meaning as a whole. The authorship of the Sifra time and again wishes to show that prior documents, the Mishnah or Tosefta, cited verbatim, require the support of exegesis of Scripture for important propositions, presented in the Mishnah and the Tosefta not on the foundation of exegetical proof at all. In the main, moreover, the authorship of Sifra tends not to attribute its materials to specific authorities, and most of the pericopae containing attributions are shared with Mishnah and Tosefta. As we should expect, just as in Mekhilta Attributed to R. Ishmael, Sifra contains a fair sample of pericopae which do not make use of the forms common in the exegesis of specific scriptural verses and, mostly, do not pretend to explain the meaning of verses, but rather resort to forms typical of Mishnah and Tosefta. When Sifra uses forms other than those in which its exegeses are routinely phrased, it commonly, though not always, draws upon materials also found in Mishnah and Tosefta. It is uncommon for Sifra to make use of nonexegetical forms for materials peculiar to its compilation. To state matters simply, Sifra quotes Mishnah or Tosefta, but its own materials follow its distinctive, exegetical forms.

Let me give one example of a commonplace composition of Sifra. What we find very routinely is simply an exegesis of a verse of Scripture, and out of the result we can discern neither premise nor presupposition of the kind that interests us in this study:

LXXI

I.1	A.	"And the priest shall put on his linen garment, and put his linen breeches upon his body":
	B.	It is to be the linen garment in accord with appropriate measure [not too long or too short].
	C.	It is to be a garment made of linen.
	D.	It is to be a garment that is new.
	E.	It is to be a garment that is doubled up.
I.2	A.	It is to be a garment with which he does not put on other garments.
	B.	Might one suppose that while he should not put on other garments made of linen, he may put on garments made of wool?
	C.	Scripture says, "linen garment."
	D.	Might one suppose that while he may not put on other holy garments, he may nonetheless put on other garments that are not consecrated?
	E.	Scripture says, "...and put his linen breeches upon his body."
I.3	A.	Why does Scripture say, "...he will put on..."?

B. "To encompass the priest's turban and girdle," the words of R. Judah.

C. R. Dosa says, "It is to encompass the garments of the high priest, indicating that they are suitable for use for a common priest."

D. Rabbi gives two answers to this view: "Is it indeed the case that the girdle of the high priest is the same as the girdle of the ordinary priest?

E. "Furthermore, should garments that are used for a more weighty matter of sanctification [the Day of Atonement] go and be used for a less weighty matter of sanctification [merely removing the ashes from the altar]?

F. "If so, why does Scripture say, '...he will put on...'?

G. "It is to indicate that that is so even though they are in tatters."

So far as I can see, nothing in the foregoing tells us what prior conclusions had to have been in mind to yield the issue or its resolution. True, we have to assume a variety of propositions concerning the character and authority of Scripture (as much as of the Mishnah); but none of these propositions is particular to this passage, or indeed, even to the document that presents it. The formal character of the document therefore proves unpromising for a search for (to use wildly incommensurate language) "the Judaism that is taken for granted."

Every example of a complex form, that is, a passage in which we have more than a cited verse and a brief exposition of its meaning, may be called "dialectical," that is, the mode of moving or developing an idea through questions and answers, sometimes implicit, but commonly explicit. What "moves" is the argument, the flow of thought, from problem to problem. The dialectics of Sifra differ in form and purpose from that of the Talmuds. Here, the movement is generated by the raising of contrary questions and theses. There are several subdivisions of the dialectical exegesis, so distinctive as to be treated by themselves. But all exhibit a flow of logical argument, unfolding in questions and answers, characteristic, in the later literature, of the Talmud. One important subdivision of the stated form consists of those items, somewhat few in number but all rather large in size and articulation, intended to prove that logic alone is insufficient, and that only through revealed law will a reliable view of what is required be attained. The polemic in these items is pointed and obvious; logic (DYN) never wins the argument, though at a few points flaws in the text seem to suggest disjunctures in the flow of logic. To clarify these general remarks, let us now address a particular chapter of Sifra and out of its details form a theory of the repertoire of forms on which our authorship has drawn.

Parashat Vayyiqra Dibura Denedabah Parashah 7

I.1 A. ["If his offering to the Lord is a burnt-offering of birds, he shall choose [bring near] his offering from turtledoves or pigeons. The priest shall bring it to the altar, pinch off its head, and turn it into smoke on the altar; and its blood shall be drained out against the side of the altar. He shall remove its crop with its contents and cast it into the place of the ashes, at the east side of the altar. The priest shall tear it open by its wings, without severing it, and turn it into smoke on the altar, upon the wood that is on the fire. It is a burnt-offering, an offering by fire, of pleasing odor to the Lord" (Lev. 1:14-17)]:

B. "[The priest] shall bring it [to the altar]":
C. What is the sense of this statement?
D. Since it is said, "he shall choose [bring near] his offering from turtledoves or pigeons," one might have supposed that there can be no fewer than two sets of birds.
E. Accordingly, Scripture states, "[The priest] shall bring it [to the altar]" to indicate, [by reference to the "it,"] that even a single pair suffices.

Reduced to its simplest syntactic traits, the form consists of the citation of a clause of a verse, followed by secondary amplification of that clause. We may call this commentary form, in that the rhetorical requirement is citation plus amplification. Clearly, the form sustains a variety of expressions, for example, the one at hand: "what is the sense of this statement...since it is said...accordingly Scripture states...." But for our purposes there is no need to differentiate within the commentary form.

I.2   A.   "The priest shall bring it to the altar, pinch off its head":
      B.   Why does Scripture say, "The priest...pinch off..."?
      C.   This teaches that the act of pinching off the head should be done only by a priest.
      D.   But is the contrary to that proposition not a matter of logic:
      E.   if in the case of a beast of the flock, to which the act of slaughter at the north side of the altar is assigned, the participation of a priest in particular is not assigned, to the act of pinching the neck, to which the act of slaughter at the north side of the altar is not assigned, surely should not involve the participation of the priest in particular!
      F.   That is why it is necessary for Scripture to say, "The priest...pinch off...,"
      G.   so as to teach that the act of pinching off the head should be done only by a priest.
I.3   A.   Might one compose an argument to prove that one should pinch the neck by using a knife?
      B.   For lo, it is a matter of logic.
      C.   If to the act of slaughter [of a beast as a sacrifice], for which the participation of a priest is not required, the use of a correct utensil is required, for the act of pinching the neck, for which the participation of a priest indeed is required, surely should involve the requirement of using a correct implement!
      D.   That is why it is necessary for Scripture to say, "The priest...pinch off...."

I.4   A.   Said R. Aqiba, "Now would it really enter anyone's mind that a nonpriest should present an offering on the altar?

      B.   "Then why is it said, 'The priest...pinch off...'?

      C.   "This teaches that the act of pinching the neck must be done by the priest using his own finger [and not a utensil]."

I.5   A.   Might one suppose that the act of pinching may be done either at the head [up by the altar] or at the foot [on the pavement down below the altar]?

      B.   It is a matter of logic:

      C.   If in the case of an offering of a beast, which, when presented as a sin-offering is slaughtered above [at the altar itself[but when slaughtered as a burnt-offering is killed below [at the pavement, below the altar], in the case of an offering of fowl, since when presented as a sin-offering it is slaughtered down below, surely in the case of a burnt-offering it should be done down below as well!

      D.   That is why it was necessary for Scripture to make explicit [that it is killed up by the altar itself:] "The priest shall bring it to the altar, pinch off its head, and turn it into smoke on the altar."

      E.   The altar is explicitly noted with respect to turning the offering into smoke and also to pinching off the head.

      F.   Just as the offering is turned into smoke up above, at the altar itself, so the pinching off of the head is to be done up above, at the altar itself.

The form at hand is to be characterized as a dialectical exegetical argument, in which we move from point to point in a protracted, yet very tight, exposition of a proposition. The proposition is both implicit and explicit. The implicit proposition is that "logic" does not suffice. The explicit proposition concerns the subject matter at hand. We may identify the traits of this form very simply: citation of a verse or clause + a proposition that interprets that phrase, then "it is a matter of logic" followed by the demonstration that logic is insufficient for the determination of taxa.

2.   A.   "[turn it into smoke on the altar;] and its blood shall be drained out":

      B.   Can one describe matters in such a way?

      C.   Specifically, after the carcass is turned into smoke, can one drain out the blood?

      D.   But one pinches the neck in accord with the way in which one turns it into smoke:

      E.   Just as we find that the turning of the carcass into smoke is done up to the head by itself and then the body by itself, so in the act of pinching the neck, the head is by itself and the body is by itself.

3.   A.   And how do we know that in the case of turning a carcass into smoke, the head is done by itself?

      B.   When Scripture says, "The priest [shall tear it open by its wings, without severing it,] and turn it into smoke on the altar" (Lev. 1:17),

      C.   lo, the turning of the body into smoke is covered by that statement.

      D.   Lo, when Scripture states here, "pinch off its head, and turn it into smoke on the altar," it can only mean that the head is to be turned into smoke by itself.

      E.   Now, just as we find that the turning of the carcass into smoke is done up to the head by itself and then the body by itself, so in the act of pinching the neck, the head is by itself and the body is by itself.

Nos. 2, 3 present in a rather developed statement the simple exegetical form. The formal requirement is not obscured, however, since all we have is the citation of a clause followed by secondary amplification. This version of commentary form obviously cannot be seen as identical to the other; but so far as the dictates of rhetoric are concerned, there is no material difference, since the variations affect only the secondary amplification of the basic proposition, and in both cases, the basic proposition is set forth by the citation of the verse or clause followed by a sentence of two of amplification. Now we come to a simple example of how the Mishnah is introduced:

4.   A.   How does the priest do it?

      B.   **The priest went up on the ramp and went around the circuit. He came to the southeastern corner. He would wring off its head from its neck and divide the head from the body. And he drained off its blood onto the wall of the altar [M. Zeb. 6:5B-E].**

      C.   **If one did it from the place at which he was standing and downward by a cubit, it is valid. R. Simeon and R. Yohanan ben Beroqah say, "The entire deed was done only at the top of the altar" [T. Zeb. 7:9C-D].**

What we have now is the verbatim citation of a passage of the Mishnah or of the Tosefta, joined to its setting in the exegetical framework of Sifra by some sort of joining formula. Mishnah citation form requires only appropriate joining language. Among the three forms of the document, my estimate is that somewhat over half of all completed units of discourse follow commentary form, a quarter, dialectical form, and a fifth, citation form.

Logic of Coherent Discourse

Just as a limited and fixed pattern of formal preferences characteristic of the document as a whole, so a simple logical program, consisting of three logics of cogent discourse, served for every statement. Sifra's authorship made choices about how cogent and coherent statements would be made to hold together in its document. Counting each entry as a single item presents a gross and simple picture of the proportions of the types of logics we have catalogued.

TYPE OF LOGIC	NUMBER OF ENTRIES	PERCENTAGE OF THE WHOLE
Propositional	73	30.4%
Teleological	1	0.4%
Fixed Associative	43	17.9%
Methodical Analytical	123	51.0%
	240	99.7%

The operative logics are mainly propositional, approximately 82 percent, inclusive of propositional, teleological, and methodical analytical compositions. An authorship intending what we now call a commentary will have found paramount use for the logic of fixed association. That logic clearly served only a modest purpose in the context of the document as a whole. Our authorship developed a tripartite program. It wished to demonstrate the limitations of the logic of hierarchical classification, such as predominates in the Mishnah; that forms a constant theme of the methodical analytical logic. It proposed, second, to restate the Mishnah within the context of Scripture, that is, to rewrite the Written Torah to make a place for the Oral Torah. This is worked out in the logic of propositional discourse. And, finally, it wished in this rewriting to re-present the whole Torah as a cogent and unified document. Through the logic of fixed association it in fact did re-present the Torah. The three logics correspond, in their setting within the inner structure of cogent discourse. What the authorship of Sifra wished to prove was that a taxonomy resting on the traits of things without reference to Scripture's classifications cannot serve. They further wished to restate the Oral Torah in the setting of the Written Torah. And, finally, they wished to accomplish the whole by rewriting the Written Torah. The dialectical form accomplished the first purpose, the citation form the second, and the commentary form the third. There is an exact correspondence between the logics of the document and its rhetorical forms.

Topical Program

As we realize, for its topical program the authorship of Sifra takes the book of Leviticus. For propositions Sifra's authorship presents episodic and ad hoc sentences. If we ask how these sentences form propositions other than amplifications of points made in the book of Leviticus itself, and how we may restate those propositions in a coherent way, nothing sustained and coherent emerges. Sifra does not constitute a propositional document transcending its precipitating text. But, as we have now seen in detail, that in no way bears the implication that the document's authorship merely collected and arranged this and that about the book of Leviticus. For three reasons, we must conclude that Sifra does not set forth propositions in the way in which the Rabbah compilations and Sifré to Deuteronomy do.

First, in general there is no topical program distinct from that of Scripture. Sifra remains wholly within Scripture's orbit and range of discourse, proposing only to expand and clarify what it found within Scripture. Where the authorship moves beyond Scripture, it is not toward fresh theological or philosophical thought, but rather to a quite different set of issues altogether, concerning Mishnah and Tosefta. When we describe the topical program of the document, the blatant and definitive trait of Sifra is simple: the topical program and order derive from Scripture. Just as the Mishnah defines the topical program and order for Tosefta, the Yerushalmi, and the Bavli, so Scripture does so for Sifra. It follows that Sifra takes as its structure the plan and program of the Written Torah, by contrast to the decision of the framers or compilers of Tosefta and the two Talmuds.

Second, for sizable passages, the sole point of coherence for the discrete sentences or paragraphs of Sifra's authorship derives from the base verse of Scripture that is subject to commentary. That fact corresponds to the results of form-analysis and the description of the logics of cogent discourse. While, as we have noted, the Mishnah holds thought together through propositions of various kinds, with special interest in demonstrating propositions through a well-crafted program of logic of a certain kind, Sifra's authorship appeals to a different logic altogether. It is one which I have set forth as fixed associative discourse. That is not a propositional logic – by definition.

The third fundamental observation draws attention to the paramount position, within this restatement of the Written Torah, of the Oral Torah. We may say very simply that, in a purely formal and superficial sense, a sizable proportion of Sifra consists simply in the association of completed statements of the Oral Torah with the exposition of the Written Torah, the whole *re*-presenting as one whole Torah the Dual Torah received by Moses at Sinai (speaking within the Torah myth). Even at the very surface we observe a simple fact. Without the Mishnah or the Tosefta, our authorship would have had virtually nothing to say about one passage after another of the Written Torah. Far more often than citing the Mishnah or the Tosefta verbatim, our authorship cites principles of law or theology fundamental to the Mishnah's treatment of a given topic, even when the particular passage of the Mishnah or the Tosefta that sets forth those principles is not cited verbatim.

It follows that the three basic and definitive topical traits of Sifra, are, first, its total adherence to the topical program of the Written Torah for order and plan; second, its very common reliance upon the phrases or verses of the Written Torah for the joining into coherent discourse of discrete thoughts, for example, comments on, or amplifications of, words or phrases; and third, its equally profound dependence upon the Oral Torah for its program of thought: the problematic that defines the issues the authorship wishes to explore and resolve.

That brings us to the positive side of the picture. While Sifra in detail presents no paramount propositions, as a whole it demonstrates a highly distinctive and vigorously demonstrated proposition. We should drastically misunderstand the document if the miscellaneous character of the parts obscured the powerful statement made by the whole. For while in detail we cannot reconstruct a topical program other than that of Scripture, viewed in its indicative and definitive traits of rhetoric, logic, and implicit proposition, Sifra does take up a well-composed position on a fundamental issue, namely, the relationship between the Written Torah, represented by the book of Leviticus, and the Oral Torah, represented by the passages of the Mishnah deemed by the authorship of Sifra to be pertinent to the book of Leviticus. As we noted at the outset, Sifra joins the two Torahs into a single statement, accomplishing a re-presentation of the Written Torah in topic and in program and in the logic of cogent discourse, and within that rewriting of the Written Torah, a re-presentation of the Oral Torah in its paramount problematic and in many of its substantive propositions. Stated simply, the Written Torah provides the form, the Oral Torah, the content. What emerges is not merely a united, Dual Torah, but *The* Torah, stated whole and complete, in the context defined by the book of Leviticus.

All of this bears obvious implications for our inquiry here. It is clear that Sifra will provide us only episodically and anecdotally with access to premises and presuppositions that speak, to begin with, for its authors and compilers. I remind readers that, as noted in the Preface, we focus solely upon those compositions or composites of Sifra independent of the Mishnah and of the passage of Scripture at hand and bypass the ones that cite and gloss the Mishnah or Scripture, since these latter items, which form a huge portion of the whole, cannot tell us about premises but only about received principles; where Sifra paraphrases Scripture or cites the Mishnah and claims to find a verse that says the same thing, we find two facts. First, Sifra engages in a large-scale polemic of its own. Second, while recapitulating what it has learned elsewhere, the authorship of Sifra tells us, as to matters of premise and presupposition, nothing of its own. I do not include the ubiquitous exercises in explaining why logic does not suffice but Scripture is required; at the passages I do cite for their premises, we find more often than not that secondary, but necessary, exercise.

II. Unarticulated Premises: The Givens of Religious Conduct

I find nothing relevant.

III. Unarticulated Premises: The Givens of Religious Conviction

1. Before God speaks to someone, he calls to him first:

I

I.1 A. "The Lord called [to Moses] and spoke [to him from the tent of meeting, saying, 'Speak to the Israelite people and say to them']" (Lev. 1:1):

B. He gave priority to the calling over the speaking.

C. That is in line with the usage of Scripture.

D. Here there is an act of speaking, and in connection with the encounter at the bush [Ex. 3:4: "God called to him out of the bush, 'Moses, Moses'"], there is an act of speaking.

E. Just as in the latter occasion, the act of calling is given priority over the act of speaking [even though the actual word, "speaking" does not occur, it is implicit in the framing of the verse], so here, with respect to the act of speaking, the act of calling is given priority over the act of speaking.

2. Gentiles do not lay hands on offerings that they present in the Temple:

III

I.1 A. "Speak to the Israelite people [and say to them, 'When any [Hebrew: Adam] of you presents an offering of cattle to the Lord, he shall choose his offering from the herd or from the flock. If his offering is a burnt-offering from the herd, he shall offer a male without blemish; he shall offer it at the door of the tent of meeting, that he may be accepted before the Lord;] he shall lay [his hand upon the head of the burnt-offering, and it shall be accepted for him to make atonement for him]'" (Lev. 1:2):

B. "He shall lay his hand": Israelites lay on hands, gentiles do not lay on hands.

3. Proselytes lay on hands, being classified as Adam in the way Israelites are:

III

III.1 A. "[Speak to the Israelite people and say to them, 'When] any man [Hebrew: Adam] of you [presents an offering of cattle to the Lord, he shall choose his offering from the herd or from the flock]":

B. "Adam" encompasses within the rule proselytes as well.

C. "...of you" excludes from the rule apostates.

4. The atonement effected by the offering concerns failure properly to perform religious duties for which concrete performance of actions is required:

VI

IV.1 A. "...and it shall be accepted for him [to make atonement for him]" (Lev. 1:2):

B. This teaches that the Omnipresent accepts it.

C. In what connection does the Omnipresent accept it?

D. If you claim that it is accepted for those matters on account of which people are liable to the death penalty inflicted by an earthly court, the death penalty inflicted at the hands of heaven, extirpation at the hands of heaven, forty stripes, sin-offerings or guilt-offerings, lo, in the case of all of those transgressions, the pertinent penalty is specified in context [so the vague statement at hand cannot apply].

E. So in what connection does the Omnipresent accept it?

F. It is in connection with the violation of requirements to perform certain actions or not to perform certain actions involving the concrete performance of actions [that the burnt-offering brought as a freewill-offering serves to attain atonement and acceptance].

G. R. Simeon says, 'and it shall be accepted for him' and for his sacrifice,

H. "[meaning,] 'even though he did not lay on hands, the sacrifice still effects atonement.'"

IV. Matters of Philosophy, Natural Science and Metaphysics

Apart from the issues of the theory of classification to which the document as a whole is devoted, I find nothing of philosophical interest.

15

Sifra Section Vayyiqra Dibura Dehobah

I. Unarticulated Premises: The Givens of Religious Conduct

There are numerous halakhic rulings, but all of them, so far as I can see, paraphrase either the Mishnah or Scripture.

II. Unarticulated Premises: The Givens of Religious Conviction

1. Gentiles are not eligible to bring a sin-offering, even if they inadvertently violate the religious duties that pertain to the children of Noah; but Israelites, including proselytes and slaves (purchased as gentiles and converted) do have to do so:

1. A. ["And the Lord said to Moses, 'Say to the people of Israel, "If anyone sins unwittingly in any of the things which the Lord has commanded not to be done, and does any one of them..."'" (Lev. 4:1-12):]
   B. Israelites bring a sin-offering, but gentiles do not bring a sin-offering.
   C. It is not necessary to say that [they do not have to bring a sin-offering for inadvertently violating] religious duties that were not assigned to the children of Noah, but even for violating religious duties concerning which the children of Noah were commanded, they do not have to bring a sin-offering on that account.
2. A. "Say to the people of Israel": I know that the sin-offering is owing only from Israelites.
   B. How do I know that it is owing also from proselytes and bondmen?
   C. Scripture says, "If anyone [sins unwittingly]."

2. The apostate is excluded from the offering that expiates unwitting sin deriving from community action:

XLIX

II.1   A.   "...from among the populace":
        B.   excluding an apostate.
        C.   R. Simeon b. Yosé says in the name of R. Simeon, "What is the sense of the clause of Scripture, 'unwittingly incurs guilt by doing any of the things which by the Lord's commandments ought not to be done'? This refers to one who, were he informed, would simply refrain from carrying out the transgression, thus excluding an apostate, who, were he informed, would not refrain from carrying out the transgression. [There can be no issue that such a one violating the law does not do so either unwittingly or by reason of the inappropriate instruction of the court.]"

3.   Performing a religious duty at the right time, when it is due, is much valued by heaven:

LXII

I.1   A.   "And if his means do not suffice for two turtledoves or two pigeons, he shall bring as his offering for that of which he is guilty a tenth of an ephah [of choice flour for a sin-offering; he shall not add oil to it or lay frankincense on it, for it is a sin-offering. He shall bring it to the priest and the priest shall scoop out of it a handful as a token portion of it and turn it into smoke on the altar, with the Lord's offerings by fire; it is a sin-offering. Thus the priest shall make expiation on his behalf for whichever of these sins he is guilty, and he shall be forgiven. It shall belong to the priest, like the meal-offering]" (Lev. 5:7-13).
       B.   R. Judah says, "Performing a religious duty when it is due is held in special esteem, for the person brings the tenth ephah right away, and he is not allowed to wait until he gets rich so that he can bring a sheep or a she-goat."
       C.   R. Eliezer says, "Performing a religious duty when it is due is held in special esteem, for in the matter of pledges of one's valuation, the person presents the sela right away, and he is not allowed to wait until he gets rich so that he can bring fifty selas."
       D.   R. Simeon says, "Performing a religious duty when it is due is held in special esteem, for turning the sacrificial fat into smoke is valid throughout the night, and on account of that rite the prohibitions of the Sabbath are overridden should they pertain, and people are not allowed to wait to perform the right and present the fats at the end of the Sabbath."

III. Matters of Philosophy, Natural Science and Metaphysics

I find nothing pertinent.

16

Sifra to Sav

I. Unarticulated Premises: The Givens of Religious Conduct

I see no candidates for inclusion.

II. Unarticulated Premises: The Givens of Religious Conviction

1. Gentiles do not present a wave-offering:

XCIV

I.1   A.   ["The Lord said to Moses, 'Say to the people of Israel, "He who offers the sacrifice of his peace-offerings to the Lord shall bring his offering to the Lord; from the sacrifice of his peace-offerings he shall bring with his own hands the offerings by fire to the Lord; he shall bring the fat with the breast, that the breast may be waved as a wave-offering before the Lord"'" (Lev. 7:28-38).]

       B.   ["Say to the people of Israel":]

       C.   The children of Israel present a wave-offering, and idolators do not present a wave-offering.

2. Nor do women do so:

I.2   A.   ["Say to the people of Israel":]

       B.   [Since "children" uses the Hebrew for "sons," we conclude that] the sons of Israel wave offerings, and the daughters of Israel do not wave offerings.

       C.   The children of Israel present a wave-offering, and idolators do not present a wave-offering.

3. But proselytes and freed slaves do so, being fully Israelite:

I.3   A.   I know only that the waving is done by sons of Israel. How do I know that the law encompasses proselytes and freed slaves?

       B.   Scripture says, "who offers the sacrifice."

III. Matters of Philosophy, Natural Science and Metaphysics

I find nothing.

17

Sifra to Shemini

I. Unarticulated Premises: The Givens of Religious Conduct

I see nothing generative.

II. Unarticulated Premises: The Givens of Religious Conviction

This parashah is exceptionally rich in theological propositions:

1. The offerings in the Temple atone for sin, and all Israelites bear the burden of sin and require atonement:

XCIX

I.5 A. "...and he said to Aaron, Take a bull calf for a sin-offering":

B. This teaches that Moses said to Aaron, "Aaron, my brother, even though the Omnipresent has been reconciled to accept atonement for your sins, you still have to put an answer into Satan's mouth.

C. "Send a present before you before you enter the sanctuary, lest he hate you when you come into the sanctuary, and lest you suppose I alone require atonement [but not the Israelites at large]."

D. The Israelites, too, require atonement, as it is said, "And speak to the Israelites, saying, Take a he-goat for a sin-offering" (Lev. 9:3).

E. How come the Israelites have to present an offering more than Aaron?

F. He said to them, "As to you, you bear responsibility both at the outset [with the incident of Joseph, which brought Israel down to Egypt], and also at the end [with the incident with the golden calf].

G. "At the outset: 'They slaughtered a kid' (Gen. 37:31) [in connection with the affair with Joseph, dipping the ornamented tunic in the blood].

H. "At the end: 'They made for themselves a molten calf' (Ex. 32:8).

I. "Let a kid come and effect atonement for the matter of the kid, and let a calf come and effect atonement for the matter of the molten calf."

I.6   A.   "...and an ox and a ram for peace-offerings":

      B.   The reason for the two different species of offering is that the original sin occurred with two different species.

      C.   For it is said, "They made for themselves a molten calf."

      D.   And elsewhere: "They exchanged their glory for the image of a bull that feeds on grass" (Ps. 106:20).

      E.   Let the bull come and make atonement for the deed involving the bull.

      F.   Let the calf come and make atonement for the deed involving the calf.

I.7   A.   [Moses said to them,] "You should know that the Omnipresent has become reconciled with you, to accept atonement for your sins.

      B.   "As to the sin concerning which you are frightened, it has already been sacrificed before the Omnipresent, as it is said, 'to sacrifice before the Lord.'"

      C.   Said the Israelites before Moses, "But how can a city celebrate the king without seeing his face?"

      D.   He said to them, "It is on that very stipulation: 'for today the Lord will appear to you.'"

2.   Sin comes about because of the impulse to do evil:

XCIX

II.2   A.   "...and all the congregation stood near and stood before the Lord":

      B.   All of them came near with great jubilation and stood before him.

      C.   It is like the case of a king who got mad at his wife and divorced her. After some days he was reconciled with her.

      D.   She immediately girded her loins and tied her kerchiefs and she served him with an excess of enthusiasm.

      E.   So Israel, when they saw that the Omnipresent was reconciled to accepting atonement for their sins, they all came near with jubilation and stood before him.

      F.   That is the meaning of the statement: "...and all the congregation stood near and stood before the Lord."

II.3   A.   "And Moses said, 'This is the thing which the Lord commanded you to do'":

      B.   Moses said to the Israelites, "Remove that impulse to do evil from your hearts, so that all of you will be at one in awe and at one in commitment to serve before the Omnipresent.

      C.   "Just as he is unique in the world, so let your service be unique before him.

      D.   "So it is said, 'Cut away therefore the thickening about your hearts and stiffen your necks no more' (Deut. 10:16).

      E.   "On what account? 'For the Lord your God is God supreme and Lord supreme, the great, the mighty, and the awesome God' (Deut. 10:17).

      F.   "And if you do this, then, 'the glory of the Lord will appear to you.'"

3. God takes up residence in the Temple, which is where God and Israel meet; Israel's sin is atoned for; God forgives Israel in accepting the offerings:

2. A. For all of the seven days of consecration, Moses would carry out the assigned tasks,

B. But the Presence of God did not come to rest on his account, until Aaron came and carried out the tasks of service in the priestly garments of the high priest.

C. Then the Presence of God came to rest on his account,

D. in line with this verse: "for today the Lord will appear to you."

3. A. What does Scripture mean by "and it came to pass"?

B. This teaches that on high there was rejoicing before God as on the day on which heaven and earth were created in the works of creation.

C. For so Scripture says, "and it came to pass that there was evening and there was morning" (Gen. 1:5).

D. And here, too: "And it came to pass."

4. A. When Moses saw that the Israelites had finished the work of making the tabernacle, Moses came and bestowed a blessing on them,

B. as it is said, "And Moses saw all the work, and behold, they had done it; as the Lord had commanded, so had they done it. And Moses blessed them" (Ex. 39:43).

C. What is the blessing that he bestowed on them?

D. He said, "May the Presence of God come to rest on the works of your hands."

E. R. Meir says, "Thus he blessed them: 'May the Lord, the God of your fathers, add to you a thousand times as you are,'

F. "and they responded, 'Let the favor of the Lord our God be upon us, and establish you the work of our hands upon us, yes, the work of our hands establish you it' (Ps. 90:17)."

5. A. And concerning that moment Scripture says, "Come out, daughters of Jerusalem, you daughters of Zion, come out and welcome King Solomon" (Song 3:11).

B. ["Daughters of Zion"] yields "children who are most distinguished" [since the word for "distinguish" uses the letters for the word for "Zion"].

C. "...welcome King Solomon":

D. The king who possesses peace [the word for "peace" and the word for "Solomon" use the same letters].

E. "...wearing the crown with which his mother has crowned him [on his wedding day, on his day of joy]" (Song 3:11):

F. This crown refers to the tent of meeting, which is decorated in blue, purple, scarlet, and marble."

G. "...his mother":

H. "His mother" refers only to Israel, as it is said, "[Listen to me, my people,] and give ear to me, my nation" (Isa. 51:4). [The word for "nation" and the word for "mother" share the same letters.]

6. A. "...on his wedding day, [his day of joy]" (Song 3:11):

B. It is the day on which the Presence came to rest on the house."

C.   "...his day of joy":
D.   the day on which new fire came down from on high and licked the burnt-offering and fat upon the altar.

7. A.   "Then Aaron lifted up his hands toward the people and blessed them":
B.   At that moment he acquired possession of the gifts that are given to the priesthood, he acquired possession of the raising up of the hands in the priestly blessing,
C.   both for himself and for the coming generations, until the dead shall live.

4. Israel is holy to God and holy like God: separate; Israel's vocation is to sanctify itself by accepting the yoke of the Torah's religious duties (commandments):

CXXI

II.3 A.   "For I am the Lord who brought you up out of the land of Egypt, to be your God; you shall therefore be holy, for I am holy" (Lev. 11:41-45):
B.   Just as I am holy, so are you holy. Just as I am separate, so you be separate.

II.4 A.   "You shall not defile yourselves with any swarming things that crawl upon the earth":
B.   even though it does not reproduce through sexual activity.

II.5 A.   "For I am the Lord who brought you up out of the land of Egypt":
B.   It was on this stipulation that I brought you up out of the land of Egypt, on the condition that you accept on yourselves the yoke of the religious duties.
C.   For whoever accepts the yoke of the religious duties also affirms the exodus from Egypt, but whoever rejects the yoke of the commandments rejects the exodus from Egypt.

II.6 A.   "...to be your God":
B.   whether you like it or not.

II.7 A.   "...you shall therefore be holy, for I am holy":
B.   Just as I am holy, so are you holy. Just as I am separate, so you be separate.

III. Matters of Philosophy, Natural Science and Metaphysics

There is nothing relevant.

18

Sifra to Tazria

I. Unarticulated Premises: The Givens of Religious Conduct

The laws that are treated are specific to the passage, resting on no broader premises.

II. Unarticulated Premises: The Givens of Religious Conviction

1. Only Israelites are subject to uncleanness after giving birth; gentiles do not produce that differentiated level of uncleanness:

CXXI

I.1 A. ["The Lord spoke to Moses, saying, Speak to the Israelite people thus": (Lev. 12:1-8)]
   B. "...Israelite people":
   C. In this matter, the Israelite people are engaged, but idolators are not engaged in this matter.

I.2 A. "...Israelite people":
   B. I know only that born-Israelites are covered by the law.
   C. How do I know that subject to it are also women – proselytes and bondswomen, whether freed or not?
   D. Scripture says, "...a woman."

III. Matters of Philosophy, Natural Science and Metaphysics

The parashah presents nothing of philosophical interest.

19

Sifra to Negaim

I. Unarticulated Premises: The Givens of Religious Conduct

I cannot identify a relevant statement.

II. Unarticulated Premises: The Givens of Religious Conviction

1. It was only from the giving of the Torah that Israel became subject to certain forms of uncleanness; prior to that time, these sources of uncleanness proved ineffective:

CXXVII

II.1   A.   "When there will be" (Lev. 12:2) –

         B.   From the [time at which this law is] proclaimed [namely, Sinai] onward.

         C.   And is it not logical?

         D.   It [Scripture] has declared unclean with reference to those afflicted with flux [Lev. 15:1ff.: Zabim] and has declared unclean with reference to plagues.

         E.   Just as in the case of those afflicted with flux, it declared clear [such appearances of uncleanness as occurred] before the pronouncement [of the Torah], so in reference to plagues, it declared clear [such appearances of uncleanness as occurred] on them before the pronouncement.

III. Matters of Philosophy, Natural Science and Metaphysics

The parashah contains nothing relevant.

20

Sifra to Mesora

I. Unarticulated Premises: The Givens of Religious Conduct

The legal corpus derives entirely from the Mishnah.

II. Unarticulated Premises: The Givens of Religious Conviction

1. The uncleanness affecting houses applies only after the Israelites entered the land and took up their permanent residences. Prior to that time it did not apply to their housing:

CLV

I.1 A. "When you will come" (Lev. 14:34) – Might one think [the law applied] once they had come to the TransJordan?

B. Scripture says, "to the land" (Lev. 14:34) – to the land which is [set aside and] distinctive.

C. Might one think this law applied once they had come to Ammon and Moab?

D. Scripture says, "which I shall give to you" (Lev. 14:34) – and not Ammon and Moab [which do not belong to you].

I.2 A. "...as a possession" (Lev. 14:34) – after they will conquer it.

B. How do you know that once they had conquered it, but before they had divided it, once they had divided it among the families, but before they had divided it among the houses of the fathers, so that each one did not yet recognize his own property –

C. might one think that [under these circumstances] they should be susceptible to plagues?

D. Scripture says, "And he will come to him to whom the house belongs" (Lev. 14:35) – until each one shall know that which is his.

III. Matters of Philosophy, Natural Science and Metaphysics

There is nothing to examine.

21

Sifra to Zabim

I. Unarticulated Premises: The Givens of Religious Conduct

All I see are secondary reprises of available rules.

II. Unarticulated Premises: The Givens of Religious Conviction

1. Gentiles are excluded from this form of uncleanness:

CLX

I.1 B. Israelites are susceptible to uncleanness through flux, and gentiles are not susceptible to uncleanness through flux.

C. **And even if they [gentiles] are not susceptible to uncleanness through flux, they impart uncleanness like (K instead of B) Zabs.**

D. **And on their account they burn heave-offering.**

E. **And on their account are they [who touch gentiles] [T.2:1: *not*] liable for entering the sanctuary [while unclean on that account].**

F. Since [Scripture speaks of] people of Israel, I know only that Israelites [are susceptible to uncleanness through flux]. How do I know that I should encompass proselytes and slaves?

G. Scripture says, "Speak to the people of Israel and say to them, [When any] man [has a discharge from his body, the discharge is unclean" (Lev. 15:2)].

H. "I know only that man [is susceptible to uncleanness through flux].

I. "How do I know that I should encompass the woman and child?

J. "Scripture says, 'any man' (Lev. 15:2)," the words of R. Judah.

K. And R. Simeon [*sic!* b. b. Nid.: *Ishmael*] son of R. Yohanan b. Beroqah says, "Lo, Scripture says, '[When there will be] flux [from his body], his flux [will be unclean]' (Lev. 15:2).

L. "[This refers both] to male and to female.

M. "[In respect to] the male, [it means] any sort of male, whether adult or child, [with respect to] female, [it means] whether adult or child."

2. Flux uncleanness commenced with the revelation of the Torah; prior to that time, that form of uncleanness was null:

CLX

II.1 A. "When there will be" ["When any man has a discharge" (Lev. 15:2)] –

B. From the pronouncement [of the Torah] and thereafter.

III. Matters of Philosophy, Natural Science and Metaphysics

The question is inappropriate here.

22

Sifra to Aharé Mot

I. Unarticulated Premises: The Givens of Religious Conduct

The *parashah* is rich in theology but contains nothing concerning law that is remarkable.

II. Unarticulated Premises: The Givens of Religious Conviction

1. We differentiate among sins by reason of the attitude that accompanies them; those done deliberately differ in character and penalty from those done inadvertently:

CLXXXIV

2.   E.   Scripture says, "[because of the uncleannesses of the people of Israel] and because of their transgressions,"] and "transgressions" refers to acts of rebellion [that is, sins done deliberately].

        F.   And so Scripture uses the word, "The king of Moab has transgressed [deliberately] against me" (2 Kgs. 3:7).

        G.   And also: "Libnah likewise fell away at that time" (2 Kgs. 8:22, which uses the same word).

        H.   "Sins" ["all their sins"] fall into the category of acts of rebellion which are not subject to expiation through an offering.

2. Intentionality governs the definition of labor; an act of labor that is random or inconsequential is null:

CLXXXV

II.1   A.   "...and shall do no work":

        B.   Might one suppose that a person should not cut greens, make the beds, rinse glasses?

        C.   It is a matter of logic:

        D.   We find a reference here to acts of labor, and we find in connection with the building of the tabernacle reference to acts of labor.

E.   Just as acts of labor involved in the works of the tabernacle are those that involve a well-considered plan, so acts of labor covered here are those that involve a well-considered plan [Hillel: acts of labor that are regarded as important and not incidental].

F.   Just as acts of labor in the setting of the work of the tabernacle are acts of labor that are completed, so I know only that acts of labor that are completed are what are forbidden here:

G.   One should not write on a tablet, weave a garment, or complete a sieve.

H.   How do I know that one should not write even two letters, weave two knots, make even two squares of a sieve or a sifter?

I.   Scripture refers not only to "work" but "no work," which serves as an inclusionary statement.

J.   I know only that prohibited are acts of labor that are optional. How do I know that acts of labor that fall into the category of religious duties also are forbidden?

K.   For example, how do I know that one should not write two letters in scrolls, phylacteries, mezuzot; that one should not weave two knots even for priestly breeches or the veil?

L.   Scripture refers not only to "work" but "no work," which serves as an inclusionary statement.

M.   I know only that prohibited are acts of labor on account of which one is liable to extirpation. But how do I know that acts of labor on account of which one is not liable to extirpation also are forbidden on the Day of Atonement?

N.   For example, how do I know that one should not write even a single letter, weave even a single knot, make even a single square on a sieve or a sifter?

O.   Scripture refers not only to "work" but "no work," which serves as an inclusionary statement.

P.   I know that the prohibition extends only to acts of labor, the genus of which produces liability to extirpation. How do I know that one is prohibited from performing acts of labor, the genus of which does not produce liability to extirpation?

Q.   How do I know that on the Day of Atonement one should not climb a tree, ride on a beast, paddle on water, knock, splash, or dance?

R.   Scripture says, "It is a Sabbath of solemn rest," [so prohibiting acts that one may not perform merely as an aspect of solemn rest but not because they fall into the afore-listed classifications].

S.   I know only that the prohibition extends to optional actions that are forbidden as matters of Sabbath rest.

T.   How do I know that the law covers even actions that involve religious duties but that are forbidden as matters of Sabbath rest?

U.   How do I know, for example, that one should not pledge the valuation of someone [in the setting of Lev. 27:1ff.], or declare something *herem*, raise up or designate priestly rations, tithe, sanctify, issue a writ of divorce, carry out a rite of refusal, go through the ritual of loosening the shoe, enter into levirate marriage, redeem produce in the fourth year after its planting or second tithe?

V.   Scripture says, "It is a Sabbath of solemn rest."

3. Gentiles are not liable for actions carried on outside of the cult for which Israelites are culpable; proselytes and slaves are classed as Israel:

CLXXXVII

I.1   A.   ["And the Lord said to Moses, Say to Aaron and his sons and to all the people of Israel, This is the thing which the Lord has commanded. If any man of the house of Israel kills an ox or a lamb or a goat in the camp, or kills it outside the camp and does not bring it to the door of the tent of meeting, to offer it as a gift to the Lord before the tabernacle of the Lord, bloodguilt shall be imputed to that man" (Lev. 17:1-7).]

      B.   ["...the people of Israel":] the people of Israel are liable on the counts of slaughtering or offering up outside [of the temple],

      C.   but gentiles are not liable on the counts of slaughtering or offering up outside [of the temple].

      D.   And not this alone, but gentiles are permitted to make a high place anywhere and to make offerings to Heaven.

I.2   A.   Since [Scripture refers to] "people of Israel," I know only that the law covers Israelites.

      B.   How do I know that the law encompasses proselytes and slaves?

      C.   Scripture says, "Say to them."

CLXXXIX

I.1   A.   "And you shall say to them, [Any man of the house of Israel or of the strangers that sojourn among them who offers a burnt-offering or sacrifice and does not bring it to the door of the tent of meeting, to sacrifice it to the Lord, that man shall be cut off from his people]" (Lev. 17:8-9):

      B.   ["You shall say to them"] in accord with all that is stated in this passage.

      C.   "...Israel": this refers to Israelites.

      D.   "...strangers": this refers to proselytes.

      E.   "...that sojourn": encompasses the wives of proselytes.

      F.   "...among them": encompasses women and slaves.

4. God is creator, merciful, judge, and is reliable to mete out punishment and reward as appropriate:

CXCIII

I.1   A.   ["The Lord spoke to Moses saying, Speak to the Israelite people and say to them, I am the Lord your God. You shall not copy the practices of the land of Egypt where you dwelt, or of the land of Canaan to which I am taking you; nor shall you follow their laws. My rules alone shall you observe and faithfully follow my laws: I the Lord am your God. You shall keep my laws and my rules, by the pursuit of which man shall live: I am the Lord" (Lev. 18:1-30).]

      B.   "The Lord spoke to Moses saying, Speak to the Israelite people and say to them, I am the Lord your God":

C. "I am the Lord," for I spoke and the world came into being.

D. "I am full of mercy."

E. "I am judge to exact punishment and faithful to pay recompense."

F. "I am the one who exacted punishment from the generation of the Flood and the men of Sodom and Egypt, and I shall exact punishment from you if you act like them."

5. The moment of the Exodus involved the most despicable generation of the most despicable nations, the Egyptians and the Canaanites:

CXCIII

I.2   A. And how do we know that there was never any nation among all of the nations that practiced such abominations, more than did the Egyptians?

      B. Scripture says, "You shall not copy the practices of the land of Egypt where you dwelt."

      C. And how do we know that the last generation did more abhorrent things than all the rest of them?

      D. Scripture says, "You shall not copy the practices of the land of Egypt."

      E. And how do we know that the people in the last location in which the Israelites dwelt were more abhorrent than all the rest?

      F. Scripture says, "...where you dwelt, you shall not do."

      G. And how do we know that the fact that the Israelites dwelt there was the cause for all these deeds?

      H. Scripture says, "You shall not copy...where you dwelt."

I.3   A. How do we know that there was never a nation among all the nations that did more abhorrent things than the Canaanites?

      B. Scripture says, "You shall not copy the practices...of the land of Canaan [to which I am taking you; nor shall you follow their laws]."

      C. And how do we know that the last generation did more abhorrent things than all the rest of them?

      D. Scripture says, "You shall not copy the practices of the land of Canaan."

      E. And how do we know that the people in the place to which the Israelites were coming for conquest were more abhorrent than all the rest?

      F. Scripture says, "...to which I am taking you."

      G. And how do we know that it is the arrival of the Israelites that caused them to do all these deeds?

      H. Scripture says, "or of the land of Canaan to which I am taking you; nor shall you follow their laws."

CXCIV

II.7   A. "You shall not copy the practices of the land of Egypt where you dwelt":

      B. Scripture makes the point that the practices of the Egyptians were the most corrupt of those of all peoples,

      C. and that place in which Israel dwelt was the most corrupt in the land of Egypt.

II.8   A.   "...or of the land of Canaan to which I am taking you":

        B.   Now was it not perfectly well-known that they were coming to the land of Canaan?

        C.   Why does Scripture make this point, saying "or of the land of Canaan to which I am taking you"?

        D.   But Scripture so makes the point that the practices of the Canaanites were the most corrupt of those of all peoples,

        E.   and that place to which the Israelites were planning to go was the most corrupt of all.

II.9   A.   "You shall not copy the practices of the land of Egypt where you dwelt, or of the land of Canaan to which I am taking you":

        B.   Scripture thereby treats as analogous the practices of the Egyptians and the practices of the Canaanites.

        C.   What were the practices of the Canaanites?

        D.   They were flooded with idolatry, fornication, murder, pederasty, and bestiality.

        E.   So the practices of the Egyptians were the same.

        F.   Then why did the Egyptians receive their punishment forty years ahead of the Canaanites?

        G.   It was as a reward for their paying honor to that righteous man, as it is said, "Hear us, my lord, you are the elect of God among us" (Gen. 23:6).

        H.   and further: "[The name of Hebron was formerly Kiriath-arba;] he was the great man among the Anakites. And the land had rest from war" (Josh. 14:15).

6.   There is a world to come, in which the full recompense for what is done in this world is rewarded or punished:

II.10   A.   "...shall live":

        B.   in the world to come.

        C.   And should you wish to claim that the reference is to this world, is it not the fact that in the end one dies?

        D.   Lo, how am I to explain, "...shall live"?

        E.   It is with reference to the world to come.

II.11   A.   "I the Lord am your God":

        B.   faithful to pay a reward.

7.   Gentiles as much as Israelites are subject to the laws governing sexual relations:

CXCIV

I.1   A.   "None of you [shall come near anyone of his own flesh to uncover nakedness; I am the Lord]":

        B.   [Since the Hebrew for "none of you" is, "a man, a man,"] why is it that Scripture says, "a man, a man"?

        C.   It serves to encompass gentiles, who are admonished against incest like Israelites.

8.   Israel is elect by reason of accepting the Torah:

CXCIV

II.1   A.   "The Lord spoke to Moses saying, Speak to the Israelite people and say to them, I am the Lord your God":

      B.   R. Simeon b. Yohai says, "That is in line with what is said elsewhere: 'I am the Lord your God [who brought you out of the land of Egypt, out of the house of bondage]' (Ex. 20:2).

      C.   "'Am I the Lord, whose sovereignty you took upon yourself in Egypt?'

      D.   "They said to him, 'Indeed.'

      E.   "'Indeed you have accepted my dominion.'

      F.   "'They accepted my decrees: "You will have no other gods before me."'

      G.   "That is what is said here: 'I am the Lord your God,' meaning, 'Am I the one whose dominion you accepted at Sinai?'

      H.   "They said to him, 'Indeed.'

      I.   "'Indeed you have accepted my dominion.'

      J.   "'They accepted my decrees: "You shall not copy the practices of the land of Egypt where you dwelt, or of the land of Canaan to which I am taking you; nor shall you follow their laws."'"

9.   Some of the laws of the Torah are logical, and if they had not been written in the Torah, it would have been logical to write them:

CXLIV

II.11 A.   "You shall keep my laws":

      B.   This refers to matters that are written in the Torah.

      C.   But if they had not been written in the Torah, it would have been entirely logical to write them,

      D.   for example, rules governing thievery, fornication, idolatry, blasphemy, murder,

      E.   examples of rules that, had they not been written in the Torah, would have been logical to include them.

      F.   Then there are those concerning which the impulse to do evil raises doubt, the nations of the world, idolators, raise doubt,

      G.   for instance, the prohibition against eating pork, wearing mixed species, the rite of removing the shoe in the case of the deceased childless brother's widow, the purification rite for the person afflicted with the skin ailment, the goat that is sent forth –

      H.   cases in which the impulse to do evil raises doubt, the nations of the world, idolators, raise doubt.

      I.   In this regard Scripture says, "I the Lord have made these ordinances, and you have no right to raise doubts concerning them."

10.   A gentile who keeps the Torah is in the status of the high priest:

CXCIV

II.15 A.   "...by the pursuit of which man shall live":

      B.   R. Jeremiah says, "How do I know that even a gentile who keeps the Torah, lo, he is like the high priest?

C.   "Scripture says, 'by the pursuit of which man shall live.'"

D.   And so he says, "'And this is the Torah of the priests, Levites, and Israelites,' is not what is said here, but rather, 'This is the Torah of the man, O Lord God' (2 Sam. 7:19)."

E.   And so he says, "'open the gates and let priests, Levites, and Israelites enter it' is not what is said, but rather, 'Open the gates and let the righteous nation, who keeps faith, enter it' (Isa. 26:2)."

F.   And so he says, "'This is the gate of the Lord. Priests, Levites, and Israelites...' is not what is said, but rather, 'the righteous shall enter into it' (Ps. 118:20).

G.   And so he says, "'What is said is not, 'Rejoice, priests, Levites, and Israelites,' but rather, 'Rejoice, O righteous, in the Lord' (Ps. 33:1)."

H.   And so he says, "It is not, 'Do good, O Lord, to the priests, Levites, and Israelites,' but rather, 'Do good, O Lord, to the good, to the upright in heart' (Ps. 125:4)."

I.   "Thus, even a gentile who keeps the Torah, lo, he is like the high priest."

11. There are forbidden deeds that one may do to save one's life, if the situation is not public; but in public one must opt for martyrdom:

CXCIV

II.16 A.   "...by the pursuit of which man shall live":

B.   not that he should die by them.

C.   R. Ishmael would say, "How do you know that if people should say to someone when entirely alone, 'Worship an idol and do not be put to death,' the person should worship the idol and not be put to death?

D.   "Scripture says, 'by the pursuit of which man shall live,' not that he should die by them."

E.   "But even if it is in public should he obey them?

F.   "Scripture says, '[You shall faithfully observe my commandments; I am the Lord.] You shall not profane my holy name, that I may be sanctified in the midst of the Israelite people – I the Lord who sanctified you, I who brought you out of the land of Egypt to be your God, I the Lord' (Lev. 22:31-32).

G.   "If you sanctify my name, then I shall sanctify my name through you.

H.   "For that is just as Hananiah, Mishael, and Azariah did.

I.   "When all of the nations of the world at that time were prostrate before the idol, while they stood up like palm trees.

J.   "And concerning them it is stated explicitly in tradition: 'Your stately form is like the palm' (Song 7:8).

K.   "'I say, let me climb the palm, let me take hold of its branches; [let your breasts be like clusters of grapes, your breath like the fragrance of apples, and your mouth like choicest wine]' (Ps. 7:9).

L.   "'This day I shall be exalted in the sight of the nations of the world, who deny the Torah.

M.   "'This day I shall exact vengeance for them from those who hate them.

N.   "'This day I shall resurrect the dead among them.'

O.   "I am the Lord":

P.   "I am judge to exact punishment and faithful to pay a reward.

III. Matters of Philosophy, Natural Science and Metaphysics

I see nothing relevant.

23

Sifra to Qedoshim

I. Unarticulated Premises: The Givens of Religious Conduct

The expositions of the law all prove either paraphrastic or secondary to the Mishnah, so far as I can see.

II. Unarticulated Premises: The Givens of Religious Conviction

1. Israel is holy, that is, separate, like God; the sanctification of Israel also represents the sanctification of God; but God remains sanctified even if Israel does not; it is Israel's task to imitate God:

CXCV

I.1 A. "And the Lord said to Moses, Say to all the congregation of the people of Israel, You shall be holy, [for I the Lord your God am holy. Every one of you shall revere his mother and his father, and you shall keep my sabbaths; I am the Lord your God. Do not turn to idols or make for yourselves molten gods; I am the Lord your God]" (Lev. 19:1-4):

B. This teaches that this chapter was stated in the assembly of all Israel.

C. And why was it stated in the assembly of all Israel?

D. It is because most of the principles of the Torah depend upon its contents.

I.2 A. "You shall be holy":

B. "You shall be separate."

I.3 A. "You shall be holy, for I the Lord your God am holy":

B. That is to say, "if you sanctify yourselves, I shall credit it to you as though you had sanctified me, and if you do not sanctify yourselves, I shall hold that it is as if you have not sanctified me."

C. Or perhaps the sense is this: "If you sanctify me, then lo, I shall be sanctified, and if not, I shall not be sanctified"?

D. Scripture says, "For I...am holy," meaning, I remain in my state of sanctification, whether or not you sanctify me.

E.　Abba Saul says, "The king has a retinue, and what is the task thereof? It is to imitate the king."

2.　Man and woman are equally obligated to carry out the Torah, but there are commandments that a woman, by reason of her imputed situation, is unable to carry out:

CXCV

II.1　A.　"Every one [Hebrew: man] [of you shall revere his mother and his father, and you shall keep my sabbaths]":

　　　B.　I know only that a man [is subject to the instruction].

　　　C.　How do I know that a woman is also involved?

　　　D.　Scripture says, "...shall revere" [using the plural].

　　　E.　Lo, both genders are covered.

II.2　A.　If so, why does Scripture refer to "man"?

　　　B.　It is because a man controls what he needs, while a woman does not control what she needs, since others have dominion over her.

3.　It is the intentionality of the human being that renders objects into gods. If one treats an object as an idol, it is an idol:

CXCV

I.9　A.　"Do not turn to idols or make for yourselves molten gods":

　　　B.　"To begin with, they are idols. But if you turn to them, you make them into gods."

4.　One should not harbor ill intent toward the other, but one also should express in so many words one's rebuke:

CC

III.1　A.　"You shall not hate your brother in your heart, [but reasoning, you shall reason with your neighbor, lest you bear sin because of him. You shall not take vengeance or bear any grudge against the sons of your own people, but you shall love your neighbor as yourself: I am the Lord]" (Lev. 19:17-18).

　　　B.　Might one suppose that one should not curse him, set him straight, or contradict him?

　　　C.　Scripture says, "in your heart."

　　　D.　I spoke only concerning hatred that is in the heart.

III.2　A.　And how do we know that if one has rebuked him four or five times, he should still go and rebuke him again?

　　　B.　Scripture says, "reasoning, you shall reason with your neighbor."

　　　C.　Might one suppose that that is the case even if one rebukes him and his countenance blanches?

　　　D.　Scripture says, "lest you bear sin."

5.　The Golden Rule is the foundation of the Torah, that is, Judaism:

CC

III.7　A.　"...But you shall love your neighbor as yourself: [I am the Lord]":

B. R. Aqiba says, "This is the encompassing principle of the Torah."
C. Ben Azzai says, "'This is the book of the generations of Adam' (Gen. 5:1) is a still more encompassing principle."

6. The Torah is phrased in accord with the rules of ordinary human speech:

CCVI

I.1 A. ["The Lord said to Moses, Say to the people of Israel" (Lev. 20:1-5).]
B. "Say to the people of Israel":
C. "And speak to the people of Israel" (Ex. 30:31).
D. "Say to the people of Israel" (Lev. 20:1).
E. "Speak to the people of Israel" (Ex. 14:2).
F. "Command the people of Israel" (Lev. 24:2).
G. "And you will command the people of Israel" (Ex. 27:20).
H. R. Yosé says, "The Torah uses the speech of ordinary mortals, utilizing many kinds of phrases, and all of them are there to be interpreted."

7. Israel's claim to the holy land is eternal, because Israel was given the Torah to keep; Israel is to be separate from the nations; Israel should keep the Torah not by reason of desire but by reason of obligation:

CCVII

II.1 A. "You shall therefore keep all my statutes and all my ordinances and do them; [that the land where I am bringing you to dwell may not vomit you out. And you shall not walk in the customs of the nation which I am casting out before you; for they did all these things, and therefore I abhorred them. But I have said to you, You shall inherit their land, and I will give it to you to possess, a land flowing with milk and honey. I am the Lord your God who have separated you from the peoples. You shall therefore make a distinction between the clean beast and the unclean, and between the unclean bird and the clean; you shall not make yourselves abominable by beast or by bird or by anything with which the ground teems, which I have set apart for you to hold unclean. You shall be holy to me, for I the Lord am holy and have separated you from the peoples, that you should be mine" (Lev. 20:22-26).]
B. This serves to assign both keeping and doing to the ordinances, and keeping and doing to the statutes.

II.2 A. "...That the land where I am bringing you to dwell may not vomit you out":
B. "For I am bringing you there only so that you will inherit it, not like the Canaanites, who kept the place intact until your arrival."

II.3 A. "And you shall not walk in the customs of the nation [which I am casting out before you]":
B. this refers to the Egyptians.
C. "...Which I am casting out before you":
D. this refers to the Canaanites.

II.4 A. "...For they did all these things, [and therefore I abhorred them]":

	B.	This teaches that the Canaanites were flooded with these things.
	C.	"I sent them into exile only on account of these things."
II.5	A.	"...And therefore I abhorred them":
	B.	"I abhorred them like someone who is repelled by his food."
II.6	A.	"But I have said to you, You shall inherit their land:
	B.	"You are worthy of disinheriting them, for you were the first to open [up and choose the Holy One (Hillel)],
	C.	as it is said, "A garden locked is my own, my bride, a fountain locked, a sealed-up spring" (Song 4:12).
II.7	A.	"...And I will give it to you to possess":
	B.	as an inheritance for eternity.
	C.	Now might you say, "You have in hand to give us only what belongs to someone else,"
	D.	is it not, in fact, your own, for it is only the portion assigned to Shem, and you are the descendants of Shem,
	E.	while they [the Canaanites] are the descendants only of Ham, so what are they doing in it?
	F.	They were simply keeping the place until you got there.
II.8	A.	"I am the Lord your God who has separated you from the peoples":
	B.	"See how vast is the difference between you and the idolatrous nations!
	C.	"One of them fixes up his wife and hands her over to someone else [for sexual relations], a man fixes up himself and gives himself to someone else [for sexual relations]."
II.9	A.	"You shall therefore make a distinction between the clean beast and the unclean":
	B.	Scripture should say, "between a cow and an ass." For has the matter at hand not already been spelled out? Why therefore does it say, "You shall therefore make a distinction between the clean beast and the unclean"?
	C.	The sense is, between what is clean for you and what is unclean for you,
	D.	specifically, between the one the greater part of the gullet of which has been cut and the one only half of which has been cut.
	E.	And what is the difference between the greater part and half?
	F.	A hair's breadth.
II.10	A.	"...And between the unclean bird and the clean; you shall not make yourselves abominable by beast or by bird or by anything with which the ground teems, which I have set apart for you to hold unclean":
	B.	that is, to subject such to a prohibition.
II.11	A.	"You shall be holy to me, for I the Lord am holy":
	B.	"Just as I am holy, so you be holy.
	C.	"Just as I am separate, so you be separate."
II.12	A.	"...And have separated you from the peoples, that you should be mine":
	B.	"If you are separated from the nations, lo, you are for my Name, and if not, lo, you belong to Nebuchadnezzar, king of Babylonia, and his associates."

II.13   A.   R. Eleazar b. Azariah says, "How do we know that someone should not say, 'I do not want to wear mixed fibers, I don't want to eat pork, I don't want to have incestuous sexual relations.'

B.   "Rather: 'I do want [to wear mixed fibers, I do want to eat pork, I do want to have incestuous sexual relations.] But what can I do? For my father in heaven has made a decree for me!'

C.   "So Scripture says, 'and have separated you from the peoples, that you should be mine.'

D.   "So one will turn out to keep far from transgression and accept upon himself the rule of Heaven."

8.   Israel consecrates itself by giving up idolatry in particular; God is reliable both in penalizing sin and in rewarding right behavior:

CCVIII

I.2   A.   "Consecrate yourselves, therefore, and be holy":

B.   This refers to the sanctification achieved through separation from idolatry.

C.   Or perhaps it refers to the sanctification involved in carrying out all religious duties?

D.   When Scripture says, "You shall be holy" (Lev. 19:1), lo, we find reference to the sanctification involved in carrying out all the religious duties.

E.   What then is the sense of the statement, "Consecrate yourselves, therefore, and be holy, for I am the Lord your God"?

F.   This refers to the sanctification achieved through separation from idolatry.

I.3   A.   "...For I am the Lord your God":

B.   I am the Judge for exacting penalty and faithful to pay a reward.

I.4   A.   "Keep my statutes and do them":

B.   I know only the matters that Scripture has spelled out in detail.

C.   How do I derive the rest of the details of the passage?

D.   Scripture says, "Keep my statutes and do them."

I.5   A.   "I am the Lord who sanctifies you":

B.   "Just as I am holy, so you be holy."

III. Matters of Philosophy, Natural Science and Metaphysics

No composition belongs here.

24

Sifra to Emor

I. Unarticulated Premises: The Givens of Religious Conduct

I find systematic expansion of the law, but no fresh conceptions that may be classified as premises or presuppositions.

II. Unarticulated Premises: The Givens of Religious Conviction

1. There is such a thing as an excess of punctiliousness about the law:

CXI

I.20   A.   There was the case of Joseph b. Paxes, on the foot of whom a wart came up. The physician wanted to chop it off.

       B.   He said to him, "When you have cut it so as to leave only a thread like a hair's breadth, tell me."

       C.   He chopped it off until he left only a thread like a hair's breadth and told him.

       D.   He called Nehunia, his son, and said to him, "Honia, my son, up to this point you were obligated to take care of me. From this point, go out, for a priest does not contract corpse uncleanness on account of a corpse from a living person in the case of his father."

       E.   And when the case came before sages, they said, "This is the sort of case concerning which Scripture says, 'Sometimes a righteous man perishes in spite of his righteousness' (Qoh. 7:15).

       F.   "The righteous man perishes, and his righteousness with him."

2. We distinguish three periods in human history: prior to Sinai, Sinai, and after Sinai, and different laws apply to each period, respectively:

CCXVII

II.1   A.   "Say to them":

       B.   to those who are standing before Mount Sinai.

II.2   A.   "If any one of all your descendants throughout your generations":

       B.   this teaches that the law applies for generations to come.

3. God is faithful to protect Israel and reward the keeping of the commandments. But people may not obey by reason of stipulations or conditions that must be met; obedience must be totally gratuitous. God will respond to what is freely given by giving freely, but God cannot be coerced. Divine justice is inexorable:

CCXXVII

I.3   A.   "So you shall keep my commandments and do them: [I am the Lord]":

      B.   this serves to assign to the commandments the duties of both keeping and doing them.

      C.   "I am the Lord":

      D.   faithful to pay a reward.

I.4   A.   "And you shall not profane [my holy name]":

      B.   I derive the implication from the statement, "you shall not profane," that sanctification is covered.

      C.   And when Scripture says, "but I will be hallowed," the sense is, "Give yourself and sanctify my name."

      D.   Might one suppose that that is when one is all alone?

      E.   Scripture says, "among the people of Israel."

I.5   A.   In this connection sages have said:

      B.   Whoever gives his life on condition that a miracle is done for him – no miracle will be done for him.

      C.   But if it is not on condition that a miracle be done for him, a miracle will be done for him.

      D.   For so we find in the case of Hananiah, Mishael, and Azariah, that they said to Nebuchadnezzar, "We have no need to answer you in this matter, for if so it must be, our God whom we serve is able to save us from the burning fiery furnace, and he will save us from your power, O king. But even if he does not, be it known to you, O king, that we will not serve your god or worship the statue of gold that you have set up" (Dan. 3:16-18).

      E.   And when Marianos seized Pappos and Lulianos, brothers in Laodicea, he said to them, "If you come from the people of Hananiah, Mishael, and Azariah, let your God come and save you from my power."

      F.   They said to him, "Hananiah, Mishael, and Azariah were worthy men, and Nebuchadnezzar was a king worthy of having a miracle done on his account.

      G.   "But you are a wicked king, and you are not worthy of having a miracle done on your account, and, for our part, we are liable to the death penalty inflicted by heaven, so if you do not kill us, there are plenty of agents of punishment before the Omnipresent, plenty of bears, plenty of lions, plenty of panthers, plenty of fiery snakes, plenty of scorpions, to do injury to us.

      H.   "But in the end the Omnipresent is going to demand the penalty of our blood from your hand."

      I.   They say that he did not leave there before orders came from Rome, and they chopped off his head with axes.

I.6   A.   "Who brought you out of the land of Egypt":

B.　　"I brought you out of the land of Egypt on a stipulation that you be prepared to give yourselves to sanctify my name."

I.7　A.　　"I to be your God":

B.　　like it or not.

I.8　A.　　"I am the Lord":

B.　　I am faithful to pay a reward.

4. Moses stated the Torah with great precision, each item at the right time and exactly as he was instructed:

CCXXXIX

III.1　A.　　"Thus Moses declared to the people of Israel the appointed feasts of the Lord" (Lev. 23:44):

B.　　This teaches that Moses stated to the Israelites the laws of Passover on Passover, the laws of Pentecost on Pentecost, the laws of the Festival on the Festival.

C.　　In precisely the language that he heard he stated to Israel.

III. Matters of Philosophy, Natural Science and Metaphysics

1. Taxonomic differences yield that similar categories do not follow the same rule, so if the same rule is to pertain to both classes, it must be made explicit by Scripture:

CCXI

I.10　A.　　Why does Scripture refer to "his son" and why does Scripture refer to "his daughter"?

B.　　The reason is that there are indicative traits pertaining to the son and not the daughter, and there are indicative traits pertaining to the daughter and not the son.

C.　　As to the son, the father bears responsibility in his regard for various religious duties, to circumcise him, to redeem him if he is kidnapped, to teach him Torah, to teach him a trade, to marry him off, which is not the case in regard to the daughter.

D.　　As to the daughter, the father enjoys the right to keep things that she may find and the work of her hands, as well as to annul her vows, none of which rights he possesses in the case of the son.

E.　　Accordingly, [these taxonomic differences made it] necessary to refer explicitly both to the son and to the daughter.

25

Sifra to Behar

I. Unarticulated Premises: The Givens of Religious Conduct

All the legal passages rest on the Mishnah's or the Torah's laws.

II. Unarticulated Premises: The Givens of Religious Conviction

1. All of the principles and details of the law derive from Sinai, without differentiation:

CCXLV

I.1   A.   ["The Lord said to Moses on Mount Sinai, Say to the people of Israel, When you come into the land which I give you, the land shall keep a sabbath to the Lord. Six years you shall sow your field, and six years you shall prune your vineyard and gather in its fruits; but in the seventh year there shall be a sabbath of solemn rest for the land, a sabbath to the Lord; you shall not sow your field or prune your vineyard. What grows of itself in your harvest you shall not reap, and the grapes of your undressed vine you shall not gather; it shall be a year of solemn rest for the land. The sabbath of the land shall provide food for you, for yourself and for your male and female slaves and for your hired servant and the sojourner who lives with you; for your cattle also and for the beasts that are in your land all its yield shall be for food" (Lev. 25:1-7).]

       B.   "The Lord said to Moses on Mount Sinai":

       C.   What has the topic of the Sabbatical Year of the land to do in particular with Mount Sinai [that of all subjects, this is the one that is explicitly tied to revelation at Sinai]?

       D.   Is it not the fact that all religious duties were announced at Sinai?

       E.   The point is that just as in the case of the Sabbatical Year both the governing principles and the details were announced from Sinai,

       F.   so all of the other religious duties' governing principles and details were announced from Sinai.

2. Israelites in gentile service are not to adopt idolatry, even though gentiles in Israelite service are converted to Judaism:

CCLXIX

II.5   A.   "...for I am the Lord your God. You shall keep my sabbaths and reverence my sanctuary":

     B.   It is concerning a Jew who sells himself to a gentile that Scripture speaks.

     C.   He should not say, "Since my master serves an idol, so shall I serve an idol; since my master fornicates, so shall I fornicate; since my master profanes the Sabbath day, so shall I profane the Sabbath day."

     D.   Scripture says, "You shall make for yourselves no idols.... You shall keep my sabbaths."

II.6   A.   "...and reverence my sanctuary":

     B.   In this passage Scripture has given an admonition concerning all the commandments.

II.7   A.   "...for I am the Lord your God":

     B.   faithful to pay a reward.

III. Matters of Philosophy, Natural Science and Metaphysics

I see nothing that pertains.

26

Sifra to Behuqotai

I. Unarticulated Premises: The Givens of Religious Conduct

Nothing pertains.

II. Unarticulated Premises: The Givens of Religious Conviction

1. God wants Israel to labor in the Torah, and learning in the Torah is as important as practicing the religious duties that the Torah sets forth:

CCLX

I.1   A.   ["If you walk in my statutes and observe my commandments and do them, then I will give you your rains in their season, and the land shall yield its increase, and the trees of the field shall yield their fruit. And your threshing shall last to the time of vintage, and the vintage shall last to the time for sowing; and you shall eat your bread to the full and dwell in your land securely. And I will give peace in the land, and you shall lie down and none shall make you afraid; and I will remove evil beasts from the land, and the sword shall not go through your land. And you shall chase your enemies, and they shall fall before you by the sword. Five of you shall chase a hundred, and a hundred of you shall chase ten thousand; and your enemies shall fall before you by the sword. And I will have regard for you and make you fruitful and multiply you, and will confirm my covenant with you. And you shall eat old store long kept, and you shall clear out the old to make way for the new. And I will make my abode among you, and my soul shall not abhor you. And I will walk among you and will be your God and you shall be my people. I am the Lord your God, who brought you forth out of the land of Egypt, that you should not be their slaves; and I have broken the bars of your yoke and made you walk erect" (Lev. 26:3-13).]

         B.   "If you walk in my statutes":

C. This teaches that the Omnipresent desires the Israelites to work in the Torah.

D. And so Scripture says, "O that my people would listen to me, that Israel would walk in my ways! I would soon subdue their enemies and turn my hand against their foes" (Ps. 81:13-14).

E. "O that you had hearkened to my commandments! Then your peace would have been like a river, and your righteousness like the waves of the sea; your offspring would have been like the sand, and your descendants like its grains; their name would never be cut off or destroyed from before me" (Isa. 48:18).

F. And so Scripture says, "Oh that they had such a mind as this always, to fear me and to keep all my commandments, that it might go well with them and with their children forever" (Deut. 5:29).

G. This teaches that the Omnipresent desires the Israelites to work in the Torah.

I.2 A. "If you walk in my statutes":

B. Might this refer to the religious duties?

C. When Scripture says, "and observe my commandments and do them,"

D. lo, the religious duties are covered. Then how shall I interpret, "If you walk in my statutes"?

E. It is that they should work in the Torah.

F. And so it is said, "But if you will not hearken to me."

G. Might that refer to the religious duties?

H. When Scripture says, "and will not do all these commandments,"

I. lo, the religious duties are covered.

J. If so, why is it said, "But if you will not hearken to me"?

K. It is that they should be working in the Torah.

I.3 A. And so Scripture says, "Remember the Sabbath day to keep it holy" (Ex. 20:8).

B. Might one suppose that what is involved is only to do so in your heart?

C. When Scripture says, "Observe [the Sabbath day]" (Deut. 5:12), lo, keeping it in the heart is covered.

D. How then am I to interpret "remember"?

E. It means that you should repeat with your mouth [the teachings concerning the Sabbath day].

F. And so Scripture says, "Remember and do not forget how you provoked the Lord your God to wrath in the wilderness, from the day you came out of the land of Egypt until you came to this place" (Deut. 9:7).

G. Might one suppose that what is involved is only to do so in your heart?

H. Scripture says, "and do not forget."

I. Lo, forgetting in the heart is covered.

J. How then am I to interpret "remember"?

K. It means that you should repeat with your mouth [the record of your behavior in the wilderness].

L. And so Scripture says, "[Take heed, in an attack of leprosy, to be very careful to do according to all that the Levitical priests shall direct you; as I commanded them, so you shall be careful to do.]

Remember what the Lord your God did to Miriam on the way as you came forth out of Egypt" (Deut. 24:9).

M.   Might one suppose that what is involved is only to do so in your heart?

N.   When Scripture says, "Take heed, in an attack of leprosy, to be very careful to do,"

O.   lo, forgetting in the heart is covered.

P.   How then am I to interpret "remember"?

Q.   It means that you should repeat with your mouth [the lessons to be learned in respect to Miriam].

R.   And so Scripture says, "Remember what Amalek did to you on the way as you came out of Egypt...[you shall blot out the remembrance of Amalek from under heaven; you shall not forget]" (Deut. 25:17, 19).

S.   Might one suppose that what is involved is only to do so in your heart?

T.   When Scripture says, "you shall not forget,"

U.   lo, forgetting in the heart is covered.

V.   How then am I to interpret "remember"?

W.   It means that you should repeat with your mouth [the record of Amalek].

I.4   A.   And so Scripture says, "And I will lay your cities waste."

B.   Might one suppose that that is of human settlement?

C.   When Scripture says, "And I will devastate the land,"

D.   lo, that covers human settlement.

E.   Then how am I to interpret, "And I will lay your cities waste"?

F.   It means there will be no wayfarers.

I.5   A.   And so Scripture says, "and will make your sanctuaries desolate."

B.   Might one suppose that that is desolate of offerings?

C.   When Scripture says, "and I will not smell your pleasing odors,"

D.   lo, that covers the offerings.

E.   Then how am I to interpret, "and will make your sanctuaries desolate"?

F.   They will be laid waste even of pilgrims.

I.6   A.   "If you walk in my statutes and observe my commandments and do them":

B.   One who studies in order to do, not one who studies not in order to do.

C.   For one who studies not in order to do – it would have been better for him had he not been created.

2.   Sin is what causes calamity, famine and the like:

CCLXI

I.2   A.   There was the case, in the time of Herod, in which the rain would come by night. At dawn the sun shown, the wind blew, the land dried out [so that it could be worked],

B.   and the workers would go out to their labor knowing that the things that they did were for the sake of heaven.

I.3   A.   "...then I will give you your rains in their season":

B.   on the night of the Sabbath [when no work can be done anyhow].

I.4 A. There was the case, in the time of Simeon b. Shatah, in the time of Queen Shelamsu, when it would rain from Friday night to Friday night [on a weekly basis],

B. so that the grains of wheat grew as large as beans, and the grains of barley were like olive pits, and the lentils were like golden denars.

C. Sages made a bundle of some of them and left them behind for coming generations,

D. so as to demonstrate how much sin accomplishes [in less virtuous generations].

E. This serves to illustrate the following:

F. "But your iniquities have made a separation between you and your God, and your sins have hidden his face from you, so that he does not hear" (Isa. 59:2).

G. They have held back goodness from you.

2. Nature was perfect in the time of the First Man (Adam), but sin corrupted nature:

I.5 A. "...then I will give you your rains in their season":

B. But not the rain that is coming on all other lands.

C. Then how shall I interpret, "and by you all the families of the earth shall bless themselves" (Gen. 12:3), and through your seed?

D. There will be abundance in the land of Israel and famine in all the other lands, and the others will come and buy from you, so that they will make them wealthy in capital [through trading with you].

E. That is in line with what is said in connection with Joseph:

F. "And Joseph gathered up all the money that was found in the land of Egypt and in the land of Canaan for the grain which they bought" (Gen. 47:14).

G. And so, too: "And as your days, so shall your strength be" (Deut. 33:25).

H. For all the lands will collect money and bring it to the land of Israel.

I.6 A. "...and the land shall yield its increase":

B. Not as the land does now, but as in the time of the first Adam.

C. And how do we know that the land is going to be sown and yield produce on the same day?

D. Scripture says, "He has caused his wonderful works to be remembered [the Lord is gracious and merciful. He provides food for those who fear him]" (Ps 111:4-5).

E. And so, too: "Let the earth put forth vegetation, plants yielding seed [and fruit trees bearing fruit in which is their seed...and it was so. The earth brought forth vegetation, plants yielding seed...and trees bearing fruit]..." (Gen. 1:11-12).

F. This teaches that on the same day on which the seed was sown, the produce came forth on that same day.

I.7 A. "...and the trees of the field shall yield their fruit":

B. Not as the land does now, but as in the time of the first Adam.

C. And how do we know that the trees are going to be planted and yield fruit on the same day?

D. Scripture says, "He has caused his wonderful works to be remembered [the Lord is gracious and merciful. He provides food for those who fear him]" (Ps. 111:4-5).

E. And so, too: "and fruit trees bearing fruit in which is their seed...and it was so. The earth brought forth vegetation, plants yielding seed...and trees bearing fruit]..." (Gen. 1:11-12).

F. This teaches that on the same day on which the trees are planted they will yield fruit on that same day.

3. Israel meets God in the sanctuary; in the age to come, Israel will meet God face to face:

CCLXIII

["And you shall eat old store long kept, and you shall clear out the old to make way for the new. And I will make my abode among you, and my soul shall not abhor you. And I will walk among you and I will be your God and you shall be my people. I am the Lord your God, who brought you forth out of the land of Egypt, that you should not be their slaves; and I have broken the bars of your yoke and made you walk erect":]

I.3 A. "And I will make my abode among you":

B. This refers to the house of the sanctuary.

I.4 A. "...And my soul shall not abhor you":

B. Once I shall redeem you, I shall never again reject you.

I.5 A. "And I will walk among you":

B. The matter may be compared to the case of a king who went out to stroll with his sharecropper in an orchard.

C. But the sharecropper hid from him.

D. Said the king to that sharecropper, "How come you're hiding from me? Lo, I am just like you."

E. So the Holy One, blessed be He, said to the righteous, "Why are you trembling before me?"

F. So the Holy One, blessed be He, is destined to walk with the righteous in the Garden of Eden in the coming future, and the righteous will see him and tremble before him,

G. [and he will say to them,] "[How come you're trembling before me?] Lo, I am just like you."

4. Rebellion against God takes place when those who know the Torah despise it; not hearkening means knowing that God is lord and intentionally rebelling against him:

CCLXIV

I.1 A. "But if you will not hearken to me [and will not do all these commandments, if you spurn my statutes and if your soul abhors my ordinances, so that you will not do all my commandments but break my covenant, I will do this to you: I will appoint over you sudden terror, consumption and fever that waste the eyes and cause life to pine away. And you shall sow your seed in vain, for your enemies shall eat it; I will set my face against you, and you shall be smitten before your enemies; those who hate you shall rule over you, and you shall flee when none pursues you. And if in spite of this you will not hearken to me, then I will chastise you again sevenfold for your sins, and I will break the pride of your power, and I will make your heavens like iron and your earth like brass; and your strength shall be spent in vain, for your land shall not yield its increase and the trees of the land shall not yield their fruit]":

B. "But if you will not hearken to me" means, if you will not listen to the exposition of sages.

C. Might one suppose that reference is made to Scripture [rather than sages' teachings]?

D. When Scripture says, "and will not do all these commandments," lo, reference clearly is made to what is written in the Torah.

E. Then how shall I interpret, "But if you will not hearken to me"?

F. It means, if you will not listen to the exposition of sages.

I.2 A. "But if you will not hearken":

B. What is the point of Scripture here?

C. This refers to one who knows God's lordship and intentionally rebels against it.

D. And so Scripture says, "Like Nimrod, a mighty hunter [before the Lord]" (Gen. 10:9).

E. Now what is the point of saying "before the Lord"?

F. [It really means, rebellion, for the letters of the name for Nimrod can spell out "rebel," so that] this refers to one who knows God's lordship and intentionally rebels against it.

I.3 A. And so Scripture says, "The men of Sodom were evil and sinful against the Lord greatly" (Gen. 13:13).

B. Now why does Scripture say, "against the Lord"?

C. It is because they knew God's lordship and intentionally rebelled against it.

I.4 A. "But if you will not hearken to me [and will not do all these commandments]":

B. What is the point of Scripture in saying, "will not do"?

C. You have someone who does not learn but who carries out [the teachings of the Torah].

D. In that connection, Scripture says, "But if you will not hearken to me and will not do."

E. Lo, whoever does not learn [the Torah] also does not carry it out.

F. And you have someone who does not learn [the Torah] and also does not carry it out, but he does not despise others [who do so].

G. In that connection, Scripture says, "if you spurn my statutes."

H. Lo, whoever does not learn the Torah and does not carry it out in the end will despise others who do so.

I. And you furthermore have someone who does not learn [the Torah], and also does not carry it out, and he does despise others [who do so], but he does not hate the sages.

J. In that connection, Scripture says, "and if your soul abhors my ordinances" –

K. Lo, whoever does not learn [the Torah], also does not carry it out, and whoever does despise others [who do so], in the end will hate the sages.

L. And you furthermore have someone who does not learn [the Torah], does not carry it out, despises others [who do so], and hates the sages, but who lets others carry out [the Torah].

M. Scripture says, "so that you will not do [all my commandments but break my covenant]" –

N. lo, whoever does not learn [the Torah], does not carry it out, despises others [who do so], and hates the sages, in the end will not let others carry out [the Torah].

O. Or you may have someone who does not learn [the Torah], does not carry it out, despises others [who do so], hates the sages, does not let others carry out [the Torah], but he confesses that the religious duties were spoken from Sinai.

P. Scripture says, "all my commandments" –

Q. lo, whoever does not learn [the Torah], does not carry it out, despises others [who do so], hates the sages, does not let others carry out [the Torah], in the end will deny that the religious duties were spoken from Sinai.

R. Or you may have someone who exhibits all these traits but does not deny the very Principle [of God's existence and rule].

S. Scripture says, "but break my covenant" –

T. lo, whoever exhibits all these traits in the end will deny the very Principle [of God's existence and rule].

5. The power of repentence is such that, as soon as people repent, they are forgiven forthwith:

CCLXIX

II.1 A. "But if they confess their iniquity and the iniquity of their fathers [in their treachery which they committed against me, and also in walking contrary to me, so that I walked contrary to them and brought them into the land of their enemies; if then their uncircumcised heart is humbled and they make amends for their iniquity; then I will remember my covenant with Jacob, and I will remember my covenant also with Isaac and my covenant also with Abraham, and I will remember the land. But the land shall be left by them and enjoy its sabbaths while it lies desolate without them; and they shall make amends for their iniquity, because they spurned my ordinances, and their soul abhorred my statutes. Yet for all that, when they are in the land of their enemies, I will not spurn them, neither will I abhor them so as to destroy them utterly and break my covenant with them; for I am the Lord their God; but I will for their sake remember the covenant with their forefathers whom I brought forth out of the land of Egypt in the sight of the nations, that I might be their God: I am the Lord. These are the statutes and ordinances and laws which the Lord made between him and the people of Israel on Mount Sinai by Moses]" (Lev. 26:40-46):

B. This is how things are as to repentance,

C. for as soon as they confess their sins, I forthwith revert and have mercy on them,

D. as it is said, "But if they confess their iniquity and the iniquity of their fathers in their treachery which they committed against me."

CCLXIX

II.4 A. "...if then their uncircumcised heart is humbled and they make amends for their iniquity":

B. This is how things are as to repentance,

C. for as soon as they humble their heart in repentance, I forthwith revert and have mercy on them,

D. as it is said, "if then their uncircumcised heart is humbled and they make amends for their iniquity."

6. The exile was bad for Israel and Israel remained responsible for their sin when they were in exile:

3. A. "...and brought them into the land of their enemies":

B. This is a good deal for Israel.

C. For the Israelites are not to say, "Since we have gone into exile among the gentiles, let us act like them."

D. [God speaks:] "I shall not let them, but I shall call forth prophets against them, who will bring them back to the right way under my wings."

E. And how do we know?

F. "What is in your mind shall never happen, the thought, 'Let us be like the nations, like the tribes of the countries, and worship wood and stone.' 'As I live,' says the Lord God, 'surely with a mighty hand and an outstretched arm and with wrath poured out, I will be king over you. [I will bring you out from the peoples and gather you out of the countries where you are scattered, with a mighty hand and an outstretched arm and with wrath poured out'" (Ezek. 20:33-3).

G. "Whether you like it or not, with or without your consent, I shall establish my dominion over you."

7. The merit of the patriarchs stands up for Israel:

CCLXVIII

II.5 A. "...then I will remember my covenant with Jacob, [and I will remember my covenant also with Isaac and my covenant also with Abraham]":

B. Why are the patriarchs listed in reverse order?

C. It is to indicate, if the deeds of Abraham are not sufficient, then the deeds of Isaac, and if the deeds of Isaac are not worthy, then the deeds of Jacob.

D. Each one of them is worthy that the world should depend upon his intervention.

III. Matters of Philosophy, Natural Science and Metaphysics

I found nothing that pertains.

Part Four

SIFRÉ TO NUMBERS

27

Sifré to Numbers 1-58

I. Sifré to Numbers: Forms and Program

Sifré to Numbers provides a miscellaneous reading of most of the book of Numbers, but examining the implicit propositions of the recurrent forms of the document yields a clear-cut purpose. The document follows no topical program; but it also is unlike Mekhilta attributed to R. Ishmael because of its recurrent effort to prove a few fundamental points. True, these are general and not limited to a given set of cases or issues, so that the successive compositions that comprise Sifré to Numbers yield no propositional program. But the recurrent proofs of discrete propositions that time and again bear one and the same implication do accumulate and when we see what is implicit in the various explicit exercises, we find a clear-cut and rather rich message indeed.

The document as a whole through its fixed and recurrent formal preferences or literary structures makes two complementary points. [1] Reason unaided by Scripture produces uncertain propositions. [2] Reason operating within the limits of Scripture produces truth. These two principles are never articulated but left implicit in the systematic reading of most of the book of Numbers, verse by verse. The exegetical forms stand for a single proposition: while Scripture stands paramount, logic, reason, analytical processes of classification and differentiation, secondary, nonetheless, man's mind joins God's mind when man receives and sets forth the Torah. Only when we examine the rhetorical plan and then in search of the topical program reconsider the forms of the document does this propositional program emerge.

As with Sifra, therefore, Sifré to Numbers follows no topical program distinct from that of Scripture, which is systematically clarified, as we shall see in our sample of the document below. An interest in the relations to Scripture of the Mishnah and Tosefta, a concern with the dialectics characteristic of Sifra – these occur episodically, but scarcely define the character of the document. Its topical program and order derive from Scripture. As with Sifra, here, too, as we have already noticed, the sole point of coherence for the discrete sentences or paragraphs derives from the base verse of Scripture that is subject to commentary. At the same time, if we examine the incremental message, the cumulative effect, of the formal traits of speech and thought revealed in the uniform rhetoric and syntax of the document, we may discern a propositional program that is implicit in the rhetoric and logic of the compilation. What is required here is the articulation of the general consequences of numerous specific exegetical exercises.

If our authorship met the sets of writers whose consensus stands behind Sifra and Sifré to Deuteronomy, the three groups would find it difficult to distinguish themselves, one from the next. For one principal point of emphasis we discern in our document takes an equally central role in the propositional, topical program of the other two. It is the insistence on the principle that logic alone cannot suffice, and that all law must in the end derive from the written part of the Torah. The single sustained proposition of both writings is that truth derives from Scripture, not from reason unaided by revelation. But a further proposition will attract our attention. By the very labor of explaining the meaning of verses of Scripture, the Rabbinic exegetes laid claim to participate in the work of revelation. And by distinguishing their contribution from the received text of the Torah, they announced their presence within the process of revelation. In these two ways the exegetes who made up Sifra and the two Sifrés announced not one but two fundamental propositions. The first is that God's revelation in the Written Torah takes priority. The second is that man's reason in the exegesis of the Written Torah enjoys full and legitimate place in the unfolding of the lessons of Sinai. No one can doubt that our authorship concurs on both principles.

The rhetorical form of both documents underlines the topical program contained in the first of the two propositions. For if I want to underline over and over again the priority of not proposition, hence reason, but process, hence the exegesis of Scripture, my best choice is an obvious one. Begin at all points with a verse of Scripture and demonstrate that only by starting with the word choices and propositions of that verse of Scripture, all further progress of interpretation commences. But the second proposition, that man (then, now: man and woman) has a place in the process of revealing the Torah of Sinai, comes to expression in the careful separation of the cited verse of the Written Torah from the contribution of the contemporary exegete.

In that formal preference, too, the authorship made a major point and established – if implicitly – a central syllogism: God's will follows the rules of reason. Man can investigate the consequences of reason as expressed in God's will. Therefore man can join in the labor of exploring God's will in the Torah.

Consequently, the authorships of all three Midrash compilations make their powerful case by their rhetorical program, which relies first and foremost on the citation and gloss of a verse of Scripture, as much as by their proposition and syllogism: only by Scripture does truth gain certainty. The appeal to Scripture, however, comes once the proposition is established, and that appeal then dictates the rhetoric and topic alike. Only when we know what question we bring to Scripture may we devise appropriate formal and programmatic policies for our Midrash exegesis and Midrash compilation alike. A second formal preference in all three documents, in addition to the exegetical form, makes the same point. The other form involves citation of a passage of the Mishnah followed by an extensive discourse on how the verse of Scripture that pertains to the topic of that Mishnah passage must contribute its facts, revealed at Sinai, if we wish to know the truth. Reason alone, which is systematically tested through a sequence of propositions shown to fail, will not serve.

The rhetorical plan of Sifra and Sifré to Numbers shows that the exegetes, while working verse by verse, in fact have brought a considerable program to their reading of the book of Leviticus. The authorships of Sifra and the two Sifrés share that program, when they cite a verse of Scripture and then a passage of the Mishnah. The proposition then in all three writings concerns the interplay of the Oral Torah, represented by the Mishnah, with the Written Torah, represented by the book of Leviticus or Numbers or Deuteronomy. That question demanded, in their view, not an answer comprising mere generalities. They wished to show their results through details, masses of details, and, like the rigorous philosophers that they were, they furthermore argued essentially through an inductive procedure, amassing evidence that in its accumulation made the point at hand.

The syllogism about the priority of the revelation of the Written Torah in the search for truth is nowhere expressed in so many words, because the philosopher exegetes of the Rabbinic world preferred to address an implicit syllogism and to pursue or to test that syllogism solely in a sequence of experiments of a small scale. Sifra's and the two Sifrés' authorships therefore find in the Mishnah and Tosefta a sizable laboratory for the testing of propositions. We have therefore to ask: At what points do Sifra's and the two Sifrés' authorships and those of the Mishnah and Tosefta share a common agenda of interests, and at what points does one compilation introduce problems, themes, or questions unknown to the other?

The answers to these questions for the three Midrash compilations are various. The one for Sifra will show that Sifra and Mishnah and Tosefta form two large concentric circles, sharing a considerable area in common. Sifra, however, exhibits interests peculiar to itself. On the criterion of common themes and interests, Mishnah and Tosefta and Sifra exhibit a remarkable unity. The authorships of the two Sifrés in diverse measure join in that united front on a basic issue. The authorship of Sifré to Numbers, for its part, took up a pentateuchal book that in no way focuses upon the topics paramount, also, in the Mishnah and the Tosefta, in the way in which the book of Leviticus covers subjects that take a prominent position in the later law codes. Consequently, we cannot find in Sifré to Numbers a counterpart to the stress on the matters we have located in Sifra. Still, the established polemic about the priority of Scripture over unaided reason does take its place. Accordingly, we can show that Sifra and the two Sifrés join together in a single species of the genus, Midrash compilation.

Rhetoric

These forms encompass all of the literary structures of Sifré to Numbers. They are exemplified in the catalogue that follows.

EXTRINSIC EXEGETICAL FORM: The form consists of the citation of an opening verse, followed by an issue stated in terms extrinsic to the cited verse. That is to say, no word or phrase of the base verse (that is, the cited verse at the beginning) attracts comment. Rather a general rule of exegesis is invoked. C then introduces a broad range of items not at all subject to attention in the verse at hand. The formal traits: [1] citation of a base verse from Numbers, [2] a generalization ignoring clauses or words in the base verse, [3] a further observation without clear interest in the verse at hand. But the whole is linked to the theme of the base verse – and to that alone. So an extrinsic exegetical program comes to bear. One example of the form involves syllogistic argument on the meaning of words or phrases, in which the base verse of Numbers occurs as one among a set of diverse items, as in the following instance:

I

III.1   A.   R. Judah b. Beterah says, "The effect of a commandment stated in any context serves only [1] to lend encouragement.

        B.   "For it is said, 'But command Joshua and encourage and strengthen him' (Deut. 3:28).

        C.   "Accordingly, we derive the lesson that strength is granted only to the strong, and encouragement only to the stout of heart."

D. R. Simeon b. Yohai says, "The purpose of a commandment in any context is only [2] to deal with the expenditure of money, as it is said, 'Command the children of Israel to bring you pure oil from beaten olives for the lamp, that a light may be kept burning continually outside the veil of the testimony in the tent of meeting. Aaron shall keep it in order from evening to morning before the Lord continually; it shall be a statute forever throughout your generations' (Lev. 24:2). 'Command the people of Israel that they put out of the camp every leper and every one having a discharge, and every one that is unclean through contact with the dead' (Num. 5:1-2). 'Command the children of Israel that they give to the Levites from the inheritance of their possession cities to dwell in, and you shall give to the Levites pasture lands round about the cities' (Num. 35:2). 'Command the people of Israel and say to them, "My offering, my food for my offerings by fire, my pleasing odor you shall take heed to offer to me in its due season"' (Num. 28:2). Lo, we see in all these cases that the purpose of a commandment is solely to bring about the expenditure of money.

E. "There is one exception, and what is that? It is this verse: 'Command the people of Israel and say to them, "When you enter the land of Canaan, this is the land that shall fall to you for an inheritance, the land of Canaan in its full extent"' (Num. 34:2).

F. "You must give encouragement to them in the matter of the correct division of the land."

G. And Rabbi [Judah the Patriarch] says, "The use of the word 'commandment' in all passages serves only for the purpose of [3] imparting an admonition [not to do a given action], along the lines of the following: 'And the Lord God commanded the man, saying, "You may freely eat of every tree of the garden, but of the tree of the knowledge of good and evil you shall not eat"' (Gen. 2:16)."

INTRINSIC EXEGETICAL FORM: in this form, the verse itself is clarified. In the first instance, the exegesis derives from the contrast with another verse that makes the same point. But the formal trait should not be missed. It is that the the focus is on the base verse and not on a broader issue. We may call this an intrinsic exegetical form, in that the focus of exegesis is on the verse, which is cited and carefully spelled out. We shall know that we have it when the base verse is cited, clause by clause or in other ways, and then given an ample dose of attention. Since the present category presents numerous variations, we shall subdivide as we go along. The key words of the species of the genus at hand will supply the basis for differentiation, as will be clear throughout. In the first example, the exegesis asks the purpose of a given passage, and the form requires the citation of base verse plus "For what purpose is this passage presented?"

I

I.1   A.   "The Lord said to Moses, 'Command the people of Israel that they put out of the camp [every leper and every one having a discharge, and every one that is unclean through contact with the dead]'" (Num. 5:1-2).

       B.   For what purpose is this passage presented?

       C.   Because it is said, "But the man who is unclean and does not cleanse himself, [that person shall be cut off from the midst of the assembly, since he has defiled the sanctuary of the Lord, because the water for impurity has not been thrown upon him, he is unclean]" (Num. 19:20).

       D.   Consequently, we are informed of the penalty [for contaminating the sanctuary]. But where are we informed of the admonition not to do so?

       E.   Scripture accordingly states, "Command the people of Israel that they put out of the camp every leper and every one having a discharge, and every one that is unclean through contact with the dead" (Num. 5:1-2).

       F.   Lo, here is an admonition that unclean persons not come into the sanctuary ["out of the camp"] in a state of uncleanness. [Consequently, the entire transaction – admonition, then penalty – is laid forth.]

In another version, we find the rudiments of a dialectical argument, that is, a proposition is announced, then challenged, and the argument moves in its own direction. Here we have the citation of a word or clause in the base verse, followed by a declarative sentence explaining the purpose and meaning of the cited passage. Then we ask, "You say this, but perhaps it means that." Then we proceed to justify the original statement. This is a fine example of the dialectical exegesis of an intrinsic character.

I

II.1   A.   "Command" (Num. 5:2):

       B.   The commandment at hand is meant both to be put into effect immediately and also to apply for generations to come.

       C.   You maintain that the commandment at hand is meant both to be put into effect immediately and also to apply for generations to come.

       D.   But perhaps the commandment is meant to apply only after a time [but not right away, at the moment at which it was given].

       E.   [We shall now prove that the formulation encompasses both generations to come and also the generation to whom the commandment is entrusted.] Scripture states, "The Lord said to Moses, 'Command the people of Israel that they put out [of the camp every leper and every one having a discharge, and every one that is unclean through contact with the dead. You shall put out both male and female, putting them outside the camp, that they may not defile their camp, in the midst of which I dwell.'] And the people of Israel did so and drove them outside the camp, as the Lord said to Moses, 'so the people of Israel did'" (Gen. 5:1-4). [The verse itself makes explicit the fact that the requirement applied forthwith, not only later on.]

F. Lo, we have learned that the commandment at hand is meant to be put into effect immediately.

G. How then do we derive from Scripture the fact that it applies also for generations to come? [We shall now show that the same word used here, "command," pertains to generations to come and not only to the generation at hand.]

H. Scripture states, "Command the children of Israel to bring you pure oil from beaten olives [for the lamp, that a light may be kept burning continually outside the veil of the testimony in the tent of meeting. Aaron shall keep it in order from evening to morning before the Lord continually; it shall be a statute forever throughout your generations]" (Lev. 24:2).

I. Lo, we here derive evidence that the commandment at hand is meant both to be put into effect immediately and also to apply for generations to come, [based on the framing of the present commandment].

J. How, then, do we drive evidence that all of the commandments that are contained in the Torah [apply in the same way]? [We wish now to prove that the language, "command," always bears the meaning imputed to it here.]

K. R. Ishmael maintained, "Since the bulk of the commandments stated in the Torah are presented without further amplification, while in the case of one of them [namely, the one at hand], Scripture has given explicit details, that commandment [that has been singled out] is meant both to be put into effect immediately and also to apply for generations to come. Accordingly, I apply to all of the other commandments in the Torah the same detail, so that in all cases the commandment is meant both to be put into effect immediately and also to apply for generations to come."

Dialectics governs yet another exegetical form. It consists of a sequence of arguments about the meaning of a passage, in which the focus is upon the base verse, and a sequence of possibilities is introduced to spell out the meaning of that verse. At issue is not the power of logic but the meaning of the base verse, but that issue is pursued through an argument of many stages.

I

IV.1 A. "[The Lord said to Moses, 'Command the people of Israel that] they put out of the camp [every leper and every one having a discharge, and every one that is unclean through contact with the dead']" (Num. 5:1-2).

B. Is it from the [innermost] camp, of the Presence of God, or should I infer that it is only from the camp of the Levites?

C. Scripture states, "...they put out of the camp." [The sense is that they are to be put outside of the camp of the Presence.]

D.   Now even if Scripture had not made the matter explicit, I could have proposed the same proposition on the basis of reasoning [that they should be put outside of the camp of the Presence]:

E.   If unclean people are driven out of the camp that contains the ark, which is of lesser sanctity, all the more so should they be driven out of the camp of the Presence of God, which is of greater sanctity.

F.   But if you had proposed reasoning on that basis, you would have found yourself in the position of imposing a penalty merely on the basis of reason [and not on the basis of an explicit statement of Scripture, and one does not impose a penalty merely on the basis of reason].

G.   Then why is it stated: "...they put out of the camp"?

H.   Making that matter explicit in Scripture serves to teach you that penalties are not to be imposed merely on the basis of logic [but require explicit specification in Scripture]. [That is, Scripture made a point that reason could have reached, but Scripture made the matter explicit so as to articulate a penalty applicable for violating the rule.]

I.   [Rejecting that principle,] Rabbi says, "It is not necessary for Scripture to make the matter explicit, since it is a matter of an argument a fortiori:

J.   "If the unclean people are driven out of the camp that contains the ark, which is of lesser sanctity, all the more so should they be driven out of the camp of the Presence of God, which is of greater sanctity.

K.   "Then why is it stated: '...they put out of the camp every leper and every one having a discharge, and every one that is unclean through contact with the dead'?

L.   "[By specifying that all three are put out of the camp,] Scripture thereby served to assign to them levels or gradations [of uncleanness, with diverse rules affecting those levels, as will now be spelled out. Since we know that that rule applies to the ostracism of the leper, the specification that the others also are to be put out of the camp indicates that a singular rule applies to each of the category. If one rule applied in common, then the specification with respect to the leper alone would have sufficed to indicate the rule for all others.]"

M.   [We review the distinctions among several gradations of uncleanness affecting human beings, inclusive of the three at hand: the leper, the one having a discharge, and the one unclean through contact with the dead.] "The Lord said to Moses, 'Command the people of Israel that they put out of the camp every leper and every one having a discharge, and every one that is unclean through contact with the dead'" (Num. 5:1-2).

N.   Shall I then draw the conclusion that all three of those listed [the leper, the one affected by a discharge, the one unclean with corpse uncleanness] are to remain in the same locale [in relationship to the Temple]?

O.   With respect to the leper, Scripture states explicitly, "He shall dwell by himself; outside of the camp shall be his dwelling" (Lev. 13:46).

P.   Now the leper fell into the same category as the others, and he has been singled out from the general category, thereby serving to impose a single rule on the category from which he has been singled out.

Q.   [And this is the rule applicable to the leper and hence to the others from among whom he has been singled out:] Just as in the case of the leper, who is subject to a most severe form of uncleanness, and who also is subjected to a more severe rule governing ostracism than that applying to his fellow, so all who are subject to a more severe form of uncleanness likewise are subject to a more severe rule of ostracism than that applying to his fellow.

R.   On this basis sages listed distinctions that apply to those that are unclean [since a different rule applies to each of them, in descending order of severity, as is now spelled out]:

S.   To any object that one affected by a flux imparts uncleanness, a leper imparts uncleanness. A leper is subject to a more severe rule, however, in that a leper imparts uncleanness through an act of sexual relations.

T.   To any object that one unclean with corpse uncleanness imparts uncleanness, one affected by a flux imparts uncleanness. But a more severe rule affects one affected by a flux, in that he imparts uncleanness to an object located far beneath a rock in the deep [imparting uncleanness to that deeply buried object merely by the application of the pressure of his weight, while one unclean with corpse uncleanness does not impart uncleanness merely by pressure of his weight alone].

U.   To any object that one unclean by reason of waiting for sunset after immersion imparts uncleanness one unclean by corpse uncleanness imparts uncleanness. A more severe rule applies to one unclean by corpse uncleanness, for he imparts uncleanness to a human being [which is not the case of one who is unclean by reason of waiting for sunset after his immersion].

V.   What is made unfit by one who has not yet completed his rites of atonement following uncleanness and purification is made unfit by one who awaits for sunset to complete his process of purification. A more strict rule applies to one awaiting sunset for the completion of his rite of purification, for he imparts unfitness to food designated for priestly rations [while the one who has completed his rites of purification but not yet offered the atonement sacrifice on account of his uncleanness does not impart unfitness to priestly rations that he may touch].

The dominant form of Sifra, the demonstration of the fallacy of logic uncorrected by exegesis of Scripture, produces in Sifré to Numbers yet another moving, or dialectical, exegetical form, but while the basic trait is familiar – a sequence of shifts and turns in the possibility of interpretation, all of them subjected to close logical scrutiny – the purpose is different. And the purpose comes to expression not in content, particular to diverse passages, but in form.

The formal indicator is the presence of the question, in one of several versions: Is it not a matter of logic? That is the never failing formal indicator. From that clause we invariably move on to a set of arguments of a highly formalized character on taxonomic classification: What is like, or unlike? What is like follows a given rule, what is unlike follows the opposite rule, and it is for us to see whether the likenesses or unlikenesses prevail. (When Ishmael's name occurs, they prevail, and when Aqiba's occurs, they do not. But these seem rather conventional.) The argument is formalized to an extreme, and there are very few variations among our document's exempla of this form, though one – the matter of length – should not be missed. The exegesis of the verse at hand plays no substantial role, beyond its initial introduction. What is critical is the issue of the reliability of logic. The base verse before us contributes virtually nothing and in no way serves as the foundation for the composition at hand.

Still another form familiar from Sifra, an inquiry into the scriptural basis for a passage of the Mishnah, occurs. The sole important difference from Sifra, of course, is that in Sifré to Numbers, this form is merely occasional, not indicative of the program of the document as a whole. What we have is simply a citation of the verse plus a law in prior writing (Mishnah, Tosefta) which the verse is supposed to sustain. The formal traits require [1] citation of a verse, with or without comment, followed by [2] verbatim citation of a passage of the Mishnah or the Tosefta.

I

IX.1 A. "[You shall put out both male and female, putting them outside the camp,] that they may not defile their camp, [in the midst of which I dwell]":

B. On the basis of this verse, the rule has been formulated:

C. **There are three camps, the camp of Israel, the camp of the Levitical priests, and the camp of the Presence of God. From the gate of Jerusalem to the Temple mount is the camp of Israel, from the gate of the Temple mount to the Temple courtyard is the camp of the Levitical priesthood, and from the gate of the courtyard and inward is the camp of the Presence of God [T. Kel. 1:12].**

A variation on the foregoing presents a statement of a rule, in which the Mishnah or Tosefta is not cited verbatim. That is the undefined side. But the rule that is presented is not intrinsic to the verse at hand, in that the verse does not refer in any way to the case or possibility framed as the issue. In that case we do not have a clear-cut exegesis of the verse in its own terms. But we also do not have an example of the linking of Scripture to the Mishnah. An example of this type follows:

III

I.1 A. "[And the Lord said to Moses, 'Say to the people of Israel, When a man or woman commits any of the sins that men commit by breaking faith with the Lord, and that person is guilty,] he shall

confess his sin which he has committed, [and he shall make full
restitution for his wrong, adding a fifth to it, and giving it to him to
whom he did the wrong.']" (Num. 5:5-10).

B.   But [in stressing, "his sin," Scripture makes it clear that he does not
have to make confession] for what his father did.

C.   For if one said to him, "Give me the bailment that I left with your
father," and he says, "You left no bailment," [and the other says,] "I
impose an oath on you," and the first says, "Amen,"

D.   [and if] after a while the [son] remembers [that a bailment indeed
had been left and must be handed over] –

E.   should I conclude that the son is liable [to make confession, not
merely to hand over the bailment]?

F.   Scripture says, "he shall confess his sin which *he* has committed,"
but he does not make confession for what his father did.

The prooftext serves for a proposition given in apodictic form. The point
is that the son does not confess the father's sin, though he has to make up
for it. Scripture then yields the stated law by its stress. We shall now
derive laws from the verses at hand to cover further such situations.

Logic of Coherent Discourse

The paramount logic that joins composition to composition is, of
course, fixed associative. The same serves for a fair number of
composites; a very small number are shaped into propositional
statements. In all, the document relies principally on the sequence of
verses of the book of Numbers for the joining of its compositions.

Topical Program

Let us now characterize the formal traits of Sifré to Numbers as a
commentary, since, as noted at the outset, it is here that we identify the
implicit propositional program of the document's compilers and the
writers of the bulk of its compositions. These we have reduced to two
classifications, based on the point of origin of the verses that are
catalogued or subjected to exegesis: exegesis of a verse in the book of
Numbers in terms of the theme or problems of that verse, hence, intrinsic
exegesis; exegesis of a verse in Numbers in terms of a theme or polemic
not particular to that verse, hence, extrinsic exegesis.

THE FORMS OF EXTRINSIC EXEGESIS: The implicit message of the
external category proves simple to define, since the several extrinsic
classifications turn out to form a cogent polemic. Let me state the
recurrent polemic of external exegesis.

THE SYLLOGISTIC COMPOSITION: Scripture supplies hard facts,
which, properly classified, generate syllogisms. By collecting and
classifying facts of Scripture, therefore, we may produce firm laws of

history, society, and Israel's everyday life. The diverse compositions in which verses from various books of the Scriptures are compiled in a list of evidence for a given proposition – whatever the character or purpose of that proposition – make that one point. And given their power and cogency, they make the point stick.

THE FALLIBILITY OF REASON UNGUIDED BY SCRIPTURAL EXEGESIS: Scripture alone supplies reliable basis for speculation. Laws cannot be generated by reason or logic unguided by Scripture. Efforts at classification and contrastive analogical exegesis, in which Scripture does not supply the solution to all problems, prove few and far between (and always in Ishmael's name, for whatever that is worth). This polemic forms the obverse of the point above. So when extrinsic issues intervene in the exegetical process, they coalesce to make a single point. Scripture stands paramount, logic, reason, analytical processes of classification and differentiation, secondary. Reason not built on scriptural foundations yields uncertain results. The Mishnah itself demands scriptural bases.

THE FORMS OF INTRINSIC EXEGESIS: What about the polemic present in the intrinsic exegetical exercises? This clearly does not allow for ready characterization. As we saw, at least three intrinsic exegetical exercises focus on the use of logic, specifically, the logic of classification, comparison and contrast of species of a genus, in the explanation of the meaning of verses of the book of Numbers. The internal dialectical mode, moving from point to point as logic dictates, underlines the main point already stated: logic produces possibilities, Scripture chooses among them. Again, the question, why is this passage stated?, commonly produces an answer generated by further verses of Scripture, for example, this matter is stated here to clarify what otherwise would be confusion left in the wake of other verses. So Scripture produces problems of confusion and duplication, and Scripture – and not logic, not differentiation, not classification – solves those problems.

To state matters simply: Scripture is complete, harmonious, perfect. Logic not only does not generate truth beyond the limits of Scripture but also plays no important role in the harmonization of difficulties yielded by what appear to be duplications or disharmonies. These forms of internal exegesis then make the same point that the extrinsic ones do.

In so stating, of course, we cover all but the single most profuse category of exegesis, which we have treated as simple and undifferentiated: [1] verse of Scripture or a clause, followed by [2] a brief statement of the meaning at hand. Here I see no unifying polemic in favor of, or against, a given proposition. The most common form also proves the least pointed: X bears this meaning, Y bears that meaning, or, as we have seen, citation of verse X, followed by, [what this means is].... Whether simple or elaborate, the upshot is the same. What can be at issue when no polemic expressed in the formal traits of syntax and logic finds its way to the surface? What do I do when I merely clarify a phrase? Or, to frame the question more logically: What premises must validate my *intervention*, that is, my willingness to undertake to explain the meaning of a verse of Scripture? These justify the labor of intrinsic exegesis as we have seen its results here:

1. My independent judgment bears weight and produces meaning. I – that is, my mind – therefore may join in the process.

2. God's revelation to Moses at Sinai requires my intervention. I have the role, and the right, to say what that revelation means.

3. What validates my entry into the process of revelation is the correspondence between the logic of my mind and the logic of the document.

Only if I think in accord with the logic of the revealed Torah can my thought processes join issue in clarifying what is at hand: the unfolding of God's will in the Torah. To state matters more accessibly: if the Torah does not make statements in accord with a syntax and a grammar that I know, I cannot so understand the Torah as to explain its meaning. But if I can join in the discourse of the Torah, it is because I speak the same language of thought: syntax and grammar at the deepest levels of my intellect.

4. Then to state matters affirmatively and finally: Since a shared logic of syntax and grammar joins my mind to the mind of God as revealed in the Torah, I can say what a sentence of the Torah means. So, too, I can amplify, clarify, expand, revise, rework: that is to say, create a commentary. So the work of commenting upon the Written Torah bears profound consequence for the revelation of the Torah, the sage becoming partner with God in the giving of the Torah. In that conclusion, we find ourselves repeating the main point that Sifra yields in the description of Rabbinic literature as a whole.

We consider two large segments of the document, the treatment of Naso and Beha'alotekha, which occupy approximately one half of the whole, Nos. 1-115.

II. Unarticulated Premises: The Givens of Religious Conduct

The legal passages are expounded, but nothing new emerges.

III. Unarticulated Premises: The Givens of Religious Conviction

The composite contains a fair number of familiar conceptions, all of them important, which are taken for granted as facts. These include the following:

1. God's Presence remains with Israel even when they are unclean; uncleanness comes about by reason of sin. So even though Israel sins, God's Presence remains with them:

I

X.1   A.   "'[You shall put out both male and female, putting them outside the camp, that they may not defile their camp,] in the midst of which I dwell.' [And the people of Israel did so and drove them outside the camp, as the Lord said to Moses, so the people of Israel did]" (Num. 5:3-4).

  B.   So beloved is Israel that even though they may become unclean, the Presence of God remains among them.

  C.   And so Scripture states, "...who dwells with them in the midst of their uncleanness" (Lev. 16:16).

  D.   And further: "...by making my sanctuary unclean, which [nonetheless] is in their midst " (Lev. 15:31).

  E.   And it further says: "...that they may not defile their camp, in the midst of which I dwell" (Num. 5:3-4).

  F.   And it further says, "You shall not defile the land in which you live, in the midst of which I dwell, for I the Lord dwell in the midst of the people of Israel" (Num. 35:34).

X.2   A.   R. Yosé the Galilean says, "Come and take note of how great is the power of sin. For before the people had laid hands on transgression, people afflicted with flux and lepers were not located among them, but after they had laid hands on transgression, people afflicted with flux and lepers did find a place among them.

  B.   "Accordingly, we learn that these three events took place on one and the same day: [transgression, the presence of those afflicted with flux, the development of leprosy among the people]."

X.3   A.   R. Simeon b. Yohai says, "Come and take note of how great is the power of sin. For before the people had laid hands on transgression, what is stated in their regard?

  B.   "'Now the appearance of the glory of the Lord was like a devouring fire on the top of the mountain in the sight of the people of Israel' (Ex. 24:17).

  C.   "Nonetheless, the people did not fear nor were they afraid.

  D.   "But once they had laid hands on transgression, what is said in their regard?

  E.   "'And when Aaron and all the people of Israel saw Moses, behold, the skin of his face shone, and they were afraid to come near him' (Ex. 34:30)."

2. Israel is to be praised, for they did precisely what Moses instructed them to do:

I

IX.1   A.   "[You shall put out both male and female, putting them outside the camp, that they may not defile their camp, in the midst of which I dwell.' And the people of Israel did so and drove them outside the camp, as the Lord said to Moses,] so the people of Israel did" (Gen. 5:3-4):

       B.   This statement, ["...And the people of Israel did so,"] serves to recount praise for the Israelites, for just as Moses instructed them, so did they do.

XI.2   A.   Scripture states, "...as the Lord said to Moses, so the people of Israel did."

       B.   What this teaches is that even the unclean people did not register opposition [but accepted the decree without complaint].

3.   Punishment is just, and therefore, punishment pertains to the responsible party or part, and so, too, when good is bestowed, it is just:

XVIII

I.1   A.   "And when he has made her drink the water, [then, if she has defiled herself and has acted unfaithfully against her husband, the water that brings the curse shall enter into her and cause bitter pain,] and her body shall swell, and her thigh shall fall away, [and the woman shall become an execration among her people. But if the woman has not defiled herself and is clean, then she shall be free and shall conceive children]" (Num. 5:23-28).

       B.   I know only that her body and thigh are affected. How do I know that that is the case for the rest of her limbs?

       C.   Scripture states, "...the water that brings the curse shall enter into her."

       D.   So I take account of the phrase, "...the water that brings the curse shall enter into her."

       E.   Why then [if all the limbs are affected equally] does Scripture specify her body and her thigh in particular?

       F.   As to her thigh, the limb with which she began to commit the transgression – from there the punishment begins.

       G.   Along these same lines:

       H.   "And he blotted out everything that sprouted from the earth, from man to beast" (Gen. 7:23).

       I.   From the one who began the transgression [namely Adam], the punishment begins.

       J.   Along these same lines:

       K.   "...and the men who were at the gate of the house they smote with piles" (Gen. 19:11).

       L.   From the one who began the transgression the punishment begins.

       M.   Along these same lines:

       N.   "...and I shall be honored through Pharaoh and through all of his force" (Ex. 14:4).

       O.   Pharaoh began the transgression, so from him began the punishment.

P. Along these same lines:
Q. "And you will most certainly smite at the edge of the sword the inhabitants of that city" (Deut. 134:15).
R. From the one who began the transgression, the punishment begins.
S. Along these same lines is the present case:
T. the limb with which she began to commit the transgression – from there the punishment begins.
U. Now does this not yield an argument a fortiori:
V. If in the case of the attribution of punishment, which is the lesser, from the limb with which she began to commit the transgression – from there the punishment begins,
W. in the case of the attribute of bestowing good, which is the greater, how much the more so!

4. There is life after death; there is the world to come; the Torah gives light; God is gracious to Israel;

XL

I.1 A. "[The Lord said to Moses, 'Say to Aaron and his sons: "Thus shall you bless the people of Israel. You shall say to them:] 'The Lord bless you and keep you, [the Lord make his face to shine upon you and be gracious to you, the Lord lift up his countenance upon you and give you peace.' So shall they put my name upon the people of Israel, and I will bless them]'"'" (Num. 6:22-27):

B. "The Lord bless you" with the blessing spelled out in the Torah: "Blessed shall you be in the city and blessed shall you be in the field. Blessed shall be the fruit of your body and the fruit of your ground and the fruit of your beasts, the increase of your cattle and the young of your flock. Blessed shall be your basket and your kneading trough. Blessed shall you be when you come in and blessed shall you be when you go out" (Deut. 28:3-6).

C. "And all these blessings will come upon you and overtake you" (Deut. 28:2) – when? "When you obey the word of the Lord your God" (Deut. 28:2).

I.2 A. "The Lord bless you":
B. With property.
C. "And keep you":
D. With property.

I.3 A. R. Nathan says, "'The Lord bless you' with property, 'and keep you' in good health."
B. R. Isaac says, "'And keep you' from the evil impulse."
C. And so Scripture says, "For the Lord will be your confidence and will keep your foot from being caught" (Prov. 3:26).

I.4 A. Another interpretation of "...and keep you":
B. So that others will not rule over you.
C. And so Scripture says, "The sun shall not smite you by day, nor the moon by night." "Behold, he who keeps Israel will neither slumber nor sleep. The Lord is your keeper; the Lord is your shade on your right hand." "The Lord will keep you for all evil; he will keep your life. The Lord will keep your going out and your coming in from this time forth and for ever more" (Ps. 121).

I.5   A.   Another interpretation of "...and keep you":

          B.   He will keep you from demons.

          C.   And so Scripture says, "For he will give his angels charge of you, to guard you in all your ways" (Ps. 91:11).

I.6   A.   Another interpretation of "...and keep you":

          B.   He will keep the covenant made with your fathers.

          C.   And so Scripture says, "The Lord your God will keep with you the covenant and the steadfast love which he swore to your fathers to keep" (Deut. 7:12).

I.7   A.   Another interpretation of "...and keep you":

          B.   He will keep the foreordained end for you.

          C.   And so Scripture says, "The oracle concerning Dumah. One is calling to me from Seir, 'Watchman, what of the night? watchman, what of the night?' The watchman says, 'Morning comes, and also the night. If you will inquire, inquire; come back again'" (Isa. 21:11-12).

I.8   A.   Another interpretation of "...and keep you":

          B.   He will keep your soul at the hour of death.

          C.   And so Scripture says, "...the life of my lord shall be bound in the bundle of the living in the care of the Lord your God" (1 Sam. 25:29).

          D.   May I infer that that is the case for righteous and wicked alike?

          E.   Scripture says, "...and the lives of your enemies he shall sling out as from the hollow of a sling" (1 Sam. 25:29).

I.9   A.   Another interpretation of "...and keep you":

          B.   He will keep your foot from Gehenna.

          C.   And so Scripture says, "He will guard the feet of his faithful ones, but the wicked shall be cut off in darkness" (1 Sam. 2:9).

I.10   A.   Another interpretation of "...and keep you":

          B.   He will guard you in the world to come.

          C.   And so Scripture says, "They who wait for the Lord shall renew their strength, they shall mount up with wings like eagles" (Isa. 40:31).

IV. Matters of Philosophy, Natural Science and Metaphysics

I find nothing that pertains to this part of our inquiry.

28

Sifré to Numbers 59-115

I. Unarticulated Premises: The Givens of Religious Conduct

The legal passages are derivative.

II. Unarticulated Premises: The Givens of Religious Conviction

1. Israel's virtue lies in doing what Moses commanded them; in obedience lies virtue:

LXVII

II.1   A.   "...According to all that the Lord commanded Moses, so the people of Israel did":

B.   This now tells us Israel's virtue, for whatever Moses told them, they did.

LXXII

II.1   A.   "...Make for yourself two silver trumpets":

B.   "When Scripture says, '...for yourself,' it means that the material should come from your own property.

C.   "When Scripture says, 'And they shall take for you...,' it means that the material comes from the community treasury," the words of R. Josiah.

D.   R. Jonathan says, "All the same are both expressions. Scripture speaks of the material's coming from community property. What then is the sense of 'make for yourself' or 'and they shall take for you'?

E.   "When the Israelites carry out the will of the Omnipresent, then 'they shall take for you...,' but when the Israelites do not carry out the will of the Omnipresent, then, 'Take for yourself.'

F.   "'...Make for yourself,' then means, 'I desire what is yours more than what is theirs' [because of their misconduct]."

2. There will be an eschatological war of Gog and Magog, after which Israel will be saved and there will be no further period of subjugation:

LXXVI

II.1 A. "[And when you go to war in your land] against the adversary who oppresses you, [then you shall sound an alarm with the trumpets]" (Num. 10:1-10):

B. Scripture speaks of the [eschatological] war of Gog and Magog.

C. You maintain that Scripture speaks of the [eschatological] war of Gog and Magog.

D. But perhaps it speaks only of any wars that are mentioned in the Torah?

E. Scripture says, "...that you may be remembered before the Lord your God, and you shall be saved from your enemies."

F. Thus you may argue: go and find a war in which Israel is saved, but after which there is no period of subjugation?

G. You can find only the war of Gog and Magog.

H. And so Scripture says, "And the Lord will go forth and make war against those nations" (Zech. 14:3).

II.2 A. What is the meaning of [the phrase in that same context], "And the Lord will be king over all the earth"?

B. R. Aqiba says, "I know only that war is involved [at the end of history]. How do I know that there are also the troubles of blight and mildew, hard labor and ships floundering in the sea? Scripture says, '...against the adversary who oppresses you,' referring to every sort of misfortune – may it not come into the world!"

3. When God remembers Israel, it is for good; God saves Israel when he remembers them:

II.3 A. "...Then you shall sound an alarm with the trumpets [that you may be remembered before the Lord your God, and you shall be saved from your enemies]":

B. R. Aqiba says, "Now is it the trumpets that bring up God's memory? And is it not the blood [of the sacrifices] that calls to mind [Israel's merit]?

C. "But the point is that if the Israelites can sound [the trumpets] and do not do so, I credit it to them as if they have not been brought to memory before the Omnipresent. [But if they fail to do so because they cannot do so, it is another matter altogether.]"

II.4 A. "...That you may be remembered before the Lord your God, [and you shall be saved from your enemies]":

B. Lo, whenever the Israelites are called to memory, they are called to memory only for salvation.

4. When Israel accepts God as king, then they get mercy from him and will be remembered by him, on the New Year, when the ram's horn is sounded:

LXXVII

IV.1   A.   "...[They shall serve you for remembrance before your God;] I am the Lord your God" (Num. 10:1-10):

       B.   Why is this statement made?

       C.   Since Scripture says, "Speak to the children of Israel, saying, 'In the seventh month on the first day of the month you shall have a Sabbath of memorial of the sounding of the trumpet'" (Lev. 23:24), but a sounding of the trumpet in remembrance of God's sovereignty we have not inferred.

       D.   Scripture then states, "The Lord his God is with him, the sounding of the trumpet for a king is with him" (Num. 23:21).

       E.   This refers, then, to the sounding of the ram's horn and [of the trumpet] for God's sovereignty.

       F.   R. Nathan says, "It is not necessary to prove it in that way, for lo, it is said, 'And you shall sound the trumpets,' lo, a reference to the ram's horn, 'They shall serve you for remembrance before your God,' this refers to [sounding the trumpets for] remembrance, 'I am the Lord your God,' now encompassing sounding the horn for God's sovereignty."

IV.2   A.   If so, why [in the New Year liturgy] have sages placed [verses referring to] the sounding of the ram's horn for God's sovereignty first, then for remembrance second, and finally for the ram's horn blasts?

       B.   The sense is: first of all accept him as king over you, then seek mercy from him, so that you will be remembered by him, and how? With the ram's horn of freedom.

       C.   And the ram's horn serves only for freedom, as it says, "And it shall come to pass, in that day, that the great ram's horn will be sounded" (Isa. 27:13).

       D.   But I do not know who will sound it.

       E.   Scripture says, "The Lord God will sound the ram's horn" (Zech. 9:14).

       F.   But we still do not know whence the sound of the horn comes forth.

       G.   This accords with the following: "Hark, an uproar from the city, a voice from the temple! The voice of the Lord, rendering recompense to his enemies" (Isa. 66:6).

5.   The following protracted passage is important, since it shows us how the premise that those who come near to God are brought by God nearer still, and, further, if an Israelite carries out the Torah, he or she is brought still closer to God:

LXXVIII

I.1   A.   "And Moses said to Hobab the son of Reuel, [the Midianite, Moses' father-in-law, 'We are setting out for the place of which the Lord said, "I will give it to you." Come with us and we will do you good; for the Lord has promised good to Israel.' But he said to him, 'I will not go; I will depart for my own land and to my kindred.' And he said, 'Do not leave us, I pray you, for you know how we are to encamp in the wilderness, and you will serve as eyes for us. And if you go with us, whatever good the Lord will do to us, the same will we do to you.' So they set out from the mount of the Lord three days' journey; and the ark of the covenant of the Lord went before them three days' journey to seek out a resting place for them. And the cloud of the Lord was over them by day, whenever they set out from the camp. And whenever the ark set out, Moses said, 'Arise, O Lord, and let your enemies be scattered, and let them that hate you flee before you.' And when it rested, he said, 'Return O Lord to the ten thousand thousands of Israel']" (Num. 10:29-36):

B. His name was both Hobeb and Reuel, for it is said, "And the women went to Reuel, their father" (Ex. 2:18).

C. When Scripture says, "Now Heber the Kenite had parted company with the Kenites, the descendants of Hobab, Moses' father-in-law" (Judg. 4:11), it indicates that his name was Hobab, not Reuel. Why then does Scripture say, "And the women went to Reuel, their father" (Ex. 2:18)?

D. It indicates that children call their grandfather father.

E. R. Simeon b. Menassia says, "His name was Reuel, meaning, 'friend of God.' For it is said, 'And Aaron and all the elders of Israel came to eat bread with the father-in-law of Moses before God' (Ex. 18:12)."

F. R. Dosetai says, "His name was Keni, and why was he called Keni? Because he abandoned the deeds of Kenites, matters on which account they cause jealousy in the Omnipresent, as it is said, 'They roused my jealousy with a god of no account, with their false gods they provoked me' (Deut. 32:21).

G. "And it further says, '...where stands the image of Lust to arouse lustful passion' (Ezek. 8:3)."

H. R. Yosé says, "His name was Keni, and why was he called Keni? Because he acquired for himself heaven, earth, and the Torah."

I. R. Ishmael b. R. Yosé says, "His name was Reuel, and why was he called Reuel? Because he was a friend of God, as it is said, 'Your friend and the friend of the father do not abandon' (Prov. 27:10)."

J. R. Simeon b. Yohai says, "He had two names, Hobab and Jethro, Jethro because he had to his credit a passage of the Torah, as it is said, 'And you shall yourself search for capable God-fearing men among all the people' (Ex., 18:21). Now had that matter not been handed over to Moses from Sinai [so why did he need Jethro's advice]? For it is said, 'Now do this and God will so command you' (Ex. 18:19), So why did it escape Moses' sight? It was so as to assign merit to a meritorious person? It was so that the credit should go to Jethro.

K. "He was called Hobab because he loved the Torah. For we find in no other proselyte that someone cherished the Torah more than did Jethro.

L. "And just as Jethro loved the Torah, so we find that his descendants loved the Torah, as it is said, 'Go and speak the words of the Lord to the Rechabites' (Jer. 35:2). Since the house was going to be destroyed, it was regarded as if it had been destroyed now: 'You shall not build houses or sow seed or plant vineyards; you shall have none of these things. Instead you shall remain tent dwellers all your lives, so that you may live long in the land where you are sojourners. We have honored all the commands of our forefather Jonadab son of Rechab and have drunk no wine all our lives....We have not built houses to live in nor have we possessed vineyards or sown fields' (Jer. 35:7-9). Now because they obeyed the command of Jonadab their father, the Omnipresent raised up from them scribes, as it is said, 'The clans of the scribes living at Jabez: Tirathites, Shimeathites, and Suchathites. These were Kenites who were connected by marriage with the ancestor of the Rechabites' (1 Chr. 2:55).

M.   "They were called Tirathites, because they heard the alarm note [which in Hebrew uses the same consonants] from Mount Sinai, because they were full of fear and fasted, because they did not shave their hair, because they lived at the door of the gates of Jerusalem.

N.   "They were called Shimeathites because they obeyed the commandment of their father.

O.   "They were called Suchathites because they did not anoint [using the same consonants] with oil.

P.   "They were called 'living at Jabez' because they left Jericho and went to Jabez, to Adar, to study Torah from him, as it is said, 'Jabez called upon the God of Israel and said, "I pray you, bless me and grant me wide territories. May your hand be with me, and do me no harm, I pray you, and let me be free from pain." And God granted his petition' (1 Chr. 4:10). The one did not have someone with whom to study, and the other did not have anyone to teach. The ones who did not have someone with whom to study came to him who did not have anyone to teach, as it is said, 'The descendants of Moses' father-in-law, the Kenite, went up with the men of Judah from the Vale of Palm Trees to the wilderness of Judah which is in the Negeb of Arad and settled among the Amalekites' (Judg. 1:16).

Q.   "And how do we know that the descendants of Jethro are the descendants of Jonadab son of Rechab? As it is said, 'These were Kenites who were connected by marriage with the ancestor of the Rechabites' (1 Chr. 2:55).

R.   "What reward did they receive? 'To the Rechabites Jeremiah said, "These are the words of the Lord of Hosts, the God of Israel: 'Because you have kept the command of Jonadab your ancestor and obeyed all his instructions and carried out all that he told you to do, therefore these are the words of the Lord of Hosts, the God of Israel: Jonadab son of Rechab shall not want a descendant to stand before me for all time'"' (Jer. 35:18-19)."

S.   R. Joshua says, "Now do proselytes go into the inner sanctum? And is it not the case that no [mere] Israelite can go into the sanctum? But they took seats on the sanhedrin and taught rulings of the Torah."

T.   And some say that some of their daughters married priests, so their grandsons offered sacrifices on the altar.

U. Now, lo, it is an argument a fortiori: now if these, who brought themselves near, were brought still closer by the Omnipresent, Israelites who carry out the Torah all the more so!

V. And so, too, you find in the case of Rahab the whore. For what does it say in her regard?

W. "...The clans of the guild of linen workers at Ashbea, Jokim, the men of Kozeba, Joash, and Saraph, who fell out with Moab and came back to Bethlehem" (1 Chr. 4:21).

X. It was linen working for they hid the spies in flax.

Y. "...At Ashbea": for the spies took an oath to her [the word for oath and Ashbea use the same consonants].

Z. R. Eliezer says, "This refers to Rahab the whore, who kept an inn [a whorehouse]. Eight priests and eight prophets descended from Rahab the whore, and these are they: Jeremiah, Hilkiah, Sariah, Menassiah, Baruch, Neriah, Hanamel, and Shallum."

AA. R. Judah says, "Also Huldah the prophetess descended from the descendants of Rahab the whore, as it is said, 'So Hilkiah the priest, Ahikam, Akbor, Shaphan, and Asaiah went to Huldah the prophetess, wife of Shallum son of Tikvah, son of Harhas, the keeper of the wardrobe, and consulted her at her home in the second quarter of Jerusalem' (1 Kgs. 22:14).

BB. "And it further says, 'Lo, when we come to the land, you shall tie a red thread...' (Josh. 2:18).

CC. "Now it is an argument a fortiori: here is someone who comes from a people of whom it is said, 'You shall not keep alive a single soul' (Deut. 20:16). But because she brought herself near, the Omnipresent brought her near, if an Israelite carries out the Torah, all the more so.

DD. "So, too, you find with the Gibeonites: '...the clans of the guild of linen workers at Ashbea, Jokim, the men of Kozeba, Joash, and Saraph, who fell out with Moab and came back to Bethlehem' (1 Chr. 4:21). It was Jokim, for Joshua carried out for them the covenant, and Kozeba, for they deceived Joshua and said to him, 'Your servants have come from a most distant land,' while in fact they came from the Land of Israel itself.

EE. "Now it is an argument a fortiori: now if these, who derived from a people that were to be wiped out, because they brought themselves near, the Omnipresent brought them nearer still, if an Israelite carries out the Torah, all the more so.

FF. "So, too, you find with Ruth the Moabite. What did she say to her mother-in-law? 'Your people will be my people, and your God, my God, where you die, there I shall die' (Ruth 1:15-17).

GG. "The Omnipresent said to her, 'You have not lost. Lo, sovereignty will be yours in this world, and sovereignty will be yours in the world to come.

HH. "And as to Joash and Saraph, 'who arrived in Moabite country'? Joash and Saraph are 'Mahlon and Chilion' [Ruth 1:2]. Joash is so called because they despaired of redemption, Joash because they despaired of the teachings of the Torah. Saraph was so called because they burned their children for idolatry.

II.   "'They arrived in the Moabite country and there they stayed...'
        (Ruth 1:2): for they married Moabite women.

JJ.   "'They arrived in the Moabite country and there they stayed...': for
        they abandoned the Land of Israel and settled in the fields of Moab.

KK.   "'The records are ancient. [They were the potters,] and those who
        lived at Netaim [and Gederah were there on the king's service]' (1
        Chr. 4:23):

LL.   "This refers to Solomon, who was like a sapling in his dominion.

MM.   "'And Gederah' refers to the sanhedrin, which went into session
        and fenced in the teachings of the Torah.

NN.   "'...On the king's service': it was in his service that they took up
        residence there.

OO.   "And how do you know that Ruth the Moabite did not die before
        she saw Solomon, her grandson, as a judge in session and judging
        the case of the whores? As it is said, '...were there on the king's
        service.'

PP.   "Now it is an argument a fortiori: now if this one, who derived
        from the people concerning whom it is said, 'You shall not marry
        among them, and they shall not marry among you' (1 Kgs. 11:2),
        because she brought herself near, the Omnipresent drew her still
        nearer, if an Israelite carries out the Torah, all the more so.

QQ.   "And if you would argue that that was not the case in Israel, lo,
        Scripture says, 'And the king of Egypt said to the Hebrew midwives
        [Shiphrah and Puah]...' (Ex.. 1:15).

RR.   "Shiphrah was Jochebed, and Puah was Miriam [Moses' mother
        and sister], Shiphrah was so called because she was fecund,
        Shiphrah because she would adorn the newborn child, Shiphrah
        because Israel was fecund in her time.

SS.   "Puah, because she would moan and weep for her brother, as it is
        said, 'And his sister stood off at a distance to know what would
        become of him' (Ex. 2:4).

TT.   "'And he said, "When you are attending the Hebrew women in
        childbirth, watch as the child is delivered, and if it is a boy, kill him,
        if it is a girl, let her live."...They did not do what the king of Egypt
        had told them....So God made the midwives prosper and the people
        increased in numbers and in strength. God gave the midwives
        homes and families of their own, because they feared him' (Ex. 1:18-
        21).

UU.   "Now I do not know what these houses are. When Scripture states,
        'Solomon had taken twenty years to build the two houses, the
        house of the Lord and the royal palace' (1 Kgs. 9:10), the house of
        the Lord refers to the priesthood, and the house of the king,
        sovereignty. Jochebed had the merit of acquiring the priesthood,
        and Miriam, the royal house, as it is said, 'Coz was the father of
        Anub and Zobebah, and the clans of Aharhel, son of Harum' (1 Chr.
        4:8). Aharhel is the same as Miriam, as it is said, 'And all the
        women went forth after her' (Ex. 15:20). '...Son of Harum' refers to
        Jochebed, as it is said, 'Everything subject to the herem in Israel will
        belong to you' (Num. 18:14). Miriam married Caleb, as it is said,
        'When Azubah died, Caleb married Ephrath, who bore him Hur' (1
        Chr. 2:19).

VV. "'The descendants of Caleb: the sons of Hur, [the eldest son of Ephrathah: Shobal, the founder of Kiriath jearim, Salma, the founder of Bethlehem, and Hareph, the founder of Beth gader; Shobal, the founder of Kiriath jearim was the father of Reaiah, and the ancestor of half the Manahethites]' (1 Chr. 4:50-52). And Scripture further states, 'David was the son of a man of Ephratah of Bethlehem in Judah' (1 Sam. 17:12).

WW. "So David turns out to be one of the grandchildren of Miriam.

XX. "Lo, whoever brings himself near, Heaven draws him still closer."

6. Who hates Israel hates God:

LXXXIV

IV.1 A. "...and let them that hate you flee before you":

B. And do those who hate [come before] him who spoke and brought the world into being?

C. The purpose of the verse at hand is to say that whoever hates Israel is as if he hates him who spoke and by his word brought the world into being.

D. Along these same lines: "In the greatness of your majesty you overthrow your adversaries" (Ex. 15:7).

E. And are there really adversaries before him who spoke and by his word brought the world into being? But Scripture thus indicates that whoever rose up against Israel is as if he rose up against the Omnipresent.

F. Along these same lines: "Do not forget the clamor of your foes, the uproar of your adversaries, which goes up continually" (Ps. 74:23).

G. "For lo, your enemies, O Lord" (Ps. 92:10).

H. "For those who are far from you shall perish, you put an end to those who are false to you" (Ps. 73:27).

I. "For lo, your enemies are in tumult, those who hate you have raised their heads" (Ps. 83:2). On what account? "They lay crafty plans against your people, they consult together against your protected ones" (Ps. 83:3).

J. "Do I not hate those who hate you, O Lord? And do I not loathe them that rise up against you? I hate them with perfect hatred, I count them my enemies" (Ps. 139:21-22).

K. And so, too, Scripture says, "For whoever lays hands on you is as if he lays hands on the apple of his eye" (Zech. 2:12).

7. When people are in want, they depend on God, and it is good for people to need God:

LXXXV

1. A. "When the dew fell upon the camp in the night, the manna fell with it" (Num. 11:7-9):

2. B. Along these same lines, R. Simeon says, "On what account did the manna not come down for Israel on one day a year? It was so that they should turn their hearts to their father in heaven.

C. "One may draw a parable. To what may the matter be compared? To a king who made a decree for his son that he should provide a living for his son all together on only one day a year, and he would greet his father only at the time that he was there to collect his living. One time the king went and made a decree that he would provide his living every day. The son said, 'Even if I greet father only at the time that he provides my living, it is enough for me.'

D.   "So the case with Israel: If someone had five sons or five daughters, he would sit and stare, saying 'Woe is me, maybe the manna will not come down tomorrow! We'll all die of starvation. May it be your pleasure that it will come down.' So it turned out that they set their hearts heavenward."

E.   Along these same lines R. Dosetai b. R. Yosé says, "On what account did the Omnipresent not create hot springs in Jerusalem like the hot springs in Tiberias? It is so that someone should not say to his fellow, 'Let's go up to Jerusalem. Now if we go up only to take a single bath, it would be enough for us!' So as a result the pilgrimage would not be for a proper motive."

8.   Idolatry is the sin of denying God and the entirety of the Torah:

CXI

I.3   A.   "...Which the Lord has spoken to Moses":

B.   How do you know that whoever confesses to belief in idolatry denies the Ten Commandments?

C.   Scripture says, "...which the Lord has spoken to Moses," and elsewhere, "And God spoke all these words, saying" (Ex. 20:1). "God spoke one word..." (Ps. 62:12). "Are not my words like fire, says the Lord" (Jer. 23:29). So, too, in respect to that concerning which Moses was commanded Scripture says, "...all that the Lord God commanded through the hand of Moses."

D.   How do we know that that same rule applies also to all matters concerning which the prophets were commanded?

E.   Scripture says, "...from the day that the Lord gave commandment [and onward throughout your generations]."

F.   And how do we know that that is the case also concerning the commandments entrusted to the patriarchs?

G.   Scripture says, "...and onward throughout your generations."

H.   And whence did the Holy One, blessed be He, begin to entrust commandments to the patriarchs?

I.   As it is said, "And the Lord God commanded Adam" (Gen. 2:16).

J.   Scripture thereby indicates that whoever confesses to belief in idolatry denies the Ten Commandments and rejects all of the commandments entrusted to Moses, the prophets, and the patriarchs.

K.   And whoever denies idolatry confesses to belief in the entirety of the Torah.

9.   Sin comes about because of wantonness:

CXV

IV.1   A.   "...Not to follow after you own heart and your own eyes":

B. This refers to heresy, along the lines of the following verse: "The wiles of a woman I find more bitter than death, her heart is a trap to catch you and her arms are fetters" (Qoh. 7:28).

C. And Scripture says, "The king will rejoice in God" (Ps. 63:12).

IV.2 A. "...And your own eyes":

B. This refers to prostitution, as it is said, "And Samson said, 'Take that one for me, for she is right in my eyes'" (Judg. 14:3).

IV.3 A. "...Which you are inclined to go after wantonly":

B. This refers to idolatry, as it is said, "And they whored after the baals" (Judg. 8:33).

IV.4 A. "...Not to follow after your own heart and your own eyes, [which you are inclined to go after wantonly]":

B. Does this indicate that the eyes follow the heart or the heart the eyes?

C. Argue in this way: do you not have the case of a blind man who may perform every despicable deed that the world contains?

D. So what does Scripture mean when it says, "...not to follow after your own heart and your own eyes, which you are inclined to go after wantonly"?

E. It teaches that the eyes follow the heart.

IV.5 A. R. Ishmael says, "Why does Scripture say, '...not to follow after your own heart and your own eyes, which you are inclined to go after wantonly'?

B. "It is because Scripture states, 'Rejoice, young man, in your youth, and follow after your heart' (Qoh. 11:9).

C. "Does this mean in the right way or merely in whatever way you want?

D. "Scripture states, '...not to follow after your own heart and your own eyes, which you are inclined to go after wantonly.'"

III. Matters of Philosophy, Natural Science and Metaphysics

I find nothing that connects with this rubric.

Part Five

SIFRÉ TO DEUTERONOMY

29

Sifré to Deuteronomy to Debarim

I. Sifré to Deuteronomy: Forms and Program

Out of cases and examples, sages in Sifré to Deuteronomy seek generalizations and governing principles. Since in the book of Deuteronomy, Moses explicitly sets forth a vision of Israel's future history, sages here examine that vision to uncover the rules that explain what happens to Israel. That issue drew attention from cases to rules, with the result that, in the book of Deuteronomy, they set forth a systematic account of Israel's future history, the key to Israel's recovery of command of its destiny. Like Sifra, Sifré to Deuteronomy pursues a diverse topical program in order to demonstrate a few fundamental propositions. The survey of the topical and propositional program of Sifré to Deuteronomy dictates what is truly particular to that authorship. It is its systematic mode of methodical analysis, in which it does two things. First, the document's compilers take the details of cases and carefully reframe them into rules pertaining to all cases. The authorship therefore asks those questions of susceptibility to generalization ("generalizability") that first-class philosophical minds raise. And it answers those questions by showing what details restrict the prevailing law to the conditions of the case, and what details exemplify the encompassing traits of the law overall. These are, after all, the two possibilities. The law is either limited to the case and to all cases that replicate this one or the law derives from the principles exemplified, in detail, in the case at hand. Essentially, as a matter of both logic and topical program, our authorship has reread the legal portions of the book of Deuteronomy and turned Scripture into what we now know is the orderly and encompassing code supplied by the Mishnah. To state matters simply, this authorship "mishna-izes" Scripture. We find in Sifré to Numbers no parallel to this dominant and systematic program of Sifré to Deuteronomy.

But in other aspects, the document presents no surprises. In the two Sifrés and Sifra we find a recurrent motif, intense here, episodic there, of how the written component of the Torah, that is, revelation in written form, serves as the sole source of final truth. Logic or reason untested against Scripture produces flawed or unreliable results. The Torah, read as rabbis read it, and that alone, proves paramount. Reason on its own is subordinate. For their search for the social rules of Israel's society, the priority of the covenant as a reliable account of the workings of reality, and the prevailing laws of Israel's history decreed by the terms of the covenant, their fundamental claim is the same. There are rules and regularities, but reason alone will not show us what they are. A systematic and reasoned reading of the Torah – the Written Torah – joined to a sifting of the cases of the Torah in search of the regularities and points of law and order – these are what will tell the prevailing rule. A rule of the Mishnah and its account of the here and now of everyday life rests upon the Torah, not upon (mere) logic. A rule of Israel's history, past, present, and future, likewise derives from a search for regularities and points of order identified not by logic alone, but by logic addressed to the Torah. So there are these modes of gaining truth that apply equally to Mishnah and Scripture. There is logic, applied reason and practical wisdom, such as sages exhibit; there is the corpus of facts supplied by Scripture, read as sages read it. These two together form God's statement upon the world today.

The topical program of the document intersects at its fundamental propositions with programs of other authorships – beginning, after all, with those of Scripture itself. The writers and compilers and compositors of Deuteronomy itself would have found entirely familiar such notions as the conditional character of Israel's possession of the land of Israel, the centrality of the covenant in Israel's relationship with God, the other nations of the world, and its own destiny, and the covenantal responsibilities and standing of Israel's leadership – surely a considerable motif in the very structure of the book of Deuteronomy itself, beginning and end in particular. The reader may well wonder how we may treat as a distinctive authorship a group of writers who simply go over ground familiar in the received literature. In some important ways the authorship of Sifré to Deuteronomy makes a statement that is very much its own. That fact becomes clear when we consider the document's rhetorical, logical, and topical characteristics.

Rhetoric

Nine recurrent patterns prove dominant in Sifré to Deuteronomy. Because of the close relationship between rhetorical conventions and logical necessities for coherent discourse, we distinguish among them by the presence of propositions, explicit, and then implicit, and how these are argued or proved:

I. Propositions Stated Explicitly and Argued Philosophically (by Appeal to Probative Facts):
1. The Proposition and Its Syllogistic Argument
2. The Proposition Based on the Classification of Probative Facts
3. The Proposition Based on the Recurrent Opinions of Sages
4. The Narrative and Its Illustrated Proposition: Parable
5. Narrative and Its Illustrated Proposition: Scriptural Story

II. Propositions Stated Implicitly but Argued Philosophically (as Above):
6. The (Implicit) Proposition Based on Facts Derived from Exegesis
7. The Priority of Exegesis and the Limitations of Logic

III. Facts That Do Not Yield Propositions Beyond Themselves:
8. Exegetical Form with No Implicit Proposition. This is one form with a clear counterpart in Sifra.

IV. Facts That Do Not Yield Propositions Particular to the Case at Hand:
9. Dialectical Exegesis with No Implicit Proposition Pertinent to the Case at Hand but with Bearing on Large-Scale Structural Issues. This form is the same as our dialectical exegetical one.

I. Propositions Stated Explicitly and Argued Philosophically

1. *The Proposition and Its Syllogistic Argument:* This form is made up of simple sentences which, in one way or another, set forth propositions and demonstrate them by amassing probative facts, for example, examples. The patterning of the individual sentences of course varies. But the large-scale rhetoric, involving the presentation of a proposition, in general terms, and then the amassing of probative facts (however the sentences are worded), is essentially uniform. What we have are two or more sentences formed into a proposition and an argument, by contrast to those that are essentially singleton sentences, rather than components of a more sustained discourse. These items ordinarily deal with matters of proper conduct or right

action, hence *halakhic* issues. There is a two-layer discourse in them, since, at the superficial level, they yield only a detail of a law, that is, thus-and-so is the rule here; but at the deep layer of thought, they demonstrate a prevailing and global proposition that applies – it is implied – throughout, and not only to a single case. Overall, rhetorical analysis draws our attention to modes of stating a middle level proposition, affecting a variety of verses and their cases, in the present list. Then we move onward, to the low level proposition that pertains only to a single case, and, finally, we turn to a global proposition that affects a broad variety of cases, left discrete, but homogenizes them. These distinctions are meant to explain the classification system represented here. The absence of a counterpart in Sifra hardly requires proof.

2. *The Proposition Based on the Classification of Probative Facts:* The prevailing pattern here is not vastly changed. This is different from the foregoing only in a minor matter. In this case we shall propose to prove a proposition, for example, the meaning of a word, by classifying facts that point toward that proposition. In the foregoing, the work of proof is accomplished through listing proofs made up of diverse facts. The difference between the one and the other is hardly very considerable, but I think we can successfully differentiate among the formal patterns through the stated criterion. However, one may reasonably argue that this catalogue and the foregoing list essentially the same formal patterns of language or argument. In many of these instances, we have a complex development of a simple exegesis, and it is at the complexity – the repeated use of a simple pattern – that the propositional form(s) reach full exposure. Sifra's authorship has no use for such a pattern.

3. *The Proposition Based on the Recurrent Opinions of Sages:* This is another variation, in that the nature of the evidence shifts, and, it follows, also the patterning of language. Here we shall have the attributive constantly present, for example, X says, and that does form an important rhetorical indicator. We may say flatly that this form is not characteristic of our authorship and accomplishes none of their goals. It is a commonplace in the Mishnah, inclusive of Tractate Abot, and in the Tosefta; large-scale compositions in the Yerushalmi and the Bavli follow the same pattern; and other large-scale compositions will be drawn together because a sequence of simple declarative sentences on diverse topics, whether or not related in theme, bears the same attributive. The omission of this pattern here therefore is noteworthy and constitutes a decision for one pattern and against another. I know of no material equivalent in Sifra.

4-5. *The Narrative and Its Illustrated Proposition. Also: Parable, Narrative and Its Illustrated Proposition: The Scriptural Story.* The construction in which a proposition is established and then illustrated in a narrative, whether parable, scriptural story, or other kind of narrative, is treated in a single rubric. The formal structural uniformity justifies doing so. We may find varieties of patterns of sentences, for example, parables as against stories. But the narrative is always marked by either, "he said to him...he said to him...," for the story, or counterpart indications of a select pattern of forming and arranging sentences, for the parable. The authorship of Sifré to Deuteronomy has resorted to a very limited repertoire of patterns of language, and "narrative," a gross and hardly refined, classification, suffices. For narratives, viewed as an encompassing formal category, do not play a large role in defining (therefore differentiating) the rhetorical logical program of our authorship. Sifra's authorship scarcely presents stories of this kind.

II. Propositions Stated Implicitly but Argued Philosophically

6. *Implicit Propositions:* These items involve lists of facts, but lack that clear statement of the proposition that the facts establish. What we have here are complexes of tightly joined declarative sentences, many of them (in the nature of things) in that atom pattern, "commentary form," but all of them joined into a much larger set of (often) highly formalized statements. Hence I characterize this form as an implicit proposition based on facts derived from exegesis. For obvious reasons, there is no counterpart in Sifra.

III. Facts That Do Not Yield Propositions Beyond Themselves

7. *Exegetical Form with No Implicit Proposition:* This simple exegetical form presents a single fact, a discrete sentence, left without further development and without association or affinity with surrounding statements – once more, "commentary form." The form is as defined: clause + phrase. In Sifra this is the single most common pattern, as we saw. But in Sifré to Deuteronomy that same form in the propositional compositions rarely occurs without development, and if I had to specify the one fundamental difference between nonpropositional exegetical form (such as we find in Sifra and Sifré to Numbers and in some measure in Sifré to Deuteronomy) and all other forms, it is in the simplicity of the one as against the complexity of the other. Or, to state matters more bluntly, excluding narrative, the sole rhetorical building block of any consequence in Sifra, Sifré to

Numbers, and Sifré to Deuteronomy is the simple exegetical one, consisting of *clause + phrase = sentence.*

What differentiates Sifra from Sifré to Deuteronomy is that here all other forms develop the simple atom of exegetical form into a complex molecule, but the "exegetical form with no implicit proposition" remains at the atomic level (if not an even smaller particle than the atom) and never gains the dimensions of a molecular composite. These therefore constitute entirely comprehensible sense units, that is, on their own, simple sentences, never formed into paragraphs, and define the lowest rhetorical form of our document. The other rhetorical forms build these simple sense units or sentences into something more complex. That fact of rhetoric accounts, also, for our having – willy-nilly – to appeal to considerations of logical cogency in our analysis of rhetoric and form.

IV. Facts That Do Not Yield Propositions Particular to the Case at Hand

8. *Dialectical Exegesis with No Implicit Proposition Pertinent to the Case at Hand but with Bearing on Large-Scale Structural Issues:* Here we deal with the same pattern that, in Sifra, we have called dialectical exegetical form. The purpose of the form in Sifra is limited to the two purposes of, first, exclusionary/inclusionary inquiry, and, second, the critique of nonscripturally based taxonomy, while in Sifré to Deuteronomy a variety of propositions will be served. This form is made up of a series of closely joined thought units or sentences. Hence they present us with two or more sentences that constitute joined, propositional paragraphs. But their rhetorical traits are so much more particular, and their net effect so much more distinctive, that I treat them as a quite distinct rhetorical phenomenon. Moreover, these are the most patterned, the most formed, of all formal compositions at hand. They require sustained exposition of a proposition, not a simple proposition plus probative facts. They all make two points, as I have already pointed out, one at the surface, the other through the deep structure. Strictly speaking, as sustained and complex forms, all of these items conform most exactly to the fundamental definition of a rhetorical form, language that coheres to a single pattern. And the pattern is one of both rhetoric and also logic.

Two such patterns are, first, the systematic analytical exercise of restricting or extending the application of a discrete rule, ordinarily signified through stereotype language; second, the demonstration that logic without revelation in the form of a scriptural formulation and exegesis produces unreliable results. There are other recurrent patterns of complex linguistic formation matched by sustained thought that conform to the indicative traits yielded by these two distinct ones. The form invariably involves either the exercise of generalization through extension or restriction of the rule to the case given in Scripture, or the demonstration that reason unaided by Scripture is not reliable. The formal traits are fairly uniform, even though the intent – the upshot of the dialectical exegesis – varies from instance to instance. Very often these amplifications leave the base verse far behind, since they follow a program of their own, to which the base verse and its information is at best contributory. One of the ways in which this formalization of language differs from the foregoing is that the exegesis that is simple in form always is closely tied to the base verse, while the one which pursues larger-scale structural issues very frequently connects only very loosely to the base verse. Another persistent inquiry, external to any given verse and yielding, in concrete terms, no general rule at all, asks how to harmonize two verses, the information of which seems to conflict. The result is a general proposition that verses are to be drawn into alignment with one another. Here, we see, we are entirely at home. Sifra and Sifré to Deuteronomy have in common the usage of the dialectical exegetical form for pretty much the same purposes. A highly restricted repertoire of formal possibilities therefore confronted the writers of materials now collected in Sifré to Deuteronomy.

Logic of Coherent Discourse

The paramount logic of Sifré to Deuteronomy is not exegetical but propositional. Most units of cogent discourse in Sifré to Deuteronomy appeal for cogency to propositions, not to fixed associations, such as characterize commentaries and other compilations of exegeses of verses of Scripture:

Propositional units of cogent discourse		*Nonpropositional units of cogent discourse*
Fixed associative	159	13.9%
Propositional	690	60.4%
Narrative	61	5.3%
Methodical Analytical	232	20.3%

More than 85 percent of all itemized units of discourse – the second, third, and fourth entries on the list – find cogency through one or another mode of propositional logic. That figure is confirmed by yet another. Of the propositional units of cogent discourse, 70.1 percent in fact constitute propositional discourse, 6.2 percent find cogency in narrative, and 23.6 percent in the methodical analytical mode. Our document's authorship links one sentence to another by appeal to connections of proposition, not mere theme, and only occasionally asks the structure of a verse or sequence of verses to sustain the intelligible joining or two or more sentences into a coherent and meaningful statement.

Do the rhetoric and logic of our document derive from the (supposed) purpose of the authorship of forming a commentary? Not at all. To the contrary, in general, the logic of our document is sustained, propositional, mostly philosophical, and not that of commentary. What holds things together for our authorship does not rely upon the verse at hand to impose order and cogency upon discourse. The authorship of this document ordinarily appeals to propositions to hold two or more sentences together. If, by definition, a commentary appeals for cogency to the text that the commentators propose to illuminate, then ours is a document that is in no essential way a commentary. The logic is not that of a commentary, and the formal repertoire shows strong preference for other than commentary form. So far as commentary dictates both its own rhetoric and its own logic, this is no commentary. It is, in fact, a highly argumentative, profoundly well-crafted and cogent set of propositions. We may indeed speak of a message, a topical program, such as, in general, a commentary that in form appeals to a clause of a verse and a phrase of a sentence, and in logic holds things together through fixed associations, is not apt to set forth. A commentary makes statements about meanings of verses, but it does not make a set of cogent statements of its own. I have now shown that in rhetoric and in logic Sifré to Deuteronomy takes shape in such a way as to yield a statement, or a set of cogent statements. Such a document as ours indicates that an authorship has found a need for propositions to attain cogency or impart connections to two or more sentences, calls upon narrative, demands recurrent methodical analyses. The text that is subjected to commentary only occasionally is asked to join sentence to sentence.

Let us now compare Sifra and Sifré to Deuteronomy, to show that these observations indeed do effect the differentiation of otherwise closely aligned documents.

Sifra

Type of Logic	Number of entries	Percentage of the whole
Propositional	73	30.4%
Narrative/teleological	1	0.4%
Fixed Associative	43	17.9%
Methodical Analytical	123	51.0%
	240	99.7%

Sifré to Deuteronomy

Type of Logic	Number of entries	Percentage of the whole
Propositional	690	60.4%
Narrative/teleological	61	5.3%
Fixed Associative	59	13.9%
Methodical Analytical	232	20.3%
	1042	99.9%

In Sifré to Deuteronomy, of the propositional units of cogent discourse, 60.4 percent in fact constitute propositional discourse, 5.3 percent find cogency in narrative, and 20.3 percent in the methodical analytical mode. Since that mode presents not one but two propositions, we find ourselves on firm ground in maintaining that the logic of Sifré to Deuteronomy is a logic not of exegesis but of sustained proposition of one kind or another. The differences between Sifra and Sifré to Deuteronomy are these:

1. *Propositional logic:* Sifré to Deuteronomy contains two times the proportion of propositional compositions. Sifré to Deuteronomy is a highly propositional compilation, while Sifra is not.

2. *Teleological logic:* Sifré to Deuteronomy contains thirteen times the proportion of narrative compositions than does Sifra. Since teleological logic is propositional in its foundation, that disproportion is readily understood.

3. *Fixed associative logic:* The two documents make use of approximately the same proportions of this mode of stringing sentences or facts together, 17.9 percent against 13.9 percent, a differential of 1.2 times the proportion in Sifra over Sifré to Numbers. That does not seem to me a significant difference, given the rough-and-ready mode of classification employed at this stage in the work.

4. *Methodical analytical logic:* Sifra's authorship presents *two and a half* times the proportion of completed units of thought held together by the logic of systematic methodical analysis than does that of Sifré to Deuteronomy. The message of Sifra depends upon repetition of a single highly abstract proposition expressed in concrete terms. Hence the repetition of the same inquiry over a sizable number of diverse entries makes the point Sifra's authorship wishes to make. Sifré to Deuteronomy makes its points as propositions, not as repeated demonstrations of fundamental

attributes of thought, such as is the paramount medium of thought and expression of Sifra.

The authorship of Sifra has a very clear notion of precisely the questions it wishes persistently to address and it follows that program through the majority of the pericopes of its document. These questions then form the distinctive trait of mind of Sifra in comparison to Sifré to Deuteronomy. The resort to teleological logic in both documents is negligible in proportion to the whole. The utilization of fixed associative logic is pretty much in equal proportions; and Sifré to Deuteronomy is characterized by an interest in propositional discourse, while in Sifra that mode of discourse is subsumed under the logic of fixed analysis.

Topical Program

Four principal topics encompass the document's propositions, of which the first three correspond to the three relationships into which, in sages' world, that is, Israel, entered: with heaven, on earth, and within. These yield systematic statements that concern the relationships between Israel and God, with special reference to the covenant, the Torah, and the land; Israel and the nations, with interest in Israel's history, past, present, and future, and how that cyclical is to be known; Israel on its own terms, with focus upon Israel's distinctive leadership. The fourth rubric encompasses not specific ad hoc propositions, that form aggregates of proofs of large truths, but rather, prevailing modes of thought, demonstrating the inner structure of intellect, in our document yielding the formation, out of the cases of Scripture, of encompassing rules.

ISRAEL AND GOD: THE IMPLICATIONS OF THE COVENANT: The basic proposition, spelled out in detail, is that Israel stands in a special relationship with God, and that relationship is defined by the contract, or covenant, that God made with Israel. The covenant comes to particular expression, in our document, in two matters, first, the land, second, the Torah. Each marks Israel as different from all other nations, on the one side, and as selected by God, on the other. In these propositions, sages situate Israel in the realm of heaven, finding on earth the stigmata of covenanted election and concomitant requirement of loyalty and obedience to the covenant.

First comes the definition of those traits of God that our authorship finds pertinent. God sits in judgment upon the world, and his judgment is true and righteous. God punishes faithlessness. But God's fundamental and definitive trait is mercy. The way of God is to be merciful and gracious. The basic relationship of Israel to God is one of God's grace for Israel. God's loyalty to Israel endures, even when Israel sins. When Israel forgets God, God is pained. Israel's leaders, whatever their excellence, plead with God only for grace, not for their own merit. Correct attitudes in prayer derive from the need for grace, Israel having slight merit on its own account. Israel should follow only God, carrying out religious deeds as the covenant requires, in accord with the instructions of prophets. Israel should show mercy to others, in the model of God's merciful character.

Second, the contract, or covenant, produces the result that God has acquired Israel, which God created. The reason is that only Israel accepted the Torah, among all the nations, and that is why God made the covenant with Israel in particular. Why is the covenant made only with Israel? The gentiles did not accept the Torah, Israel did, and that has made all the difference. Israel recognized God forthwith; the very peace of the world and of nature depends upon God's giving the Torah to Israel. That is why Israel is the sole nation worthy of dwelling in the palace of God and that is the basis for the covenant, too. The covenant secures for Israel an enduring relationship of grace with God. The covenant cannot be revoked and endures forever. The covenant, terms of which are specified in the Torah, has duplicate terms: if you do well, you will bear a blessing, and if not, you will bear a curse.

That is the singular mark of the covenant between God and Israel. A mark of the covenant is the liberation from Egypt, and that sufficed to impose upon Israel God's claim for their obedience. An important sign of the covenant is the possession of the land. Part of the covenant is the recognition of merit of the ancestors. God promised, in making the covenant, recognition for the children of the meritorious deeds of the ancestors. The conquest of the land and inheriting it are marks of the covenant, which Israel will find easy because of God's favor. The inheritance of the land is a mark of merit, inherited from the ancestors. The land is higher than all others and more choice. All religious duties are important, those that seem trivial as much as those held to be weightier.

God always loves Israel. That is why Israel should carry out the religious duties of the Torah with full assent. All religious duties are equally precious. Israel must be whole-hearted in its relationship with God. If it is, then its share is with God, and if not, then not. But Israel may hate God. The right attitude toward God is love, and Israel should love God with a whole heart. The reason that Israel rebels against God is prosperity. Then people become arrogant and believe that their prosperity derives from their own efforts. But that is not so, and God punishes people who rebel to show them that they depend upon God. When Israel practices idolatry, God punishes them, for example, through exile, through famine, through drought, and the like. Whether or not

Israel knows or likes the fact, it is the fact that Israel therefore has no choice but to accept God's will and fulfill the covenant.

The heaven and the earth respond to the condition of Israel and therefore carry out the stipulations of the covenant. If Israel does not carry out religious duties concerning heaven, then heaven bears witness against them. That centers of course on the land of Israel in particular. Possession of the land is conditional, not absolute. It begins with grace, not merit. It is defined by the stipulation that Israel observe the covenant, in which case Israel will retain the land. If Israel violates the covenant, Israel will lose the land. When Israel inherits the land, in obedience to the covenant and as an act of grace bestowed by God, it will build the temple, where Israel's sins will find atonement. The conquest of the land itself is subject to stipulations, just as possession of the land, as an act of God's grace, is marked by religious obligations. If Israel rebels or rejects the Torah, it will lose the land, just as the Canaanites did for their idolatry.

The land is not the only, or the most important, mark of the covenant. It is the fact that Israel has the Torah which shows that Israel stands in a special relationship to God. The Torah is the source of life for Israel. It belongs to everyone, not only the aristocracy. Children should start studying the Torah at the earliest age possible. The study of the Torah is part of the fulfillment of the covenant. Even the most arid details of the Torah contain lessons, and if one studies the Torah, the reward comes both in this world and in the world to come.

The possession of the Torah imposes a particular requirement, involving an action. The most important task of every male Israelite is to study the Torah, which involves memorizing, and not forgetting, each lesson. This must go on every day and all the time. Study of the Torah should be one's main obligation, prior to all others. The correct motive is not for the sake of gain, but for the love of God and the desire for knowledge of God's will. People must direct heart, eyes, ears, to teachings of the Torah. Study of the Torah transforms human relationships, so that strangers become the children of the master of the Torah whom they serve as disciples. However unimportant the teaching or the teacher, all is as if on the authority of Moses at Sinai. When a person departs from the Torah, that person becomes an idolator. Study of the Torah prevents idolatry.

ISRAEL AND THE NATIONS: THE MEANING OF HISTORY: The covenant, through the Torah of Sinai, governs not only the ongoing life of Israel but also the state of human affairs universally. The history of Israel forms a single, continuous cycle, in that what happened in the beginning prefigures what will happen at the end of time. Events of Genesis are reenacted both in middle history, between the beginning and the end, and also at the end of times. So the traits of the tribal founders dictated the history of their families to both the here and now and also the eschatological age. Moses was shown the whole of Israel's history, past, present, future. The times of the patriarchs are reenacted in the messianic day. That shows how Israel's history runs in cycles, so that events of ancient times prefigure events now. The prophets, beginning with Moses, describe those cycles. What happens bears close ties to what is going to happen. The prophetic promises, too, were realized in temple times, and will be realized at the end of time.

The periods in the history of Israel, marked by the exodus and wandering, the inheritance of the land and the building of the temple, the destruction, are all part of a divine plan. In this age Rome rules, but in the age to come, marked by the study of the Torah and the offering of sacrifices in the temple cult, Israel will be in charge. That is the fundamental pattern and meaning of history. The Holy Spirit makes possible actions that bear consequences only much later in time. The prefiguring of history forms the dominant motif in Israel's contemporary life, and the reenacting of what has already been forms a constant. Israel therefore should believe, if not in what is coming, then in what has already been. The very names of places in the land attest to the continuity of Israel's history, which follows rules that do not change. The main point is that while Israel will be punished in the worst possible way, Israel will not be wiped out.

But the cyclical character of Israel's history should not mislead. Events follow a pattern, but knowledge of that pattern, which is provided by the Torah, permits Israel both to understand and also to affect its own destiny. Specifically, Israel controls its own destiny through its conduct with God. Israel's history is the working out of the effects of Israel's conduct, moderated by the merit of the ancestors. Abraham effected a change in God's relationship to the world. But merit, which makes history, is attained by one's own deeds as well. The effect of merit, in the nation's standing among the other nations, is simple. When Israel enjoys merit, it gives testimony against itself, but when not, then the most despised nation testifies against it.

But God is with Israel in time of trouble. When Israel sins, it suffers. When it repents and is forgiven, it is redeemed. For example, Israel's wandering in the wilderness took place because of the failure of Israel to attain merit. Sin is what causes the wandering in the wilderness. People rebel because they are prosperous. The merit of the ancestors works in history to Israel's benefit. What Israel does not merit on its own, at a given time, the merit of the ancestors may secure in any event. The best way to deal with Israel's powerlessness is through Torah study; the vigor of engagement with Torah study compensates for weakness.

It goes without saying that Israel's history follows a set time, for example, at the fulfillment of a set period of time, an awaited event will take place. The prophets prophesy concerning the coming of the day of the Lord. Accordingly, nothing is haphazard, and all things happen in accord with a plan. That plan encompasses this world, the time of the Messiah, and the world to come, in that order. God will personally exact vengeance at the end of time. God also will raise the dead. Israel has overcome difficult times and can continue to do so. The task ahead is easier than the tasks already accomplished. Israel's punishment is only once, while the punishment coming upon the nations is unremitting. Peace is worthwhile and everyone needs it. Israel's history ends in the world to come or in the days of the Messiah. The righteous inherit the Garden of Eden. The righteous in the age to come will be joyful.

God acts in history and does so publicly, in full light of day. That is to show the nations who is in charge. The Torah is what distinguishes Israel from the nations. All the nations had every opportunity to understand and accept the Torah, and all declined it; that is why Israel was selected. And that demonstrates the importance of both covenant and the Torah, the medium of the covenant. The nations even had a prophet, comparable to Moses. The nations have no important role in history, except as God assigns them a role in relationship to Israel's conduct. The nations are estranged from God by idolatry. That is what prevents goodness from coming into the world. The name of God rests upon Israel in greatest measure. Idolators do not control heaven. The greatest sin an Israelite can commit is idolatry, and those who entice Israel to idolatry are deprived of the ordinary protections of the law. God is violently angry at the nations because of idolatry. As to the nations' relationships with Israel, they are guided by Israel's condition. When Israel is weak, the nations take advantage, when strong, they are sycophantic. God did not apportion love to the nations of the world as he did to Israel.

ISRAEL AT HOME: THE COMMUNITY AND ITS GOVERNANCE: A mark of God's favor is that Israel has (or, has had and will have) a government of its own. Part of the covenantal relationship requires Israel to follow leaders whom God has chosen and instructed, such as Moses and the prophets. Accordingly, Israel is to establish a government and follow sound public policy. Its leaders are chosen by God. Israel's leaders, for example, prophets, are God's servants, and that is a mark of the praise that is owing to them. They are to be in the model of Moses, humble, choice, select, well-known. Moses was the right one to bestow a blessing, Israel were the right ones to receive the blessing.

Yet all leaders are mortal, even Moses died. The saints are leaders ready to give their lives for Israel. The greatest of them enjoy exceptionally long life. But the sins of the people are blamed on their leaders. The leaders depend on the people to keep the Torah, and Moses thanked them in advance for keeping the Torah after he died. The leaders were to be patient, honest, give a full hearing to all sides, make just decisions, in a broad range of matters. To stand before the judge is to stand before God. God makes sure that Israel does not lack for leadership. The basic task of the leader is both to rebuke and also to console the people.

The rulers of Israel are servants of God. The prophets exemplify these leaders, in the model of Moses, and Israel's rulers act only on the instruction of prophets. Their authority rests solely on God's favor and grace. At the instance of God, the leaders of Israel speak, in particular, words of admonition. These are delivered before death, when the whole picture is clear, so that people can draw the necessary conclusions. These words, when Moses spoke them, covered the entire history of the community of Israel. The leaders of Israel address admonition to the entire community at once. No one is excepted. But the Israelites can deal with the admonition. They draw the correct conclusions. Repentance overcomes sin, as at the sin of the golden calf. The Israelites were contentious, nitpickers, litigious, and, in general, gave Moses a difficult time. Their descendants should learn not to do so. Israel should remain united and obedient to its leaders. The task of the community is to remain united. When the Israelites are of one opinion below, God's name is glorified above.

THE LAWS AND LAW. THE STRUCTURE OF INTELLECT: The explicit propositional program of our document is joined by a set of implicit ones. These comprise repeated demonstration of a point never fully stated. The implicit propositions have to do with the modes of correct analysis and inquiry that pertain to the Torah. There are two implicit propositions that predominate. The first, familiar (as I shall show presently) from other compilations, is that pure reason does not suffice to produce reliable results. Only through linking our conclusions to verses of Scripture may we come to final and fixed conclusions. The implicit proposition, demonstrated many times, may therefore be stated very simply. The Torah (written) is the sole source of reliable information. Reason undisciplined by the Torah yields unreliable results. These items may occur, also, within the rubrics of the specific propositions that they contain. Some of them moreover overlap with the later catalogue, but, if so, are not listed twice.

The second of the two recurrent modes of thought is the more important. Indeed, we shall presently note that it constitutes the one substantial, distinctive statement made by our authorship. It is the demonstration that many things conform to a single structure and pattern. We can show this uniformity of the law by addressing the same questions to disparate cases and, in so doing, composing general laws that transcend cases and form a cogent system. What is striking, then, is the power of a single set of questions to reshape and reorganize diverse data into a single cogent set of questions and answers, all things fitting together into a single, remarkably well-composed structure. Not only so, but when we review the numerous passages at which we find what in the logical repertoire I called methodical analytical logic, we find a single program. It is an effort to ask whether a case of Scripture imposes a rule that limits or imparts a rule that augments the application of the law at hand.

A systematic reading of Scripture permits us to restrict or to extend the applicability of the detail of a case into a rule that governs many cases. A standard repertoire of questions may be addressed to a variety of topics, to yield the picture of how a great many things make essentially a single statement. This seems to me the single most common topical inquiry in our document. It covers most of the laws of Deuteronomy 12-26. I have not catalogued the laws of history, which generalize from a case and tell us how things always must be; the list of explicit statements of the proposition that the case at hand is subject to either restriction or augmentation, that the law prevailing throughout is limited to the facts at hand or exemplified by those facts, would considerably add to this list. The size, the repetitious quality, the obsessive interest in augmentation and restriction, generalization and limitation – these traits of logic and their concomitant propositional results form the centerpiece of the whole.

In some few units of thought I discern no distinctive message, one that correlates with others to form a proposition of broad implications. Perhaps others can see points that transcend the cases at hand. These items would correspond to ones we should expect from an authorship that remained wholly within Scripture's range of discourse, proposing only to expand and clarify what it found within Scripture. Were our document to comprise only a commentary, then the messages of Scripture, delivered within the documentary limits of Scripture – that is, verse by verse, in a sustained statement solely of what Scripture says restated in paraphrase – would constitute the whole of the catalogue of this chapter. We now see that that is far from the fact. Relative to the size of the document as a whole, these items do not seem to me to comprise an important component of the whole. They show that had our authorship wished only to amplify and restate the given, without presenting their own thought through the medium of Scripture (as through other media), they had every occasion and means of doing so. But they did so only in a limited measure. So much for the document overall. Let us now examine Sifré to Deuteronomy to Parashat Debarim and identify the important legal and theological premises, on the one side, and philosophical points of interest, on the other.

II. Unarticulated Premises: The Givens of Religious Conduct

There is nothing of halakhic interest here.

III. Unarticulated Premises: The Givens of Religious Conviction

Most of the exposition is given over to the amplification and paraphrase of the verses at hand, but there are a few points of theological interest:

1. The Messiah will be harsh toward the nations but kindly toward Israel:

I

XI.1   A.   Along these same lines [of dispute between Judah and Yosé:]

      B.   R. Judah expounded, "'The burden of the word of the Lord. In the land of Hadrach, and in Damascus, shall be his resting place, for the Lord's is the eye of man and all the tribes of Israel' (Zech. 9:1)":

      C.   "[Hadrach] refers to the Messiah, who is sharp [had] toward the nations, but soft [rakh] toward Israel."

2. God never hates Israel, but Israel sometimes hates God:

XXIV

III.1   A.   "It is because the Lord hates us":

      B.   It is impossible that the Omnipresent should hate Israel. For has it not been said, "I have loved you, said the Lord" (Mal. 1:2)?

      C.   Rather, they are the ones who hate the Omnipresent.

      D.   There is a popular saying that has it: What you think of your friend is what he thinks of you.

IV. Matters of Philosophy, Natural Science and Metaphysics

There is nothing that qualifies.

30

Sifré to Deuteronomy to Waethanan

I. Unarticulated Premises: The Givens of Religious Conduct

There is considerable exposition of law here, but I find no premises or presuppositions of note.

II. Unarticulated Premises: The Givens of Religious Conviction

1. No one's merit is sufficient, and everyone must in the end throw himself upon God's mercy and grace:

XXVI

I.1   A.   "I pleaded with the Lord at that time, saying, ['O Lord, God, you who let your servant see the first works of your greatness and your mighty hand, you whose powerful deeds no god in heaven or on earth can equal! Let me, I pray, cross over and see the good land on the other side of the Jordan, that good hill country, and the Lebanon.' But the Lord was wrathful with me on your account and would not listen to me. The Lord said to me, 'Enough, never speak to me of this matter again! Go up to the summit of Pisgah and gaze about, to the west, the north, the south, and the east. Look at it well, for you shall not go across yonder Jordan. Give Joshua his instructions and imbue him with strength and courage, for he shall go across at the head of this people, and he shall allot to them the land that you may only see.' Meanwhile we stayed on in the valley near Beth-peor']" (Deut. 4:23-29):

B.   That is in line with this verse: "The poor uses pleading, but the rich answers impudently" (Prov. 18:23):

C.   Israel had two truly excellent leaders, Moses and David, king of Israel, and their deeds were sufficient to sustain the whole world. Nonetheless, they pleaded the Holy One, blessed be He, only for nought [but grace, without appealing to their own meritorious achievements].

D.   And that produces an argument a fortiori:

E.   If these two, whose deeds were sufficient to sustain the whole world, pleaded with the Holy One, blessed be He, only for nought [but grace, without appealing to their own meritorious achievements], one who is only no more than one thousand-thousand-thousandth or ten-thousand-ten-thousandth part of the disciples of their disciples should also plead with the Holy One, blessed be He, only for nought [but grace, without appealing to their own meritorious achievements].

2.   One may serve God out of love or out of fear; loving God means bringing people to love God; one loves God with both of the impulses of the heart, to do good and to do evil; one loves God to the last breath of life:

XXXII

I.1   A.   "You shall love the Lord your God [with all your heart and with all your soul and with all your might. Take to heart these instructions with which I charge you this day. Impress them upon your children. Recite them when you stay at home and when you are away, when you lie down and when you get up. Bind them as a sign on your hand, and let them serve as a symbol on your forehead; inscribe them on the doorposts of your house and on your gates]" (Deut. 6:4-9):

    B.   Act out of love.

    C.   There is a difference between one who acts out of love and one who acts out of fear.

    D.   The one who acts out of love gets a doubled and redoubled reward, for it says, "The Lord your God you are to fear, and him you are to serve" (Deut. 10:20).

    E.   There may be someone who fears his fellow. When the latter needs him the former may leave him and go his way.

    F.   But as to you, act out of love, for there is no place for love in a state of fear, or fear in a state of love.

    G.   But matters accord solely with the prevailing condition.

XXXII

II.1   A.   Another explanation of the phrase, "You shall love the Lord your God":

    B.   Bring about love for him on the part of people, as did Abraham, your father.

    C.   That is in line with this statement: "The soul that they had made in Haran" (Gen. 12:5).

    D.   Now is it not the case that if everyone in the world got together to create a single gnat and to bring into it the breath of life, they could never do so?

    E.   But the sense is that our father, Abraham, made converts and brought them under the wings of God's presence.

XXXII

III.1   A.   "...With all your heart":

B.   [That is, with the entirety of your heart,] with both of the impulses that are yours, the one to do good, the one to do bad.

III.2   A.   Another explanation of "...with all your heart":

B.   with the whole of the heart that is in you, that your heart should not be divided against the Omnipresent.

III.3   A.   "...With all your soul":

B.   even if he takes your soul.

III.4   A.   And so Scripture says, "For your sake we are killed all day long, we are accounted as sheep for the slaughter" (Ps. 44:23).

B.   R. Simeon b. Menassia says, "And how is it possible for someone to be slaughtered all day long?

C.   "But the Holy One, blessed be He, credits it to the righteous as if they were slaughtered every day."

XXXII

IV.1   A.   Simeon b. Azzai says, "'With all your soul' – love him to the last drop of your soul."

IV.2   A.   R. Eliezer says, "Since it is said, 'with all your soul,' why is it said, 'with all your might'? And if it is said, 'with all your might,' why is it said, 'with all your soul'?

B.   "You may have someone whose physical welfare is more precious to him than his money. Therefore it is said, 'with all your soul.' And you may have someone whose money is more precious to him than his physical welfare. Therefore it is said, 'with all your might.'"

3.   One should love God in prosperity and adversity, in whatever measure God metes out to you:

XXXII

V.1   A.   R. Aqiba says, "Since it is said, 'with all your soul,' it is an argument a fortiori that we should encompass, 'with all your might.'

B.   "Why then does Scripture say, 'with all your might'?

C.   "It is to encompass every single measure that God metes out to you, whether the measure of good or the measure of punishment."

V.2   A.   So does David say, "[How can I repay the Lord for all his bountiful dealings toward me?] I will lift up the cup of salvation and call upon the name of the Lord" (Ps. 116:12-13).

B.   "I found trouble and sorrow but I called upon the name of the Lord" (Ps. 116:3-4).

V.3   A.   So does Job say, "The Lord gave and the Lord has taken away. Blessed be the name of the Lord" (Job 1:21).

B.   If that is the case for the measure of goodness, all the more so for the measure of punishment.

C.   What does his wife say to him? "Do you still hold fast your integrity? Blaspheme God and die" (Job 2:9).

D.   And what does he say to her? "You speak as one of the impious women speaks. Shall we receive good at the hand of God and shall we not receive evil?" (Job 2:10).

V.4   A.   The men of the generation of the flood were churlish as to the good, and when punishment came upon them, they took it willy-nilly.

B.   And is it not an argument a fortiori: if one who was churlish as to the good behaved with dignity in a time of punishment, we who behave with dignity in response to good should surely behave with dignity in a time of trouble.

C.   And so did he said to her, "You speak as one of the impious women speaks. Shall we receive good at the hand of God and shall we not receive evil?" (Job 2:10).

V.5   A.   And, furthermore, a person should rejoice in suffering more than in good times. For if someone lives in good times his entire life, he will not be forgiven for such sin as may be in his hand.

B.   And how shall he attain forgiveness? Through suffering.

III. Matters of Philosophy, Natural Science and Metaphysics

Nothing pertains.

31

Sifré to Deuteronomy to Eqeb

I. Unarticulated Premises: The Givens of Religious Conduct

The matter never arises.

II. Unarticulated Premises: The Givens of Religious Conviction

1. The Land of Israel is not only holier than, but also superior to, all other lands:

XXXVII

III.2 A. R. Judah says, "Now did the thirty-one kings who were in the past ever spend time in the Land of Israel?

   B. "But it is as they do things in Rome now.

   C. "For any king or ruler who did not acquire a portion in Rome says, 'I have never done a thing.'

   D. "So, too, any king or ruler who has not acquired a palace or fortification in the Land of Israel says, 'I have accomplished nothing.'"

III.3 A. "How would I give you a pleasant land":

   B. [Since the letters of the word for "pleasant" may also be read "deer," we draw the following analogy:] Just as the deer is faster than any domestic or wild beast, so the produce of the Land of Israel ripens more quickly than all of the produce of other lands.

III.4 A. Just as in the case of a deer, when you flay it, its hide cannot again contain its flesh, so the Land of Israel cannot contain the produce of the Land –

   B   when the Israelites carry out the Torah.

III.5 A. Just as a deer is easiest to digest among all domestic and wild beasts' [meat],

   B. so the produce of the Land of Israel is easiest to digest of the produce of all lands.

III.6 A. If the produce is so easy to digest, might one suppose that it is not rich?

   B. Scripture says, "A land flowing with milk and honey" (Deut. 11:9).

172

	C.	The produce is as fat as milk and sweet as honey.
	D.	So it is written, "Let me sing of my well-beloved, a song of my beloved, touching his vineyard; my well-beloved had a vineyard in a very fruitful hill" (Isa. 5:1).
III.7	A.	[With reference to the just cited prooftext, "Let me sing of my well-beloved, a song of my beloved, touching his vineyard; my well-beloved had a vineyard in a very fruitful hill (the Hebrew words may also be read 'a horn, bearing oil')" (Isa. 5:1)], just as an ox has no part higher than its horns,
	B.	so the Land of Israel is higher than all other lands.
	C.	Might one say, just as an ox has no part less valuable than its horn, so the Land of Israel is the least valuable of all lands?
	D.	Scripture to the contrary states, "a horn, bearing oil," meaning the Land of Israel is rich in oil.
	E.	This teaches you that it is higher than any other and more praiseworthy than any other.
III.8	A.	Since the Land of Israel is higher than all, it is more praiseworthy than all.
	B.	For so it is said, "We should go up at once and possess it" (Num. 13:30).
	C.	"...So they went up and spied out the land" (Num. 13:21).
	D.	"And they went up into the south" (Num. 13:22).
	E.	"And they went up out of Egypt" (Gen. 45:25).
III.9	A.	Since the house of the sanctuary is higher than all, it is more praiseworthy than all.
	B.	For so it is said, "You shall arise and go up to the place" (Deut. 17:18).
	C.	"And many peoples shall go and say, 'Come and let us go up to the mountain of the house of the Lord'" (Isa. 2:3).
	D.	"For there shall be a day, that the watchmen shall call upon the mount Ephraim: 'Arise and let us go up to Zion, to the Lord our God'" (Jer. 31:6).

Israel's residence in the Land of Israel is contingent upon their keeping the covenant of the Torah:

XXXVIII

II.6	A.	There is, therefore, a difference between your coming into this land and your coming into that land.
	B.	Coming into the land of Egypt was an optional matter, coming into the land of Israel is obligatory.
	C.	As to the land of Egypt, whether or not one carries out the will of the Omnipresent, lo, it is yours.
	D.	But the land of Israel is not that way.
	E.	If you carry out the will of the Omnipresent, lo, the land of Canaan is yours,
	F.	but if you do not carry out the will of the Omnipresent, you will go into exile from it.
	G.	And so Scripture says, "...so that the land not vomit you out if you make it unclean" (Lev. 18:25).

God cares for all lands but looks out for them only because of his love for the Land of Israel in particular, and the same is so for the nations and Israel:

XL

I.1   A.   "It is a land which the Lord your God looks after, on which the Lord your God always keeps his eye, from year's beginning to year's end" (Deut. 11:10-12):

B.   Does God look after that land alone? Does he not look after all lands?

C.   For it is said, "...to cause it to rain on a land where no man is...to satisfy the desolate and waste ground" (Job 38:26-27).

D.   Why then does Scripture say, "It is a land which the Lord your God looks after, [on which the Lord your God always keeps his eye, from year's beginning to year's end]" (Deut. 11:10-12)?

E.   It is – as it were – that he cares only for that land, but on account of caring about that land, he cares also for all other lands as well.

I.2   A.   Along these same lines: "Behold, he who keeps Israel does not slumber or sleep" (Ps. 121:4).

B.   Does God keep only Israel? Does he not keep everyone, for it is said, "In whose hand is the soul of every living thing and the breath of all mankind" (Job 12:10).

C.   Why then does Scriptures say "Behold, he who keeps Israel does not slumber or sleep" (Ps. 121:4)?

D.   It is – as it were – that he keeps Israel alone, but on account of keeping Israel, he also keeps everyone else along with them.

I.3   A.   Along these same lines: "My eyes and my heart shall be there perpetually" (1 Kgs. 9:3).

B.   But is it not also said, "The eyes of the Lord that run to and fro through the whole earth" (Zech. 4:10)?

C.   And it further says, "The eyes of the Lord are in every place, keeping watch on the evil and the good" (Prov. 15:3).

D.   Why then does Scripture state, "My eyes and my heart shall be there perpetually" (1 Kgs. 9:3)?

E.   It is – as it were – that "my eyes and my heart are only there."

I.4   A.   Along these same lines: "The voice of the Lord shakes the wilderness, the Lord shakes the wilderness of Kadesh" (Ps. 29:8).

B.   Why does Scripture say this?

C.   This [wilderness] more than the rest.

2.   Through studying the Torah with sages, Israel knows God; God is best served through the study of the Torah and prayer:

XLI

III.2   A.   ["The words of the sages are as goads" (Qoh. 12:11):] just as a goad guides an ox in its furrow to produce life sustaining crops for its master,

B.   so teachings of Torah guide a person's intellect to know the Omnipresent.

III.3   A.   And it is not as if one has heard it merely on the authority of the collegium of sages, but as if one has heard it from a formally constituted sanhedrin:

      B.   "...Masters of assemblies" (Qoh. 12:11),

      C.   and "assemblies" refers only to the sanhedrin,

      D.   as it is said, "Assemble to me seventy men of the elders of Israel" (Num. 11:16).

      E.   And it is not as if one has heard it merely from a formally constituted sanhedrin, but as if one has heard it from the mouth of Moses:

      F.   "Then his people remembered the days of old, the days of Moses" (Isa. 63:11).

      G.   And it is not as if one has heard it from Moses, but as if one has heard it from the mouth of the Omnipotent God:

      H.   "They are given from one shepherd." "Give ear, shepherd of Israel, thou who leads Joseph like a flock" (Ps. 80:2). "Hear O Israel, the Lord our God, the Lord is one" (Deut. 6:4).

XLI

VI.1   A.   "...And serving him [with all your heart and soul]":

      B.   This refers to study [of the Torah].

      C.   You say that it refers to study. But perhaps it refers only to actual service?

      D.   Lo, Scripture says, "And the Lord God took the man and put him into the Garden of Eden to work it and to guard it" (Gen. 2:15).

      E.   Now in the past what sort of work was there to do, and what sort of guarding was there to do?

      F.   But you learn from that statement that "to work it" refers to study of the Torah, and "to guard it" refers to keeping the religious duties.

      G.   And just as the service at the altar is called work, so study of the Torah is called work.

VI.2   A.   "...And serving him [with all your heart and soul]":

      B.   This refers to prayer.

      C.   You say that it refers to prayer. But perhaps it refers only to actual service?

      D.   Lo, Scripture says, "With all your heart and with all your soul" (Deut. 11:13).

      E.   Now is there a form of labor that is carried out only with the heart?

      F.   Why then does Scripture say, "...and serving him [with all your heart and soul]?"

      G.   This refers to prayer.

      H.   And so David says, "Let my prayer be set forth as incense before you, the lifting up of my hands as the evening sacrifice" (Ps. 141:23).

      I.   "And when Daniel knew that the writing was signed, he went into his house – now his windows were open in his upper chamber toward Jerusalem – and he kneeled upon his knees three times a day and prayed" (Dan. 6:11).

      J.   "O Daniel, servant of the living God, is your God, whom you serve continually, able to deliver you from the lions" (Dan. 6:21).

      K.   [The verse refers to continual service,] but is there a rite [of sacrifice] in Babylonia?

L.   What then does Scripture mean when it says, "To serve him with all your heart and with all your soul"?

M.   This refers to prayer.

N.   And just as the service at the altar is called work, so prayer is called work.

3.   People rebel against God by reason of prosperity; suffering brings them back:

XLIII

III.1 A.   "...And thus you shall eat your fill. Take care not to be lured away to serve other gods and bow to them. [For the Lord's anger will flare up against you, and he will shut up the skies so that there be no rain and the ground will not yield its produce; and you will soon perish from the good land that the Lord is assigning to you]" (Deut. 11:13-17):

B.   He said to them, "Take care lest you rebel against the Omnipresent. For a person rebels against the Omnipresent only in prosperity."

C.   For so it is said, "Lest when you have eaten and are satisfied and have built large houses and lived in them, and when your herds and your flocks multiply, and your silver and your gold" (Deut. 8:12-13).

D.   What then? "Then your heart be lifted up and you forget the Lord your God" (Deut. 8:14).

E.   Along these same lines: "For when I shall have brought them into the land which I swore to their fathers, flowing with milk and honey" (Deut. 31:20).

F.   What then? "And turned to other gods and served them" (Deut. 31:20).

G.   Along these same lines: "And the people sat down to eat and to drink" (Ex. 32:6).

H.   What then? "They have made a molten calf" (Ex. 32:8).

III.2 A.   Along these same lines in connection with the men of the generation of the flood, they rebelled against the Omnipresent only in prosperity.

B.   What is said in their regard? "Their houses are safe, without fear...their bull genders, they send forth their little ones like a flock...they spend their days in prosperity" (Job 21:9-13).

C.   This is what made them act as they did: "Depart from us, we do not desire knowledge of your ways. What is the almighty that we should serve him" (Job 21:14-15).

D.   They said, "Not even for a drop of rain do we need him, for 'There goes up a mist from the earth' (Gen. 2:6)."

E.   Said to them the Omnipresent, "In the very act of goodness which I have done for you, you take pride before me? Through that same act I shall exact a penalty from you."

F.   "And the rain was upon the earth forty days and forty nights" (Gen. 7:12).

4.   Imitating God means to be merciful and gracious to others; cleaving to the Torah is like cleaving to God:

XLIX

I.1 A. "...Walking in all his ways, and holding fast to him, [the Lord will dislodge before you all these nations; you will dispossess nations greater and more numerous than you. Every spot on which your foot treads shall be yours; your territory shall extend from the wilderness to the Lebanon, and from the River, the Euphrates, to the Western Sea. No man shall stand up to you: the Lord your God will put the dread and the fear of you over the whole land in which you set foot, as he promised you]" (Deut. 11:22-25):

    B. What are the ways of the Omnipresent?

    C. "The Lord God, merciful and gracious" (Ex. 34:6).

I.2 A. Scripture states, "And it shall come to pass that whoever shall be called by the name of the Lord shall be delivered" (Joel 3:5).

    B. How is it possible for someone to be called by the name of the Omnipresent?

    C. But since the Omnipresent is called "merciful," you, too, be merciful.

    D. The Holy One, blessed be He, is called gracious, so you, too, be gracious.

    E. For it is said, "The Lord, God, merciful and gracious" (Ps. 145:8).

    F. And give gifts for nothing.

    G. Just as the Omnipresent is called "righteous," as it is said, "For the Lord is righteous, he loves righteousness" (Ps. 11:7), so you, too, be righteous.

    H. The Omnipresent is called merciful: "For I am merciful, says the Lord" (Jer. 3:12), so you, too, be merciful.

    I. That is why it is said, "And it shall come to pass that whoever shall be called by the name of the Lord shall be delivered" (Joel 3:5).

    J. "Everyone who is called by my name" (Isa. 43:7).

    K. "The Lord has made everything for his own purpose" (Prov. 16:4).

XLIX

II.1 A. "...And holding fast to him":

    B. Now how is it possible for a person to go up to the height and to cleave to fire?

    C. And has it not been said, "For the Lord your God is a consuming fire" (Deut. 4:24)?

    D. "His throne was fiery flames" (Dan. 7:9).

    E. [But God has said,] "Cleave to sages and their disciples, and I shall credit it to you as if you had gone up to the height and taken [the Torah],

    F. "and not merely as if in peace you had gone up to the height and taken [the Torah], but as if you had made war and taken it [by struggle]."

    G. And so Scripture says, "You have ascended on high, you have taken captives" (Ps. 68:19).

II.2 A. Those who expound lore [aggadoth] say, "If you want to know the one who spoke and brought the world into existence, study lore [aggadah],

B.   "for out of that you will truly know the one who spoke and brought
the world into existence and cleave to his ways."

III. Matters of Philosophy, Natural Science and Metaphysics

This parashah contains nothing relevant.

32

Sifré to Deuteronomy to Re'eh

I. Unarticulated Premises: The Givens of Religious Conduct

This parashah contains a massive amplication of verses of Scripture pertinent to legal matters, but if any premises not already captured in the Mishnah make their appearance, I cannot identify them.

II. Unarticulated Premises: The Givens of Religious Conviction

1. Israel is to consult prophets and to seek them out:

LXII

I.1   A.   "...But look only to the site that the Lord your God will choose amidst all your tribes [as his habitation to establish his name there. There you are to go and there you are to bring your burnt-offerings and other sacrifices, your tithes and contributions, your votive- and freewill-offerings, and the firstlings of your herds and flocks. Together with your households, you shall feast there before the Lord your God, happy in all the undertakings in which the Lord your God has blessed you]" (Deut. 12:5-7):

     B.   Look only to a prophet.

     C.   Is it possible to suppose that you should wait until a prophet instructs you?

     D.   Scripture says, "As his habitation there you are to go."

     E.   Seek and find, and afterward a prophet will instruct you.

I.2   A.   Along these same lines you find the following in regard to David:

     B.   "Lord, remember for David all his afflictions, how he swore to the Lord and vowed to the Mighty One of Jacob, 'Surely I will not go to the tent of my house nor go up into the bed that is spread for me; I will not give sleep to my eyes nor slumber to my eyelids, until I find out a place for the Lord, a dwelling place for the Mighty One of Jacob'" (Ps. 132:1-5).

     C.   How on the basis of Scripture do we know that he acted only on the instruction of a prophet?

D.   As it is said, "And Gad came that day to David and said to him, 'Go up, raise an altar to the Lord in the threshing floor of Araunah the Jebusite'" (2 Sam. 24:18).

E.   And Scripture says, ""Then Solomon began to build the house of the Lord at Jerusalem in Mount Moriah, where the Lord had appeared to David his father, for which provision had been made in the place of David, in the threshing floor of Araunah the Jebusite" (2 Chr. 3:1).

2.   Israelites accept the commandments in an uneven way, some finding greater, some lesser, assent:

LXXVI

I.1   A.   "But make sure that you do not partake of the blood; [for the blood is the life, and you must not consume the life with the flesh. You must not partake of it; you must pour it out on the ground like water; you must not partake of it, in order that it may go well with you and with your descendants to come, for you will be doing what is right in the sight of the Lord]" (Deut. 12:20-25):

B.   R. Judah says, "This indicates that the Israelites were stuffed with blood before the giving of the Torah. Is it possible to suppose that after they had received it, with full assent, from Sinai, [that was still the case]? Scripture says, 'But.'"

C.   Said R. Simeon b. Azzai, "But is it not the case that three hundred religious duties requiring affirmative action, which are listed in the Torah, follow suit?

D.   "This is meant to tell you that as to the matter of blood, which is the least among all the commandments, the Scripture has admonished you, how much the more so all the rest of the commandments!'

I.2   A.   R. Simeon says, "Every religious duty which the Israelites received from Sinai with full assent they perform with full assent,

B.   "but every religious duty which they received from Mount Sinai not with full assent they do not carry out with full assent."

I.3   A.   Rabban Simeon b. Gamaliel says, "Every religious duty for which the Israelites were prepared to give their lives in the time of repression they carry out in public,

B.   "...but any religious duty for which the Israelites were not prepared to give their lives in the time of repression still is loosely in hand."

But that is not how things should be. Rather, Israel should keep all the commandments, minor and major alike:

XCVI

III.1   A.   "...For you will be heeding the Lord your God, [obeying all his commandments that I enjoin upon you this day, doing what is right in the sight of the Lord your God]" (Deut. 13:13-19):

B.   On this basis they have said:

C.   If one has begun to obey only in minor measure, in the end he will obey in full measure.

III.2   A.   "...Obeying all his commandments that I enjoin upon you this day":

B.   This indicates that a minor religious duty should be as precious to you as a principal one.

3.   God responds to Israel's actions and attitudes, and the merit of the ancestors stands Israel in good stead as well:

XCVI

II.1   A.   "...In order that the Lord may turn from his blazing anger [and show you compassion, and in his compassion increase you as he promised your fathers on oath, for you will be heeding the Lord your God, obeying all his commandments that I enjoin upon you this day, doing what is right in the sight of the Lord your God]" (Deut. 13:13-19):

B.   So long as there is idolatry, blazing anger burns against the world. When idolatry is removed, blazing anger is removed from the world.

II.2   A.   "...And show you compassion":

B.   show you mercy, not others.

C.   On this basis, Rabban Gamaliel b. Rabbi says, "So long as you show mercy to others, Heaven shows mercy to you. If you do not show mercy to others, Heaven shows you no mercy."

II.3   A.   "...Increase you [as he promised your fathers on oath]":

B.   As it is said, "And I shall multiply your seed like the stars of the heaven" (Gen. 26:4).

II.4   A.   "...[Increase you] as he promised your fathers on oath":

B.   all is on account of the merit of the ancestors.

III. Matters of Philosophy, Natural Science and Metaphysics

It is vain to expect this rubric to serve here.

33

Sifré to Deuteronomy to Shofetim

To my surprise, I find no presuppositions that are both fresh and also of legal or theological interest here, only systematic amplifications of Scripture.

34

Sifré to Deuteronomy to Ki Tese

Every line of this parashah is exegetical, and I find nothing of broader interest whatsoever.

35

Sifré to Deuteronomy to Ki Tabo

Readers will better grasp my frustration at finding nothing of consequence for our study when they examine the following. Here we find a systematic treatment of the history of Israel laid forth in the text of Deuteronomy, a passage that surely invites theological commentary (as other passages we have examined have yielded such commentary). And yet all we have is exegesis of the phrases, with a very limited program of amplification, paraphrase, and extension forming the hermeneutics of the passage. On the strength of a passage such as this, we have to call into question whether a quest for the Judaism behind the texts forms a well-conceived exercise at all:

CCCI

I.1 A. ["You shall then recite as follows before the Lord your God: 'My father was a fugitive Aramean. He went down to Egypt with meager numbers and sojourned there; but there he became a great and very populous nation. The Egyptians dealt harshly with us and oppressed us; they imposed heavy labor upon us. We cried to the Lord, the God of our fathers, and the Lord heard our plea and saw our plight, our misery, and our oppression. The Lord freed us from Egypt by a mighty hand, by an outstretched arm and awesome power, and by signs and portents. He brought us to this place and gave us this land, a land flowing with milk and honey. Wherefore I now bring the first fruits of the soil which you, O Lord, have given me.' You shall leave it before the Lord your God and bow low before the Lord your God. And you shall enjoy, together with the Levite and the stranger in your midst, all the bounty that the Lord your God has bestowed upon you and your household" (Deut. 26:1-11).]

B. "You shall then recite as follows":

C. There is a provision here for "responding," and elsewhere there is an equivalent provision [at Deut. 27:14].

184

	D.	Just as "responding" at that other passage requires use of the Holy Language, so "responding" stated here requires use of the Holy Language.
I.2	A.	In this connection sages have said, "In earlier times whoever knew how to recite [in Hebrew] would make the recitation, and whoever did not know how to recite – they would recite in his behalf.
	B.	Consequently people refrained from bringing first fruits [out of shame].
	C.	Sages made the rule that [priests] would recite in behalf of both those who knew how to make the recitation as well as those who did not know how to make the recitation.
	D.	They ruled upon the verse of Scripture, "And you shall then respond...,"
	E.	maintaining that "responding" is solely to what others say.
II.1	A.	"You shall then recite as follows before the Lord your God: 'My father was a fugitive Aramean'":
	B.	This teaches that our father, Jacob, went down to Aram only in order to perish,
	C.	and Scripture credits Laban, the Aramaean, as though he had destroyed him.
III.1	A.	"He went down to Egypt":
	B.	Might you suppose that he went down in order to assume for himself the crown of royalty?
	C.	Scripture says, "...and sojourned there."
III.2	A.	Might one suppose that it was with a large population?
	B.	Scripture says, "with meager numbers."
	C.	That is in line with this verse: "With seventy souls your fathers went down to Egypt" (Deut. 10:22).
III.3	A.	"...But there he became a great and very populous nation":
	B.	This teaches that the Israelites were distinguished there [and did not become like the Egyptians].
III.4	A.	"...And saw our plight":
	B.	That is in line with this verse: "And you have seen the stones" (Ex. 1:16).
III.5	A.	"...Our misery":
	B.	In line with this verse: "Every son that is born you will throw into the river" (Ex. 1:22).
III.6	A.	R. Judah would assign mnemonics to them.
IV.1	A.	"He brought us to this place [and gave us this land]":
	B.	This refers to the house of the sanctuary.
	C.	Or might one suppose that this refers to the land of Israel?
	D.	When Scripture says, "and gave us this land," lo, reference is made to the land of Israel.
	E.	Why then does Scripture say, "He brought us to this place"?
	F.	As a reward for our coming to this place, he has given us this land.
V.1	A.	"A land flowing with milk and honey":
	B.	Here we find the phrase, "a land flowing with milk and honey,"
	C.	and elsewhere the same phrase, "a land flowing with milk and honey," occurs [at Ex. 13:5].
	D.	Just as the phrase, "a land flowing with milk and honey," when used elsewhere refers to the territory of the five peoples, so the

phrase, "a land flowing with milk and honey," as it occurs here refers to the land of the five peoples.

V.2   A.   R. Yosé the Galilean says, "People do not bring first fruits from TransJordan, which is not an area flowing with milk and honey."

VI.1 A.   "Wherefore":
      B.   immediately.

VI.2 A.   "Lo":
      B.   with rejoicing.

VI.3 A.   "I bring":
      B.   of my own property.

VII.1 A.   "...The first fruits of the soil":
      B.   In this connection sages have ruled:
      C.   A person goes down into his fields and sees a fig that produced its first fruit, a grape cluster that produced its first fruit, a pomegranate that produced its first fruit.
      D.   He ties a string on it and says, "Lo, this falls into the classification of first fruits."

VIII.1 A. "...Which you, O Lord, have given me":
       B. In this connection sages have ruled:
       C. A guardian, slave, agent, woman, person of indeterminate gender, person bearing traits of both sexes bring first fruits but do not make the required declaration.
       D. For they are unable to say, "...which you, O Lord, have given me."

IX.1 A.   "You shall leave it before the Lord your God and bow low before the Lord your God":
      B.   This teaches that the first fruits are to be set down two times,
      C.   once at the time of the declaration, the other time at the moment of prostration.

X.1   A.   "And you shall enjoy":
      B.   with all manner of enjoyments.

X.2   A.   "...All the bounty":
      B.   this refers to song.

XI.1 A.   "...That the Lord your God has bestowed upon you and your household":
      B.   This [reference to household] teaches that a man brings first fruits in behalf of his wife's estate and makes the required declaration.

XII.1 A.   "together with the Levite and the stranger in your midst":
      B.   In this connection sages have said:
      C.   Israelite mamzers [offspring of an illegitimate union] make the confession, but proselytes and freed slaves, who have no inherited share in the land, do not do so.

The parashah has nothing of fresh halakhic concern or of theological interest.

36

Sifré to Deuteronomy to Nesabim

This parashah yields nothing of legal or theological interest in connection with the present exercise.

37

Sifré to Deuteronomy to Ha'azinu

I. Unarticulated Premises: The Givens of Religious Conduct

This category does not fit the data before us.

II. Unarticulated Premises: The Givens of Religious Conviction

1. When the Israelites are meritorious, they testify against themselves. When not, God brings inferior persons to testify against them:

CCCVI

I.1   A.   ["Give ear, O heavens, let me speak; let the earth hear the words I utter! May my discourse come down as the rain, my speech distill as the dew, like showers on young growths, like droplets on the grass. For the name of the Lord I proclaim; give glory to our God" (Deut. 32:1-3).]

    B.   "Give ear, O heavens, let me speak":

    C.   R. Meir says, "When the Israelites enjoyed merit, they would give testimony against themselves.

    D.   "So it is said, 'And Joshua said to the people, "You are witnesses against yourselves"' (Josh. 24:22).

    E.   "When they went wrong, as it is said, 'Ephraim surrounds me with lies, and the house of Israel with deceit' (Hos. 12:1),

    F.   "the tribes of Judah and Benjamin gave testimony against them.

    G.   "So it is said, 'and now, inhabitants of Jerusalem and men of Judah, judge, I ask, between me and my vineyard. What could have been done more to my vineyard' (Isa. 5:3-4).

    H.   "When the tribes of Judah and Benjamin went wrong, as it is said, 'Judah has dealt treacherously' (Mal. 2:11),

    I.   "the prophets gave testimony against them.

    J.   "So it is said, 'Yet the Lord forewarned Israel and Judah by the hand of every prophet (2 Kgs. 17:13).

    K.   "When they did wrong to the prophets, as it is said, 'But they mocked the messengers of God" (2 Chr. 36:16),

L. "the heavens gave testimony against them.

M. "So it is said, 'I call heaven and earth to witness against you this day' (Deut. 4:26).

N. "When they did wrong to heaven, as it is said, 'Do you not see what they do...the children gather wood, the fathers kindle fire, the women knead the dough, to make cakes to the queen of heaven' (Jer. 7:17-18),

O. "the earth gave testimony against them.

P. "So it is said, 'Hear, O earth, see I will bring evil' (Jer. 6:16).

Q. "When they did wrong to the earth, as it is said, 'Yes, their altars shall be as heaps in the furrows of the field' (Hos. 12:12),

R. "the roads gave testimony against them.

S. So it is said, 'Thus says the Lord, Stand in the ways and see' (Jer. 6:16).

T. "When they did wrong to the roads, as it is said, 'You have built your high place at every head of the way' (Ezek. 16:26),

U. "the gentiles gave testimony against them.

V. "So it is said, 'Therefore hear, you nations, and know, O Congregation, what is against them,' (Jer. 6:18).

W. "When they did wrong to the gentiles, as it is said, 'But our fathers mixed with the nations and learned their works' (Ps. 106:35),

X. "he called the mountains to give testimony against them.

Y. "So it is said, 'Hear, O you mountains, the Lord's controversy' (Mic. 6:2).

Z. "When they did wrong to the mountains, as it is said, 'They sacrifice upon the tops of the mountains' (Hos. 4:13),

AA. "he called the oxen to give testimony against them.

BB. "So it is said, 'The ox knows his owner...' (Isa. 1:3).

CC. "When they did wrong to the oxen, as it is said, 'Thus they exchanged their glory for the likeness of an ox that eats grass' (Ps. 106:20),

DD. "he called the fowl to give testimony against them.

EE. "So it is said, 'Yes, the stork in heaven knows her appointed times...' (Jer. 8:7).

FF. "When they did wrong to the domesticated beasts, wild beasts, and fowl, as it is said, 'So I went in and saw and behold, every detestable form of creeping things and beasts' (Ezek. 8:10),

GG. "he called the fish to give testimony against them.

HH. "So it is said, 'Or speak to the earth and it shall teach you, and the fishes of the sea shall declare you' (Job 12:8).

II. "When they did wrong to the fish, as it is said, 'And make man as the fish of the sea' (Hab. 1:14),

JJ. "he called the ant to give testimony against them: 'Go to the ant, you sluggard...which provides her bread in the summer' (Prov. 6:6-8)."

KK. R. Simeon b. Eleazar says, "Sad indeed is the man who has to learn from an ant. Had he learned and done what he learned, he would have been sad, but he had to learn from the ant's ways and did not even learn!"

2. God will forgive Israel all her sin and will remove the record of her past:

II.1   A.   The Community of Israel is going to say before the Holy One, blessed be He, "Lord of the world, lo, my witnesses are present."

        B.   For so it is said, "I call heaven and earth to witness against you this day" (Deut. 30:19).

        C.   He will say to her, "Lo, I shall remove them."

        D.   For so it is said, "For behold, I create a new heaven and a new earth" (Isa. 65:17).

        E.   She will say to him, "Lord of the world, lo, I see the places in which I did wrong, and I am ashamed."

        F.   For so it is said, "See your way in the valley..." (Jer. 2:23).

        G.   He will say to her, "Lo, I shall remove them."

        H.   For so it is said, "Every valley shall be lifted up" (Isa. 40:4).

        I.   She will say to him, "Lord of the world, lo, my [bad] name endures."

        J.   He will say to her, "Lo, I shall remove it."

        K.   For so it is said, "And you shall be called by a new name" (Isa. 62:2).

        L.   She will say to him, "Lord of the world, Lo, my name endures on account of my Baal-worship."

        M.   He will say to her, "Lo, I shall remove it."

        N.   For so it is said, "For I will take away the names of the Baalim" (Hos. 2:19).

        O.   She will then say before him, "Lord of the world, none the less, children of my house make mention of it."

        P.   He will say to her, "And they shall no more be mentioned by their name" (Hos. 2:19).

3. Israel may have rebuffed God, but God has remained steadfast toward Israel:

V.1   A.   The community of Israel is going to stand in judgment before the Omnipresent and say to him, "Lord of the world, I do not know who did bad things against whom, and who has proved deceitful to whom, whether Israel has treated the Omnipresent badly, or whether the Omnipresent has deceitfully treated Israel."

        B.   When Scripture says, "And the heavens declare his righteousness" (Ps. 50:6),

        C.   one must conclude that it is Israel that has treated the Omnipresent badly, and not the Omnipresent who treated Israel deceitfully.

        D.   And so Scripture states, "For I the Lord do not change" (Mal. 3:6).

4. Israel's fate depends wholly on Israel's obedience:

VI.1   A.   Another teaching concerning the verse, "Give ear, O heavens, let me speak":

B.   R. Judah says, "The matter may be compared to the case of a king who had two deputies in a town. He gave over to them his property and handed his son to them and said to them, "So long as my son does what I want, pamper him and give him luxuries and feed him and give him drink.

C.   "But when he does not do what I want, let him not taste a thing of what belongs to me."

D.   Along these same lines, so long as the Israelites do what the Omnipresent wants, what is written concerning them? "The Lord will open to you his good treasure, the heaven" (Deut. 28:12).

E.   When they do not do what the Omnipresent wants, what is written concerning them? "And the anger of the Lord be kindled against you, and he shut up heaven, so that there shall be no rain, and the ground shall not yield her fruit" (Deut. 11:17).

5.   Israel is subject to the Torah and cannot deny that God has given the Torah or that Israel has accepted it:

XIV.1   A.   Another teaching concerning the verse, "Give ear, O heavens, let me speak":

B.   It was because the Israelites did not carry out all of the religious duties that were assigned to them from heaven.

C.   "...Let the earth hear the words I utter!"

D.   It was because the Israelites did not carry out all of the religious duties that were assigned to them on earth.

E.   Moses thus brought to testify against Israel two witnesses who last forever and ever, as it is said, "I call to witness against you this day the heaven and the earth" (Deut. 30:19).

F.   And the Holy One, blessed be He, called to witness against you the song [that Moses was about to sing], as it is said, "Now therefore write this song for you" (Deut. 31:19).

G.   We do not then know whose testimony would endure, that of the Holy One, blessed be He, or that of Moses.

H.   When Scripture says, "This song shall testify before them as a witness" (Deut. 31:21),

I.   lo, [we learn that] it is the testimony of the Holy One, blessed be He, that confirms that of Moses, and not that of Moses that confirms the testimony of the Holy One, blessed be He.

J.   And on what account did Moses call to testify against Israel two witnesses which live and endure forever and ever?

K.   He said, "I am mortal, and tomorrow I shall be dead. What if the Israelites want to say, 'We never received the Torah'? Who will contradict them?"

L.   Therefore he called to testify against them two witnesses which live and endure forever and ever.

M.   And the Holy One, blessed be He, called the song to testify against them, saying, "This song will testify against them from below, and I from above."

N.   And how on the basis of Scripture do we know that the Omnipresent is called a witness?

O.   As it is said, "And I will come near to you to judgment, and I will be a swift witness" (Mal. 3:5).

P.   "I am he who knows and I am witness, says the Lord" (Jer. 29:23).

Q.   "And let the Lord God be witness against you, the Lord from his holy temple" (Mic. 1:2).

6. Human beings are formed of heaven and earth; Torah is what makes human beings like God in heaven; the resurrection of the dead is the principal message of the Torah:

XXVIII.2 A.   And so did R. Simai say, "All creatures that are formed from the heaven – their soul and body derives from heaven, and all creatures that are formed from the earth – their soul and their body derive from the earth,

B.   "except for the human being, whose soul is from heaven and whose body is from earth.

C.   "Therefore if a man has worked [in] the Torah and done the will of his father in heaven, lo, he is like the creatures of the upper world, as it is said, 'I said, "You are godlike beings, and all of you are sons of the Most High"' (Ps. 82:6).

D.   "But if one has not worked [in] the Torah and done the will of his father in heaven, lo, he is like the creatures of the lower world, as it is said, 'Nevertheless you shall die like Adam' (Ps. 82:7)."

XXVIII.3 A.   And so did R. Simai say, "There is no passage [in the Torah] which does not contain [clear evidence concerning] the resurrection of the dead, but we have not got the power of exegesis [sufficient to find the pertinent indication].

B.   "For it is said, 'He will call to the heaven above and to the earth, that he may judge his people' (Ps. 50:4).

C.   "'He will call to the heaven above': this refers to the soul.

D.   "'and to the earth': this refers to the body.

E.   "[Following Hammer:] 'that he may judge his people': who judges with him?

F.   "And how on the basis of Scripture do we know that Scripture speaks only of the resurrection of the dead?

G.   "As it is said, 'Come from the four winds, O breath, and breathe upon these slain, that they may live' (Ezek. 37:9)."

7. Even though creation did not work out as planned, God is utterly without flaw:

CCCVII

I.1   A.   ["The Rock – his deeds are perfect. Yes, all his ways are just; a faithful God, never false, true and upright is he. Children unworthy of him – that crooked perverse generation – their baseness has played him false. Do you thus requite the Lord, O dull and witless people? Is not he the father who created you, fashioned you and made you endure!" (Deut. 32:4-6).]

B.   "The rock": [The letters for the word 'rock' may be read to mean artist, design, and form or create, thus yielding this sense:] the artist, for he designed the world first, and formed man in it [and all of these deeds are perfect].

C.   For it is said, "The Lord God formed man" (Gen. 2:7).

I.2   A.   "...His deeds are perfect":

B.   What he does is entirely perfect with all those who are in the world, and none may complain against his deeds, even the most minor nitpicking.

C.   Nor may anyone look askance and say, "Would that I had three eyes," "would that I had three hands," "would that I had three legs," "would that I walked on my head," "would that my face were turned around toward my back," "how nice it would be for me!"

D.   Scripture states, "...His deeds are perfect."

I.3   A.   "...His deeds are perfect":

B.   [Since the word translated "perfect" can also be read as "just," we interpret as follows:] He sits as judge for every single person and gives to each what is coming to him.

I.4   A.   "...A faithful God":

B.   For he believed in the world and created it.

I.5   A.   "...Never false":

B.   For people were not created to be wicked but to be righteous, and so Scripture says, "Behold, this only have I found, that God made man upright, but they have sought out many inventions" (Qoh. 7:29).

I.6   A.   "...True and upright is he":

B.   He conducts himself in uprightness with everyone in the world.

8.   God is perfectly just and pays back what everyone does, whether in this world or in the next:

III.1   A.   Another comment concerning the verse, "The Rock – [his deeds are perfect. Yes, all his ways are just; a faithful God, never false, true and upright is he:]."

B.   ["Rock" means] "the mighty."

III.2   A.   "...His deeds are perfect":

B.   What he does is entirely perfect with all those who are in the world.

C.   The recompense of the righteous and the punishment of the wicked [are entirely correct, for] the former have gotten nothing of what is coming to them in this world, and the latter have never gotten what is coming to them in this world either.

D.   And how on the basis of Scripture do we know that the righteous have never gotten what is coming to them in this world?

	E.	As it is said, "Oh, how abundant is your goodness, which you have laid up for them who fear you" (Ps. 31:20).
	F.	And how on the basis of Scripture do we know that the wicked have never gotten what is coming to them in this world?
	G.	As it is said, "Is not this laid up in store with me, sealed up in my treasuries" (Deut. 32:34).
	H.	When does each get what is coming to him?
	I.	"...All his deeds are perfect."
	J.	[Since the word translated "perfect" can also be read as "just," we interpret as follows:] Tomorrow, when he takes his seat in the throne of justice, he sits as judge for every single person and gives to each what is coming to him.
III.3	A.	"...A faithful God":
	B.	Just in the world to come as he pays back a completely righteous person a reward for the religious duty that he did in this world,
	C.	so in this world he pays the completely wicked person a reward for every minor religious duty that he did in this world.
	D.	And in the world to come just as he exacts punishment from a completely righteous world for the transgression that he did in this world,
	E.	so in this world he exacts from the completely righteous person a penalty for every minor transgression that he did in this world.
III.4	A.	"...Never false":
	B.	When someone dies, all the person's deeds come and are spelled out before him, saying to him, "Thus-and-so did you do on such-and-such a day, and thus-and-so did you do on such-and-such a day.
	C.	"Do you confess these things?"
	D.	And he says, "Yes."
	E.	They say to him, "Sign here,"
	F.	as it is said, "The hand of every man shall seal it, so that all men may know his deeds" (Job 37:7).
III.5	A.	"...True and upright is he":
	B.	Then he justifies the decision saying, "I have been fairly judged,"
	C.	as Scripture says, "That you may justify the judgment when you speak" (Ps. 51:6).

9.   Even though Israel sins, it is still Israel:

CCCVIII

I.1	A.	[Hammer:] "Is corruption his? No, his children's is the blemish." [JPS: ...Children unworthy of him – that crooked perverse generation – their baseness has played him false. Do you thus requite the Lord, O dull and witless people? Is not he the father who created you, fashioned you and made you endure!" (Deut. 32:4-6).]
	B.	"Is corruption his? No, his children's is the blemish":

| | C. | "Even though they are covered with blemishes, they still are called his children," the words of R. Meir, |

           C.   "Even though they are covered with blemishes, they still are called his children," the words of R. Meir,

           D.   as it is said, "his children's is the blemish."

           E.   R. Judah says, "There are no blemishes in them at all, as it is said, 'there are no blemishes in his children.'"

I.2   A.   And so Scripture says, "A seed of evil-doers, children that deal corruptly" (Isa. 1:4).

           B.   If, when they do evil, they are called "children," if they did not do evil, how much the more so!

I.3   A.   Along these same lines, Scripture says, "They are wise to do evil" (Jer. 4:22).

           B.   Now this yields an argument a fortiori:

           C.   If when they do evil, they are called "wise," if they were to do good, how much the more so!

I.4   A.   Along these same lines, Scripture says, "They are sottish children" (Jer. 4:22).

           B.   If when they are sottish, they still are called children, if they were discerning, how much the more so!

I.5   A.   Along these same lines, Scripture says, "And comes to you as people come and sit before you as my people and hear your words..." (Ezek. 33:31).

           B.   Might one suppose they both hear and also do?

           C.   Scripture says, "...but do them not" (Ezek. 33:31).

           D.   Now this yields an argument a fortiori:

           E.   If when they listen but do not obey, they are called "my people," were they to listen and obey, how much the more so!

10. Israel was chosen because the nations proved unworthy; Israel chose God as much as God chose Israel; the relationship is always reciprocal:

CCCXII

I.1   A.   "For the Lord's portion is his people, [Jacob his own allotment]":

           B.   The matter may be compared to a king who had a field, which he handed over to tenant farmers.

           C.   The tenant farmers began to steal [the produce of the field that was owing to the king, so] he took it from them and handed it over to the children.

           D.   They began to conduct themselves worse than the earlier ones.

           E.   He took it from their children and handed it over to the children of the children.

           F.   They began to conduct themselves even worse than the earlier ones.

           G.   He had a son. He said to them, "Get out of what is mine. I don't want you in it. Give me my portion, which I may get it back."

           H.   So when our father, Abraham, came into the world, chaff came forth from him, Ishmael and all the children of Keturah.

           I.   When Isaac came into the world, chaff came forth from him, Esau and all the nobles of Edom.

J.   They began to conduct themselves worse than the earlier ones.

K.   When Jacob came along, no chaff came forth from him. All the sons that were born to him were proper people, as it is said, "And Jacob was a perfect man, dwelling in tents" (Gen. 25:27).

L.   Whence will the Omnipresent regain his share? It will be from Jacob: "For the Lord's portion is his people, Jacob his own allotment."

M.   And further: "For the Lord has chosen Jacob to himself" (Ps. 135:4).

I.2   A.   Still, the matter is not fully clear, for we do not know whether the Holy One, blessed be He, has chosen Jacob, or whether it is Jacob who chose the Holy One, blessed be He.

B.   Scripture says, "And Israel for his own treasure" (Ps. 135:4).

C.   Still, the matter is not fully clear, for we do not know whether the Holy One, blessed be He, has chosen Israel as his own treasure, or whether it is Israel who chose the Holy One, blessed be He.

D.   Scripture says, "And the Lord has chosen you to be his own treasure" (Deut. 14:2).'

E.   And how on the basis of Scripture do we know that Jacob, for his part, chose him?

F.   As it is said, "Not like these is the portion of Jacob" (Jer. 10:16).

11. Israel really controls its own destiny through its actions and attitudes:

CCCXXIII

I.1   A.   "Were they wise, they would think upon this, [gain insight into their future. How could one have routed a thousand or put ten thousand to flight, unless their rock had sold them, the Lord had given them up? For their rock is not like our rock, in our enemies' own estimation]" (Deut. 32:19-31):

B.   "If the Israelites would look upon the teachings of the Torah that I gave to them, no nation or kingdom would rule over them."

C.   The meaning of "this" [in the base verse] is only Torah, in line with this verse: "This is the Torah that Moses set..." (Deut. 4:44).

I.2   A.   Another teaching concerning the phrase, "Were they wise, they would think upon this":

B.   If the Israelites would look upon what their ancestor, Jacob, said to them, no nation or kingdom would rule over them.

C.   And what did he say to them? "Accept upon yourselves the rule of Heaven, and let one subdue the other in fear of Heaven, and conduct yourselves with one another through acts of unrequired love."

12. God's justice is inexorable, in this world or in the next;

CCCXXX

II.1   A.   "...And say, 'As I live forever'":

B.   The trait of the Holy One, blessed be He, is not the same as the trait of a mortal.

C.   When the ruler of a province takes over his province, if he can collect taxes from his province, he does so, and if not, he cannot collect the taxes.

D.   But that is not the way of the one who spoke and brought the world into being.

E.   If he cannot collect from those who are alive, he collects from the dead,

F.   and if he cannot collect in this world, he collects in the next.

III. Matters of Philosophy, Natural Science and Metaphysics

I find nothing to the point.

38

Sifré to Deuteronomy to Zot Habberakhah

I. Unarticulated Premises: The Givens of Religious Conduct

No legal materials occur.

II. Unarticulated Premises: The Givens of Religious Conviction

1. God offered the Torah to every nation; only Israel took it:

CCCXLIII

IV.1　A. Another teaching concerning the phrase, "He said, 'The Lord came from Sinai'":

　　　B. When the Omnipresent appeared to give the Torah to Israel, it was not to Israel alone that he revealed himself but to every nation.

　　　C. First of all he came to the children of Esau. He said to them, "Will you accept the Torah?"

　　　D. They said to him, "What is written in it?"

　　　E. He said to them, "'You shall not murder' (Ex. 20:13)."

　　　F. They said to him, "The very being of 'those men' [namely, us] and of their father is to murder, for it is said, 'But the hands are the hands of Esau' (Gen. 27:22). 'By your sword you shall live' (Gen. 27:40)."

　　　G. So he went to the children of Ammon and Moab and said to them, "Will you accept the Torah?"

　　　H. They said to him, "What is written in it?"

　　　I. He said to them, "'You shall not commit adultery' (Ex. 20:13)."

　　　J. They said to him, "The very essence of fornication belongs to them [us], for it is said, 'Thus were both the daughters of Lot with child by their fathers' (Gen. 19:36)."

　　　K. So he went to the children of Ishmael and said to them, "Will you accept the Torah?"

　　　L. They said to him, "What is written in it?"

　　　M. He said to them, "'You shall not steal' (Ex. 20:13)."

N. They said to him, "The very essence of their [our] father is thievery, as it is said, 'And he shall be a wild ass of a man' (Gen. 16:12)."

O. And so it went. He went to every nation, asking them, "Will you accept the Torah?"

P. For so it is said, "All the kings of the earth shall give you thanks, O Lord, for they have heard the words of your mouth" (Ps. 138:4).

Q. Might one suppose that they listened and accepted the Torah?

R. Scripture says, "And I will execute vengeance in anger and fury upon the nations, because they did not listen" (Mic. 5:14).

S. And it is not enough for them that they did not listen, but even the seven religious duties that the children of Noah indeed accepted upon themselves they could not uphold before breaking them.

T. When the Holy One, blessed be He, saw that that is how things were, he gave them to Israel.

IV.2 A. The matter may be compared to the case of a person who sent his ass and dog to the threshing floor and loaded up a letekh of grain on his ass and three seahs of grain on his dog. The ass went along, while the dog panted.

B. He took a seah of grain off the dog and put it on the ass, so with the second, so with the third.

C. Thus was Israel: they accepted the Torah, complete with all its secondary amplifications and minor details, even the seven religious duties that the children of Noah could not uphold without breaking them did the Israelites come along and accept.

D. That is why it is said, "The Lord came from Sinai; he shone upon them from Seir."

CCCXLIV

V.1 A. Another interpretation of the phrase, "...lover, indeed, of the people, [their hallowed are all in your hand. They followed in your steps, accepting your pronouncements]":

B. This teaches that the Holy One, blessed be He, loved Israel as he did not apportion love to any other nation or kingdom.

C. "...Their hallowed are all in your hand":

D. This refers to the souls of the righteous, who are placed in a treasury, as it is said, "And the soul of my Lord will be bound up in the bond of life with the Lord your God" (1 Sam. 25:29).

E. "They followed in your steps":

F. That is so, even if they step backward twelve mils and come forward twelve mils.

G. "...Accepting your pronouncements":

H. They accept upon themselves [your commandments]: "Whatever the Lord has spoken we shall do and hearken" (Ex. 24:7).

2. The teachings of the Torah are eternal and indistinguishible:

CCCXLIII

XI.1 A. "...Lightning flashing at them from his right, [lover, indeed, of the people, their hallowed are all in your hand]":

B. This tells us that the words of the Torah are compared to fire.

C. Just as fire is given from heaven, so words of the Torah were given from heaven, as it is said, "You yourselves have seen that I have talked with you from heaven" (Ex. 20:19).
D. Just as fire lives forever, so words of the Torah live forever.
E. Just as if a man comes close to fire, he is burned, but if he stands far from it, he is cold, so in the case of words of the Torah, so long as a person labors in them, they live for him. When he leaves off from them, they kill him.
F. Just as people make use of fire in this world and in the world to come, so people make use of words of the Torah in this world and in the world to come.
G. Just as whoever makes use of fire leaves a mark on his body, so whoever makes use of words of the Torah makes a mark on his body.
H. Just as whoever works in fire is readily distinguished among people, so disciples of sages are readily distinguished in the market by the way they walk, by the way they talk, and by the way they cloak themselves.

3. When Israel is unanimous on earth, God's name is one in heaven:

CCCXLVI

I.1   A. "Then he became King in Jeshurun, when the heads of the people assembled, the tribes of Israel together":
        B. When the Israelites are of one opinion below, then his great name is glorified above.
        C. For it is said, "Then he became King in Jeshurun." When does this come about? "...When the heads of the people assembled, the tribes of Israel together."
        D. And an assembly consists only of the chiefs of the people: "And the Lord said to Moses, 'Take all the chiefs of the people'" (Num. 25:4).

4. Israel on earth and God in heaven correspond with one another and communicate in their comparability:

CCCLV

XVII.1 A. ["O Jeshurun, there is none like God, riding through the heavens to help you, through the skies in his majesty. The ancient God is a refuge, a support are the arms everlasting. He drove out the enemy before you. By his command: Destroy. Thus Israel dwells in safety, untroubled is Jacob's abode, in a land of grain and wine, under heavens dripping dew. O happy Israel! who is like you, a people delivered by the Lord, your protecting shield, your sword triumphant. Your enemies shall come cringing before you and you shall tread on their backs" (Deut. 33:24-29).]
        B. "O Jeshurun, there is none like God":
        C. The Israelites say, "There is none like God,"
        D. and the Holy Spirit says, "O Jeshurun."
XVII.2 A. The Israelites say, "Who is like you, O Lord among the mighty" (Ex. 15:11).

> B. And the Holy Spirit says, "Happy are you, Israel, who is like you" (Isa. 33:29).

XVII.3   A. The Israelites say, "Hear O Israel, the Lord our God, the Lord is one" (Deut. 56:4).

> B. And the Holy Spirit says, "And who is like your people, Israel, a unique nation in the earth" (1 Chr. 17:21).

XVII.4   A. The Israelites say, "As an apple tree among the trees of the wood..." (Song 2:3).

> B. And the Holy Spirit says, "As a lily among thorns" (Song 2:2).

XVII.5   A. The Israelites say, "This is my God and I will glorify him" (Ex. 15:2).

> B. And the Holy Spirit says, "The people which I formed for myself" (Isa. 43:21).

XVII.6   A. The Israelites say, "For you are the glory of their strength" (Ps. 89:18).

> B. And the Holy Spirit says, "Israel, in whom I will be glorified" (Isa. 49:3).

III. Matters of Philosophy, Natural Science and Metaphysics

Nothing pertains.

Appendix

Four Approaches to the Description of Rabbinic Judaism: Nominalist, Harmonistic, Theological, and Historical

Four approaches have defined the modern and contemporary description of Rabbinic Judaism, of which the fourth has been followed in my works, culminating in my *Rabbinic Judaism: An Historical Introduction* (New York, 1996: Doubleday Anchor Reference Library).[1]

NOMINALIST: The first is the radically nominalist view that every Jew defines Judaism. Judaism is the sum of the attitudes and beliefs of all the members of an ethnic group; each member of the group serves equally well to define Judaism, with the result that questions of the social order – for example, which particular group or social entity of persons held this view, which that – are dismissed. All issues of philosophy and intellect then are dismissed, and the work of intellectual description and definition is abandoned before it is undertaken. This is the method of S.J.D. Cohen. It yields the opposite of description and forestalls all analysis and interpretation.

HARMONISTIC: If the nominalist description regards "Judaism" as the sum of everybody's personal "Judaism," the harmonistic finds its definition in the common denominator among the sum of all Judaisms. So the second is at the opposite extreme: all Jewish data – writings and

---

[1]See William Scott Green, "Ancient Judaism, Contours and Complexity," in the *James Barr Festschrift*, to whom I owe the identification and classification of the first of the four. I have elaborated my account of problems of method in the following books: *The Ecology of Religion: From Writing to Religion in the Study of Judaism* (Nashville, 1989: Abingdon) and *Studying Classical Judaism: A Primer* (Louisville, 1991: Westminster/John Knox Press).

other records – together tell us about a single Judaism, which is to be defined by appeal to the lowest common denominator among all the data. That is the view taken by E.P. Sanders in the 1992 version of his opinion. This is an approach that accomplishes description, but produces banality.

THEOLOGICAL JUDAISM: Just as the first two approaches to the description of Judaism, or of Rabbinic Judaism, ignore all questions of context and deem irrelevant the inquiry into the relationship between the ideas people held and the world in which they lived, so the third equally takes its position in the idealist, as against the social, world of interpretation. The third is the method of theological description, followed by George Foot Moore, Joseph Bonsirven, Ephraim E. Urbach, and E.P. Sanders in the 1977 version of Sanders's views. This approach provides a well-drafted description, but ignores all questions of context and social relevance. Its "Judaism" came into existence for reasons we cannot say, addressed no issues faced by ordinary people, and constituted a set of disembodied, socially irrelevant ideas, lacking history and consequence. So it can be described and even analyzed, but not interpreted.

HISTORICAL: The fourth position is the approach to description taken in this book: we work our way through the sources in the order in which, it is generally assumed, they reached closure, so finding the order and sequence in which ideas came to expression. This approach produces not only historical description and systemic analysis, but also hypotheses of interpretation on the interplay of texts and contexts, ideas and the critical issues addressed by the people who put forth those ideas. The results of the fourth approach are laid out in this book and explained in the final unit of this appendix. Mine is the sole effort at the historical description, analysis, and interpretation of Rabbinic Judaism.

Our survey therefore will identify three major problems in the approaches typified by Cohen, Sanders (1992), and Moore-Urbach-Sanders (1977). These are conceptual, contextual, and historical.

The conceptual problem is best illustrated by S.J.D. Cohen, who simply defines "Judaism" as the sum of the beliefs of all Jews. Cohen simply evades the issues of the study of religion, to which he scarcely claims to be party. He investigates religious writings without the tools of the academic study of religion.

The contextual problem affects all the others treated here; it is, alas, paralyzing but ubiquitous. To do their work everyone assumes that if a story is told, it really happened; if a saying is assigned to a named authority, he really said it, and his opinion, moreover, is shared by everybody else, so we have not his opinion but "Judaism." The operative question facing anyone who proposes to translate writing into religion –

that is, accounts of "Judaism," as George F. Moore claims to give, or "The Sages," that Ephraim E. Urbach imagines he has made, or Sanders's charming, if puerile, "harmony of the sources" – is the historical one. It is this: how you know exactly what was said and done, that is, the history that you claim to report about what happened long ago? Specifically, how do you know he really said it? And if you do not know that he really said it, how can you ask the question that you ask, which has as its premise the claim that you can say what happened or did not happen?

We shall now see how prior scholars have described Rabbinic Judaism, or just "Judaism" including Rabbinic Judaism. My view of the other three approaches to the description of Rabbinic Judaism, or of all Judaisms of antiquity, takes the form of truncated reviews of the books of their principal proponents. In the course of these reviews, I characterize the method, as to description of Judaism(s), of the scholar under discussion and explain what is wrong with that method and its results.

I. Nominalist: The Innumerable Judaisms of S.J.D. Cohen

From the Maccabees to the Mishnah. By Shaye J.D. Cohen. *Library of Early Christianity* (Philadelphia, 1987: Westminster Press).

Cohen's account reminds us of the prophetic description of Israelite religion, with its altars on every hilltop and at every street corner. For him, every Jew tells us about a Judaism, one by one. Cohen presents a textbook for college students on Judaism: "the goal of this book is to interpret ancient Judaism: to identify its major ideas, to describe its salient practices, to trace its unifying patterns, and to assess its relationship to Israelite religion and society. The book is arranged thematically rather than chronologically...." Cohen begins with a general chronology of ancient Judaism and offers definitions thereof. He proceeds to "Jews and Gentiles," covering political matters, gentile domination, in that section: the Maccabean rebellion, the rebellion against the Romans, the wars of 115-117 and 132-135; cultural: Judaism and Hellenism, covering "Hellenism," "Hellenization," and "Hellenistic Judaism" and the like; social: Jews and gentiles, anti-Judaism and "Anti-Semitism" and Philo-Judaism; then the Jewish "Religion" (his quotation marks), practices and beliefs, in which he defines "religion" (again, his quotation marks), practices, worship of God, ritual observances, ritual, ethics, and the yoke of the law, legalism, beliefs, kingship of God, reward and punishment, redemption. Then comes "the community and its institutions," dealing with the public institutions of the land of Israel, the Temple and sanhedrin, the public institutions of the diaspora, the synagogue, private organizations, sects, professional guilds, schools.

Then he treats "sectarian and normative," with attention to "sect and heresy," "focal points of Jewish sectarianism," "orthodox and normative," proto-sectarianism in the Persian period, Ezra and Nehemiah, Isaiah 65, Pharisees, Sadducees, and Essenes; other sects and groups, touching "fourth philosophy," Christians, Samaritans, Therapeutae. This is followed by "canonization and its implications," with attention to the history of the biblical canon. At the end is "the emergence of rabbinic Judaism," with the main point "from second temple Judaism to rabbinic Judaism." All of these topics – and many more not catalogued – are covered in 230 pages, with a few pages of notes, and a few more for further reading.

The book exhibits a number of substantial flaws in presentation, conception, and mode of argument. These are three, and each one is so fundamental as to turn the book into a good bit less than meets the eye. The first of the three is the one relevant to the problem of describing Rabbinic (or any other) Judaism, and the others connected to it.

First, Cohen's plan of organization yields pure chaos. Reading this book is like reading a sequence of encyclopaedia articles. That is why the first, and the principal minus is the mode of organization, which separates important components of the picture at any given moment. That is to say, in one chapter, Cohen treats "Jews and gentiles," in another, Jewish religion, yet in a quite separate chapter, "sectarianism," and so on. In that way we are denied a sense of the whole and complete picture, at any one time, of the religious worldview and way of life of the Jews in the land of Israel.

Within the chapters, too, we find the same incapacity at forming a cogent and coherent statement of the whole. "Jews and gentiles" covers, separately, matters of political, cultural, and social policy, one by one. But these of course are not separate matters and never were. Within politics we move from Jeremiah to the Persians, the Maccabees, the Romans; then on the cultural agenda, we have Judaism and Hellenism, out of phase with the foregoing. And then we come to "social: Jews and gentiles," and yet a fresh set of issues. So the book is chaotic in character. But that results from a more profound intellectual chaos, Cohen's disciplinary inadequacy.

The second principal failure of the book derives from a simple methodological incapacity. Cohen's knowledge of the study of religion is remarkably shallow, with the result that he operates with crude and unworkable definitions of principal categories and classifications. Though Cohen's prior scholarship lies in history, not in religion, he proposes to speak not of Jews' histories, or "the Jews' history" in some one place or time, but of "Judaism." By his own claim, then, he is to be judged; but he has not done his homework. He simply has not got the training in the field of the history of religion to develop an interpretive framework adequate to his task. As a result he is left to try to present cogently a vast array of diverse materials that are not cogent at all. With this he simply cannot cope, and the result is a series of rather unfortunate "definitions," which define nothing and lead nowhere.

Let me give two probative examples. In both of them he substitutes classical philology for the history of religion. Nominalism takes over when Cohen wishes to define religion. This he does by asking what the word "religio" meant in antiquity. Using the words of Morton Smith, he says, "If a contemplative person in antiquity sought systematic answers to questions about the nature of the gods and their involvement in human affairs, he would have studied philosophy, not 'religion.'" Placing religion in quotation marks does not solve any problems left unsolved by this monumentally irrelevant definition. For when *we* study religion, it is within the definition(s) of religion that we have formed and brought to evidence we have identified as pertinent. That process is in part inductive and in part deductive, but it is never defined wholly within the definitions of another language and another age. There is a vast literature, from the Enlightenment forward, on the definition of religion, a literature in philosophy, history of religions, and a range of other fields. Cohen does not seem to have followed the discussions on the nature and meaning of religion that have illuminated studies in the nineteenth and twentieth centuries, with the result that his discussion is monumentally ignorant. The result is that he does not know how to deal with the data he is trying to sift, organize, and present in a cogent way, and that accounts for the book's wild incoherence.

As to "Judaism," the word occurs on every page and in nearly every paragraph. It starts, "The goal of this book is to interpret ancient Judaism." But I do not know what Cohen means by "Judaism." Cohen recognizes, of course, that various groups of Jews formulated matters, each in its own way, lived each in its own pattern, defined each its own "Judaism." And yet from the opening lines, "Judaism" is an "it," not a "they," and Cohen tells us "its major ideas...its salient practices...its unifying patterns...its relationship to Israelite religion" (which then is another, different "it"). But that is only part of the story. Cohen recognizes that the data that fall into the category, "religion," hence "Judaism," are incoherent and diverse. He says so – but then he is stymied when he tries to justify treating many things as one thing.

Cohen states, "Second temple Judaism was a complex phenomenon. Judaism changed dramatically during the Persian, Hellenistic, Maccabean, Roman, and rabbinic periods. Generalizations that may be true for one period may not be true for another. In addition, at any given moment, Jews practiced their religion in manifold different ways. The

Jewish community of Egypt in the first century C.E. was far from uniform in practice and belief...." That then is the question. How is it answered?

Here is the clear statement of that conceptual chaos that I call Cohen's extreme nominalism: one Judaism per Jew. I underline the relevant language. "What links these diverse phenomena together and allows them all to be called *Judaism*? [Italics his.] The Jews saw (and see) themselves as the heirs and continuators of the people of pre-exilic Israel; the Jews also felt...an affinity for their fellow Jews throughout the world....This self-perception manifested itself especially in the relations of diaspora Jewry to the land of Israel and the temple....Thus, like the bumblebee which continues to fly, unaware that the laws of aerodynamics declare its flight to be impossible, the Jews of antiquity saw themselves as citizens of one nation and one religion, unaware of, or oblivious to, the fact that they were separated from each other by their diverse languages, practices, ideologies, and political loyalties. In this book I do not minimize the varieties of Jewish religious expression, but my goal is to see the unity within the diversity." That, sum and substance, is Cohen's solution. What is wrong is that Cohen's "unity" adds up to the sum of all diversities. His is the opposite of Sanders's lowest common denominator Judaism, which we shall examine presently.

As a matter of fact, Cohen's description of "Judaism" simply is wrong, because his data contradict his "method." There were groups of Jews who regarded themselves as the only Jews on earth; everyone else was not "Israel" at all. The Essenes of Qumran saw themselves in that way. But so, too, did the authorship of the Pentateuch, which treated as normative the experience of exile and return and excluded from the normative experience of their particular "Israel" the Samaritans, who had not gone into exile, and the Jews elsewhere, who never went back and who are totally ignored in the pentateuchal statement of 450 B.C. So the allegation that Cohen knows what all the Jews thought of themselves is called into question by his rather blithe failure to conduct a survey of opinion, to the degree that we know opinion at all. He seems to me to play somewhat fast and loose with facts – if there are any facts about affinities, public opinion, attitudes, and the like.

As a matter of definition, Cohen does not really answer the question of defining a single Judaism at all. Here again, the vacuity of his theoretical system – of which there is none – accounts for his failure. Historians do not ask the questions that historians of religion do. How people see themselves forms a fundamental fact for the description of their worldview – but not for the world they view. Cohen is correct to claim that the way in which a given group sees itself tells us something about their Judaism. But whether or not their views testify to other

Judaisms he does not know. The reason is that he does not explain and unpack the theology within his allegations of a mutually supportive society throughout the world. Cohen claims that "this self-perception manifested itself especially in the relations of diaspora Jewry to the land of Israel and the temple." But diaspora Jews preserved a certain distance; they gave money to the temple, but when the Jews of the land of Israel went to war, diaspora Jews remained at peace, within the same empire – and vice versa. That hardly suggests that the perceived "affinity" made much difference in public policy. What we have is an excuse for not investigating the answers to a well-asked question – but not an answer to that question. Cohen does not have the equipment to answer the question, being a historian, not a historian of religion.

This matter of Cohen's limited knowledge of the study of religion lies at the heart of the book's failure. Lest Cohen's difficulty at conceptualization seem one episode in an otherwise well-crafted work, let me point to yet another example of how Cohen dismisses as trivial a central question of definition. Cohen has, of course, to address the issue of "sects," meaning (in my language) diverse Judaisms. He has to tell us the difference between the sectarian and the normative, and, to his credit, he devotes a whole chapter to the matter. Here, too, Cohen appeals to ancient usage in the solution of a problem of conceptualization – as though anybody any more is bound to word usages of Greek or Latin. He contrasts the negative use of "sect" and "heresy," deriving from theology. "'Sects' and 'heresies' are religious groups and doctrines of which we disapprove." That is true, but only for the uninformed.

A vast literature on the definition of "sect" and "church" has been written. Cohen does not use it. Here is Cohen's definition: "A sect is a small, organized group that separates itself from a larger religious body and asserts that it alone embodies the ideals of the larger group because it alone understands God's will." A sect then seems to me in Cohen's mind to be no different from a religion, except that it is small ("small") and differs from a group that is larger ("a larger religious body"). How the sect relates to the "larger religious body" we do not know. If the "sect" dismisses the "larger group" because the sect claims alone to understand God's will, then why is the sect not a "religious body" on its own? It would seem to me to claim exactly that. Lest I appear to exaggerate the conceptual crudity at hand and to impute to Cohen opinions he does not hold, let me now cite Cohen's own words (including his italics):

> A sect must be *small* enough to be a distinctive part of a *larger religious body*. If a sect grows to the extent that it is a large body in its own right, it is no longer a sect but a "religion" or a "church." The

precise definition of "large body" and "church" is debated by
sociologists, but that question need not be treated here.

This, I submit, is pure gibberish – and so is Cohen's "Judaism." A small
group is a sect. A big one is a "religion" or a "church." What has led
Cohen to this impasse is simple. Since there is one "Judaism" we have to
figure out some way to deal with all the other Judaisms, and by calling
them "little" we can find a suitable pigeonhole for them; then we do not
have to ask how "little" is different from "big" except that it is little. So
much for his crude definitions and unworkable classifications.

II. Harmonistic: The One Judaism of Sanders (1992)

Judaism. Practice and Belief 63 B.C.E. - 66 C.E. by E.P. Sanders (London,
1992: SCM Press, and Philadelphia, 1992: Trinity Press International).

E.P. Sanders has described "Judaism" twice, one intelligently, the
other stupidly. The intellectually challenging and perspicacious one
appeared in 1977 and is dealt with below, as one of the principal
examples of theological volumes; there he distinguishes among
Judaisms, with special reference to the Dead Sea Scrolls and Rabbinic
Judaism in comparison to Paul's system, and he finds characteristics of a
single Judaism – with special reference to what he calls "covenantal
nomism" – shared among the carefully distinguished systems. That
work presents problems of a historical and hermeneutical character. In
the more recent volume, by contrast, Sanders joins all evidences
concerning Judaic religious systems into a single, harmonious "Judaism,"
the equivalent to the New Testament "harmonies of the Gospels" that
people used to put together.

Sanders claims to give us an account of one, single, comprehensive
Judaism, underscores the profound misconstruction that emerges from
the confusion of history and theology. So far as I know, Sanders must be
the first scholar in recent times to imagine that all sources produced by
Jews, anywhere, any time, by any sort of person or group, equally tell us
about one and the same Judaism. Schürer was far more critical nearly a
century ago. The other major "Judaisms" – Bousset-Gressman's or
Moore's or Urbach's, for instance – select a body of evidence and work
on that, not assuming that everything everywhere tells us about one
thing, somewhere: Judaism. True, to account for a single Christianity,
Christian theologians have also to define a single Judaism, and that
explains why Sanders has fabricated a single "Judaism" out of a mass of
mutually contradictory sources. But others did the work with greater
acumen and discernment, and, when we examine Sanders's results
closely, we see that there is less than meets the eye.

Sanders really thinks that any and every source, whoever wrote it, without regard to its time or place or venue, tells us about one and the same Judaism. The only way to see everything all together and all at once, as Sanders wishes to do, is to rise high above the evidence, so high that we no longer see the lines of rivers, the height of mountains, the undulations of plains – any of the details of the earth's true configuration. This conflation of all sources yields his fabricated Judaism. It is a "Judaism" that flourished everywhere but nowhere – Alexandria, Jerusalem, Galilee, Babylonia (to judge from the sources he mixed together); a Judaism that we find all the time but in no one period – represented equally by the historical Moses and the rabbinic one, the pseudepigraph of the third century B.C. and the first century A.D., the Dead Sea Scrolls of the second and first centuries B.C., and, where Sanders has decided, the Mishnah of the early third century A.D.

Sanders does not identify "the synagogue" where this Judaism offered up its prayers, the community that was shaped by its rules, the functioning social order that saw the world within its vision. And of course, that failure of specificity attests to the good sense of the Jews of antiquity, who cannot have affirmed everything and its opposite: the sacrifices of the Temple are valid (as many sources maintain) and also invalid (as the Dead Sea Scrolls hold); study of the Torah is critical (as the rabbinic sources adduced ad lib. by Sanders) and eschatological visions prevail (as many of the pseudepigraphic writers conceive). Philo's cool, philosophical mind and the heated imagination of visionaries form for Sanders a single Judaism, but no single corpus of evidence, deriving from a particular place, time, circumstance, and community, concurs for "Judaism." To refer to a single issue, baptism can have been for the eschatological forgiveness of sins, as John the Baptist and Jesus maintained; or it can have been for the achievement of cultic purity in an eternal rhythm of nature and cult, as the Pharisees and the Mishnah held; but not both.

Sanders sees unities where others have seen differences. The result of his Judaic equivalent of a "harmony of the Gospels" is simply a dreary progress through pointless information. Sanders's relentlessly informative discourse persistently leaves open the question, so what? Throughout this long and tedious book, readers will find themselves wondering why Sanders thought the information he set forth important, and the information he omitted unimportant. If we know that his conflationary Judaism prevailed everywhere, then what else do we know about the Judaisms to which each source in turn attests (as well)? Do all the writers subscribe to this one Judaism, so that we are supposed to read into each document what all the documents together supposedly affirm?

He elaborately tells us why he thinks various documents tell, or do not tell, what really happened; he never explains why he maintains these same documents and artifacts of archaeology, commonly so profoundly at variance with one another, all concur on a single Judaism or attest to a single Judaism. Did all these Jews pray together in the same synagogue, did they eat together at the same table, did they give their children in marriage to one another as part of the same social entity? If he thinks that they did, then he contradicts a fair part of the evidence he allegedly reviews. Certainly the members of the Essene community at Qumran, for one example, did not regard the Jerusalem Temple as holy, and the Mishnah is explicit that its faithful are not going to eat supper with other Israelites, a view on which the Gospels concur as well.

Now that capricious conflation of all the sources Sanders thinks fit together and silent omission of all the sources he rejects is something Moore, Schechter, and even Urbach never did. Urbach cited Philo but not the Dead Sea Scrolls, having decided that the one was *kosher,* the other *treif.* Sanders has decided there are no intellectual counterparts to dietary laws at all: he swallows it all and chews it up and spits out a homogenized "Judaism" lacking all specific flavor. Nor can I point to any other scholar of ancient Judaism working today who cites everything from everywhere to tell us about one and the same Judaism. The contrast between the intellectually rigorous thinking of James Dunn on defining "Judaism" in his *Partings of the Ways* and the conceptually slovenly work of Sanders on the same problem – adding up all the sources and not so much finding as inventing through mushy prose what he conceives to be the common denominator – tells the story. Sanders's *Judaism* is a mulligan stew, a four-day-old, over-cooked *tcholent* – for us plain Americans, Wonder Bread, full of air and not very tasty.

This fabrication of a single Judaism is supposed to tell us something that pertains equally to all: the Judaism that forms the basis for all the sources, the common denominator among them all. If we know a book or an artifact is "Jewish," (an ethnic term, "Judaic" being the religious category) then we are supposed automatically to know various other facts about said book or artifact. But the upshot is either too general to mean much (monotheism) or too abstract to form an intelligible statement. Let me be specific. How Philo would have understood the Dead Sea Scrolls, the authors of apocalyptic writings, those of the Mishnah passages Sanders admits to his account of Judaism from 63 B.C. to A.D. 66, we are never told. Each of these distinctive documents gets to speak whenever Sanders wants it to; none is ever brought into relationship – comparison and contrast – with any other. The homogenization of Philo, the Mishnah, the Dead Sea Scrolls, Ben Sira, apocryphal and pseudepigraphic writings, the results of archaeology, and on and on and on turns out to yield generalizations about a religion that none of those responsible for the evidence at hand would have recognized: lifeless, dull, hopelessly abstract, lacking all social relevance. After a while, readers come to realize, it hardly matters, the results reaching so stratospheric a level of generalization that all precise vision of real people practicing a vivid religion is lost.

These remarks, meant to suggest that before us is an empty, pointless compilation of this and that and the other thing, will appear harsh and extravagant until we take up a concrete example of the result of Sanders's huge labor of homogenization. To understand what goes into Sanders's picture of Judaism, let me now provide a reasonable sample (pp. 103-104), representative of the whole, the opening paragraphs of his discussion, Chapter Seven, entitled "Sacrifices":

> The Bible does not offer a single, clearly presented list of sacrifices. The legal books (Exodus, Leviticus, Numbers and Deuteronomy), we know now, incorporate various sources from different periods, and priestly practice evidently varied from time to time. There are three principal sources of information about sacrifices in the first century: Josephus, Philo and the Mishnah. On most points they agree among themselves and with Leviticus and Numbers; consequently the main outline of sacrifices is not in dispute. Josephus, in my judgment, is the best source. He knew what the common practice of the priesthood of his day was: he had learned it in school, as a boy he had watched and assisted, and as an adult he had worked in the temple. It is important for evaluating his evidence to note that his description of the sacrifices sometimes disagrees with Leviticus or goes beyond it. This is not an instance in which he is simply summarizing what is written in the Bible: he is almost certainly depending on what he had learned as a priest.
>
> Though the Mishnah is often right with regard to pre-70 temple practice, many of the discussions are from the second century: the rabbis continued to debate rules of sacrifice long after living memory of how it had been done had vanished. Consequently, in reading the Mishnah one is sometimes reading second-century theory. Occasionally this can be seen clearly. For example, there is a debate about whether or not the priest who sacrificed an animal could keep its hide if for any reason the animal was made invalid (for example, by touching something impure) after it was sacrificed but before it was flayed. The mishnah on this topic opens with an anonymous opinion, according to which the priest did not get the hide. R. Hanina the Prefect of the Priests disagreed: "Never have I seen a hide taken out to the place of burning"; that is, the priests always kept the hides. R. Akiba (early second century) accepted this and was of the view that the priests could keep the hides of invalid sacrifices. "The Sages," however, ruled the other way (*Zevahim* 12.4). R. Hanina the Prefect of the Priests apparently worked in the temple before 70, but survived its destruction and became part of the rabbinic movement. Akiba died c. 135; "the Sages" of this passage are probably his contemporaries or possibly the rabbis of the next generation. Here we see that second-century rabbis were quite willing to vote against

actual practice in discussing the behavior of the priests and the rules they followed. The problem with using the Mishnah is that there is very seldom this sort of reference to pre-70 practice that allows us to make critical distinctions: not only are we often reading second-century discussions, we may be learning only second-century theory.

Philo had visited the temple, and some of his statements about it (for example, the guards) seem to be based on personal knowledge. But his discussion of the sacrifices is 'bookish', and at some important points it reveals that he is passing on information derived from the Greek translation of the Hebrew Bible (the Septuagint), not from observation. The following description basically follows the Hebrew Bible and Josephus, but it sometimes incorporates details from other sources.

One may make the following distinctions among sacrifices:

> With regard to what was offered: meal, wine, birds (doves or pigeons) and quadrupeds (sheep, goats and cattle).
> With regard to who provided the sacrifice: the community or an individual.
> With regard to the purpose of the sacrifice: worship of and communion with God, glorification of him, thanksgiving, purification, atonement for sin, and feasting.
> With regard to the disposition of the sacrifice: it was either burned or eaten. The priests got most of the food that sacrifices provided, though one of the categories of sacrifice provided food for the person who brought it and his family and friends. The Passover lambs were also eaten by the worshippers.

Sacrifices were conceived as meals, or, better, banquets. The full and ideal sacrificial-offering consisted of meat, cereal, oil and wine (Num. 14:1-10, Ant. 3.233f.; the menu was sometimes reduced: see below).

I ask readers to stipulate that I can have cited numerous other, sizable instances of the same sort of discourse.

Now let us ask ourselves, what, exactly, does Sanders wish to tell his readers about the sacrifices in this account of *Judaism. Practice & Belief* ? He starts in the middle of things. He assumes we know what he means by "sacrifices," why they are important, what they meant, so all we require is details. He will deal with Josephus, Philo, the Mishnah, and Leviticus and Numbers. Does he then tell us the distinctive viewpoint of each? Not at all. All he wants us to know is the facts common to them all. Hence his problem is not one of description, analysis, and interpretation of documents, but a conflation of the information contained in each that he deems usable. Since that is his principal concern, he discusses "sacrifice" by telling us why the Mishnah's information is useless, except when it is usable. But Sanders never suggests to his readers what the Mishnah's discussion of sacrifice wishes to find out, or how its ideas on the subject may prove religiously engaging. It is just a rule book, so it has no ideas on the subject. So

Sanders; that is not my view. Philo is then set forth. Here, too, we are told why he tells us nothing, but not what he tells us. Then there follows the facts, the indented "with regard to" paragraphs.

Sanders did not have to tell us all about how Leviticus, Numbers, Philo and Josephus and the Mishnah concur, then about how we may ignore or must cite the several documents respectively, if his sole intent was to tell us the facts of the "with regard to..." paragraphs. And how he knows that "sacrifices were conceived...," who conceived them in this way, and what sense the words made, "worship of and communion with God, glorification of him, thanksgiving, purification, atonement for sin, and feasting," and to whom they made sense, and how other Judaisms, besides the Judaism portrayed by Philo, Josephus, the Mishnah, and so on and so forth, viewed sacrifices, or the Temple as it was – none of this is set forth. The conflation has its own purpose, which the following outline of the remainder of the chapter reveals: community sacrifices; individual sacrifices ("Neither Josephus, Philo, nor other first-century Jews thought that burnt-offerings provided God with food..."), a family at the temple, an example; the daily temple routine. In this mass of information on a subject, one question is lost: what it all meant. Sanders really does suppose that he is telling us how things were, what people did, and, in his stress on common denominator Judaism, he finds it entirely reasonable to bypass all questions of analysis and interpretation and so forgets to tell us what it all meant. His language, "worship of and communion with God, glorification of him, thanksgiving, purification, atonement for sin, and feasting" – that Protestant formulation begs every question and answers none.

But this common denominator Judaism yields little that is more than simply banal, for "common theology," for example, "The history of Israel in general, and of our period in particular, shows that Jews believed that the one God of the universe had given them his law and that they were to obey it" (p. 240). No one, obviously, can disagree, but what applies to everyone equally, in a nation so riven with division and rich in diversity, also cannot make much of a difference. That is to say, knowing that they all were monotheists or valued the Hebrew Scriptures (but which passages he does not identify, how he read them he does not say) does not tell us more than we knew about the religion of those diverse people than before. Sanders knows what people thought, because anything any Jew wrote tells us what "Jews" or most Jews or people in general thought. What makes Sanders's representation bizarre is that he proceeds to cite as evidence of what "Jews" thought opinions of Philo and Josephus, the Dead Sea Scrolls, Rabbinic Literature, and so on and so forth. The generality of scholarship understands that the Dead Sea Scrolls represent their writers, Philo speaks for Philo, Josephus says what he thinks, and the Mishnah is whatever it is and is not whatever it is not. No one, to my knowledge, until Sanders has come to the facile judgment that anything any Jew thought has to have been in the mind of all the other Jews.

But it is only with that premise that we can understand the connections Sanders makes and the conclusions about large, general topics that he reaches. His juxtapositions are in fact beyond all understanding. Let me skim through his treatment of graven images, which captures the flavor of the whole:

> Comments by Philo and Josephus show how Jews could interpret other objects symbolically and thus make physical depictions acceptable, so that they were not seen as transgressions of one of the Ten Commandments, but as symbols of the glory of the God who gave them.

There follows a reference to War 5:214. Then Sanders proceeds:

> Josephus, as did Philo, found astral and other symbolism in many other things....

Some paragraphs later, in the same context, we have:

> The sun was personified and worshipped....The most important instance was when Josiah...instituted a reform of worship...[now with reference to 2 Kgs. 23:4f]. This is usually regarded as having been a decisive rejection of other deities, but elements derived from sun worship continued. Subsequently Ezekiel attacked those who turned 'their backs to the Temple of the Lord...' (Ezek. 8:16). According to the Mishnah, at one point during the feast of Booths priests 'turned their faces to the west,' recalling that their predecessors had faced east and worshipped the sun and proclaimed that 'our eyes are turned toward the Lord' (Suk. 5:4). Despite this, the practice that Ezekiel condemned was continued by some. Josephus wrote that the Essenes 'are particularly reverent towards the divinity....'

This is continued with a citation of the Qumran Temple Scroll and then the Tosefta:

> That the Essenes really offered prayer to the sun is made more probable by a passage in the Qumran Temple Scroll.
>
> Above we noted the floor of the synagogue at Hammath that had as its main decoration the signs of the zodiac in a circle....This synagogue floor, with its blatant pagan decoration, was built at the time when rabbinic Judaism was strong in Galilee – after the redaction and publication of the Mishnah, during the years when the material in the Tosefta and the Palestinian Talmud was being produced and edited. According to the Tosefta, Rabbi Judah, who flourished in the middle of the second century, said that 'If anyone says a blessing over the sun – this is a heterodox practice (T. Ber. 6[7]). In the light of the floor, it seems he was opposing contemporary practice.

And so on and on he goes, introducing in the paragraph that follows references to Christian symbols (John 1:9, 15:1); the issue of whether "one God" meant there were no other supernatural beings (yielding a citation to Paul who was a Pharisee, with reference to Phil. 3:2-6. And so he runs on, for five hundred tedious pages. This "harmony" yields chaos.

III. Theological:
The Dogmatic Judaism of Moore, Urbach, and Sanders (1977)

Among numerous descriptions of Rabbinic Judaism, or of ancient Judaism in general, that organize themselves around theological topics, ordinarily Protestant Christian theological categories, three serve to illustrate the state of the question, the first and most influential, George F. Moore's, the Israeli version, Ephraim E. Urbach's, and the American model, E.P. Sanders in his initial statement of his views. The source of the category formation for all three is uniform. First, it does not derive from the documents of Rabbinic Judaism, which do not focus on the points of main concern to the theological dogmatics of Protestant Christianity that govern. Second, it does raise questions important to Pauline Christianity but hardly critical to Rabbinic or any other Judaism of this time. All three moreover claim to provide a historical description, but read the sources in an uncritical manner, believing all the attributions and treating as fact all the fables of all the Rabbinic documents, without discrimination.

Judaism in the First Centuries of the Christian Era. The Age of the Tannaim. By George Foot Moore (Cambridge, 1927: Harvard University Press). I-III.

Moore's description of "Judaism" invokes standard Protestant categories of dogmatic theology. Moore fails to tell us of whom he wishes to speak. So his repertoire of sources for the description of "Judaism" in the "age of the Tannaim" is awry. He makes use of sources which speak of people assumed to have lived in the early centuries of the Common Era, even when said sources derive from a much later or a much earlier time. What generates this error is the problem of dealing with a category asymmetrical to the evidence. That is, an essentially philosophical theological construct, an -ism, "Judaism," is imposed upon wildly diverse evidence deriving from many kinds of social groups and testifying to the state of mind and way of life of many sorts of Jews, who in their own day would scarcely have understood one another (for instance, Bar Kokhba and Josephus, or the teacher of righteousness and Aqiba).

So for Moore, as for the others who have described "Judaism" solely in terms of theological dogmas, without reference to the time, place, and circumstance, of those who framed these dogmas, "Judaism" is a problem of ideas, and the history of Judaism is the history of ideas abstracted from the groups that held them and from the social perspectives of said groups. This seems to me a fundamental error, making the category "Judaism" a construct of a wholly fantastic realm of thought: a fantasy, I mean. What is wrong with the philosophical theological description of "Judaism" is not only the failure to correlate ideas with the world of the people who wrote the books that contain those ideas. There are problems of a historical, and history of religions, character.

Moore's work, to begin with, is not really a work in the history of religions at all – in this instance, the developmental and formative history of a particular brand of Judaism. His research is in theology, and there is no social foundation for the theology he describes. The description of Judaism is organized in theological categories. Moore presents a synthetic account of diverse materials, focused upon a given topic of theological interest. There is nothing even rhetorically historical in the picture of opinions on these topics, no pretense of systematically accounting for development and change. What is constructed as a static exercise in dogmatic theology, not an account of the history of religious ideas and – still more urgent – their unfolding in relationship to the society of the people who held those ideas.

Moore in no way describes and interprets the religious worldview and way of life expressed, in part, through the ideas under study. He does not explore the interplay between that worldview and the historical and political context of the community envisioned by that construction of a world. So far as history attends to the material context of ideas and the class structure expressed by ideas and institutions alike, so far as ideas are deemed part of a larger social system and religious systems are held to be pertinent to the given political, social, and economic framework which contains them, Moore's account of dogmatic theology, to begin with, has nothing to do with religious history, that is the history of Judaism in the first two centuries of the Common Era.

Moore describes the Judaism his sources set forth as "normative." So far as that represents a descriptive, not an evaluative, judgment, Moore simply does not make the case. A brilliant critique of his view appeared in 1927, in the review of the work by F.C. Porter. Here is what he says:

> The Judaism which Professor Moore describes with such wealth of learning is that of the end of the second century of our era, and the sources which he uses are those that embody the interpretations and formulations of the law by the rabbis, chiefly from the fall of Jerusalem,

70 A.D., to the promulgation of the Mishnah of the Patriarch Judah, about 200 A.D. When Moore speaks of the sources which Judaism has always regarded as authentic, he means "always" from the third century A.D. onward. It is a proper and needed task to exhibit the religious conceptions and moral principles, the observances, and the piety of the Judaism of the Tannaim. Perhaps it is the things that most needed to be done of all the many labors that must contribute to our knowledge of that age. But Professor Moore calls this Judaism "normative"; and means by this, not only authoritative for Jews after the work of the Tannaim had reached its completion in the Mishnah, but normal or authentic in the sense that it is the only direct and natural outcome of the Old Testament religion. It seems therefore, that the task here undertaken is not only, as it certainly is, a definite, single, and necessary one, but that other things hardly need doing, and do not signify much for the Judaism of the age of Christian beginnings. The book is not called, as it might have been, "The Judaism of the Tannaim," but Judaism in the First Centuries of the Christian Era: The Age of the Tannaim. Was there then no other type of Judaism in the time of Christ that may claim such names as "normative," "normal," "orthodox"? The time of Deuteronomy was also the time of Jeremiah. The religion of revelation in a divinely given written law stood over against the religion of revelation in the heart and living words of a prophet. The conviction was current after Ezra that the age of prophecy had ended; the Spirit of God had withdrawn itself from Israel (I, 237). But if prophecy should live again, could it not claim to be normal in Judaism? Where, in the centuries after Ezra, are we to look for the lines of development that go back, not to Ezra and Deuteronomy, but to Jeremiah and Isaiah? R.H. Charles claims the genuine succession for his Apocalypses. The Pharisees at least had the prophets in their canon, and it is claimed by many, and by Moore, that the rabbis were not less familiar with the prophets than with the Pentateuch, and even that they had "fully assimilated" the teaching of the prophets as to the value of the cultus (II, 13), and that their conception of revealed religion "resulted no less from the teaching of the prophets than from the possession of the Law" (I, 235). Christians see prophecy coming back to Judaism in John the Baptist and in Jesus, and find in Paul the new experience that revelation is given in a person, not in a book, and inwardly to each one through the in-dwelling Spirit of God, as Jeremiah had hoped (31:31-34). And now, finally, liberal Judaism claims to be authentic and normal Judaism because it takes up the lines that Jeremiah laid down.

It would require more proof than Professor Moore has given in his section on "History" to justify his claim that the only movements that need to be traced as affecting religion are these that lead from Ezra to Hillel and Johanan ben Zakkai and Akiba and Judah the Prince. Great events happened during the three centuries from Antiochus IV to Hadrian, events which deeply affected Judaism as a religion. But of these events and their influence Moore has little to say. It is of course in connection with these events that the Apocalypses were written.

A proper description, by contrast, should invoke considerations of social circumstance and context, so as to yield a Judaism portrayed within a specific, socially circumscribed corpus of evidence.

Porter's second criticism of Moore seems to me still more telling. He points out that Moore ignores the entire legal corpus, so that his "Judaism" builds upon categories alien, and not native, to the sources at hand. A principal flaw in theological description, affecting not only Moore, but the others who follow, flows from a category formation awry to the sources; the category formation is that of Protestant Christianity, not Rabbinic Judaism. This is how Porter states matters:

> In [Moore's] actual exposition of the normative, orthodox Judaism of the age of the Tannaim comparatively little place is given to Halakah. One of the seven parts of his exposition is on observances; and here cultus, circumcision, Sabbath, festivals, fasts, taxation, and interdictions are summarily dealt with; but the other six parts deal in detail with the religion and ethics, the piety and hopes, of Judaism, matters about which the Haggada supplies most of the material, and for which authority and finality are not claimed. The tannaite (halakic) Midrash (Mechilta, etc.) contains a good deal of Haggada together with its halakic exegesis, and these books Moore values as the most important of his sources (I, 135ff.; II, 80). The principles of religion and morals do indeed control the interpretation of certain laws, so that Halakah is sometimes a source for such teachings, and "is in many instances of the highest value as evidence of the way and measure in which great ethical principles have been tacitly impressed on whole fields of the traditional law" (I, 134). This sounds as if the ethical implications constituted the chief value of the Mishnah for Moore's purposes. But these are not its chief contents. It is made up, as a whole, of opinions or decisions about the minutiae of law observance. It constructs a hedge of definitions and restrictions meant to protect the letter of the law from violation, to make its observance possible and practicable under all circumstances, and to bring all of life under its rule....
>
> The Jewish scholar, Perles, in a pamphlet with which Moore is in sympathy, criticized Bousset, in Die Religion des Judentums, for using only books such as Bacher's, on the Haggada, and for expressing a preference for haggadic sources; whereas the Halakah in its unity, in its definitive and systematic form, and its deeper grasp upon life is much better fitted to supply the basis of the structures of a history of the Jewish religion. Moore agrees with Perles' criticism of Bousset's preference for the later, haggadic, Midrashim; but it is not because they are halakic that he gives the first place to the early Midrash. "It is this religious and moral element by the side of the interpretation of the laws, and pervading it as a principle, that gives these works [Mechilta, etc.] their chief value to us" (I, 135). Perles insists on the primary importance of the Halakah, not only because it shows here and there the influence of prophetic ethics, but because throughout as it stands, it is the principal work of the rabbis, and the work which alone has the character of authority, and because, concerned as it is with ritual, cultus, and the law

(Recht), it has decisive influence upon the whole of life. This applies peculiarly to the religion of the Tannaim. The Haggada neither begins nor ends with them, so that Bousset ought not, Perles thinks, to have used exclusively Bacher's work on the Haggada of the Tannaim, but also his volumes on the Haggada of the Amoraim, as well as the anonymous Haggada which Bacher did not live to publish. It is only in the region of the Halakah that the Tannaim have a distinctive place and epoch making significance, since the Mishnah, the fundamental text of the Talmud, was their creation.

Would Perles be satisfied, then, with Moore's procedure? Would he think it enough that Halakah proper, observances, should occupy one part in seven in an exposition of the Judaism of the Tannaim, considering that in their classical and distinctive work Halakah practically fills sixty-two out of sixty-three parts? Moore agrees with Perles that there is no essential distinction between earlier and later Haggada (I, 163), and that the teachings of the Tannaim about God and man, morals and piety, sin, repentance, and forgiveness are not only also the teachings of the later Amoraim, but run backward, too, without essential change into the Old Testament itself. There is no point at which freedom and variety of opinion and belief, within the bounds, to be sure, of certain fundamental principles, came to an end, and a proper orthodoxy of dogma was set up. But orthodoxy of conduct, of observance, did reach this stage of finality and authority in the Mishnah; and the tannaite rabbis were those who brought this about. It is in accordance with Moore's chief interests in haggadic teachings that he does not confine himself to sayings of the Tannaim, but also quotes freely from the Amoraim; how freely may be seen by the list that ends Index IV.

Professor Moore's emphasis upon his purpose to present normative Judaism, definitive, authoritative, orthodox, would lead one to expect that he would give the chief place to those "jurisdic definitions and decisions of the Halakah" to which alone, as he himself sometimes says, these adjectives strictly apply. We should look for more about the Mishnah itself, about its systematic arrangement of the laws, its methods of argument and of bringing custom and tradition into connection with the written law, and more of its actual contents and total character, of those actual rules of life, that "uniformity of observance" which constituted the distinction of the Judaism of the rabbis.

It is not possible to improve on Porter's critique. The halakhic materials address the issues of the social order in relationship to the intellectual structure and system of the documents themselves. Neglecting the contents and categories of the legal documents, the Mishnah, Tosefta, Yerushalmi, and Bavli, results in ignoring the social context of a religious structure and system. For the law deals precisely with that – the construction of society, the formation of a rational, public way of life. The history of a religion should tell how a religion took shape and describe its concern for a relationship to the concrete historical context in which that religion comes to full expression. These simply are not topics which form part of the hermeneutical framework of Moore's book.

The critical issue in my view is the relationship between a religion, that is, the worldview and way of life of a coherent social group, and history, that is, the material, economic, and political circumstance of that same social group. This history in Moore simply is not addressed. True, the history of a religion and the dogmatics of that religion are going to relate to one another. But a description of dogmatics of seven centuries or more and an account of the contents thereof simply do not constitute a history of the religion which comes to formal ideological expression in dogmatic theology. So Moore did not do what the title of his book and of his professorship ("professor of the history of religion") promises, even though in his work he discusses numerous matters bearing historical implication. Moore's failure flows from two contradictory facts. First, he believes everything he reads, so his "history" is gullible. Second, he forgets the work of historians, which is to tell us not only exactly how things were, but why. His history is not history, and anyhow, it lacks all historical context.

The Sages. Their Concepts and Beliefs. By Ephraim E. Urbach. Translated from the Hebrew by Israel Abrahams (Jerusalem: The Magnes Press, The Hebrew University, 1975). Two volumes.

Ephraim E. Urbach, professor of Talmud at the Hebrew University and author of numerous articles and books on the Talmud and later Rabbinic literature, here presents a compendious work intended "to describe the concepts and beliefs of the Tannaim and Amoraim and to elucidate them against the background of their actual life and environment." The work before us has been accurately described by M.D. Heer (Encyclopaedia Judaica 16:4): "He [Urbach] outlines the views of the rabbis on the important theological issues such as creation, providence, and the nature of man. In this work Urbach synthesizes the voluminous literature on these subjects and presents the views of the talmudic authorities."

The topics are as follows: belief in one God; the presence of God in the world; "nearness and distance – Omnipresent and heaven;" the power of God; magic and miracle; the power of the divine name; the celestial retinue; creation; man; providence; written law and oral law; the commandments; acceptance of the yoke of the kingdom of heaven; sin, reward, punishment, suffering, etc.; the people of Israel and its sages, a chapter which encompasses the election of Israel, the status of the sages in the days of the Hasmoneans, Hillel, the regime of the sages after the destruction of the Temple, and so on; and redemption. The second volume contains footnotes, a fairly brief and highly selective bibliography, and alas, a merely perfunctory index. The several chapters, like the work as a whole, are organized systematically, consisting of sayings and stories relevant to the theme under discussion, together with Urbach's episodic observations and comments on them. It is clear that Urbach has taken over, but improved upon, the description of "Judaism" as dogmatic theology set forth by Moore.

Urbach's categories, like Moore's, come to him from dogmatic theology, not from the sources on which he works. For let us ask, does the worldview of the talmudic sages emerge in a way which the ancient sages themselves would have recognized? From the viewpoint of their organization and description of reality, their worldview, it is certain that the sages would have organized their card files quite differently. We know that is the case because we do not have, among the chapters before us, a single one which focuses upon the theme of one of the orders, let alone tractates, within which the rabbis divided and presented their various statements on reality, for example, Seeds, the material basis of life; Seasons, the organization and differentiation of time; Women, the status of the individual; Damages, the conduct of civil life including government; Holy Things, the material service of God; and Purities, the immaterial base of divine reality in this world. The matter concerns not merely the superficial problem of organizing vast quantities of data. The talmudic rabbis left a large and exceedingly complex, well-integrated legacy of law. Clearly, it is through that legacy that they intended to make their fundamental statements upon the organization and meaning of reality. An account of their concepts and beliefs which ignores nearly the whole of the halakhah surely is slightly awry. How Porter would have reviewed Urbach's book is readily imagined: he would have said of Urbach exactly what he said of Moore, with the further observation that Israeli Orthodox Judaism should produce greater appreciation for the halakhic embodiment of theology than Urbach here shows.

Not only so, but Urbach's "Judaism" is, to say the least, eclectic. And it is not historical in any conventional sense. Urbach's selection of sources for analysis is both narrowly canonical and somewhat confusing. We often hear from Philo, but seldom from the Essene Library of Qumran, still more rarely from the diverse works assembled by R.H. Charles as the apocrypha and pseudepigrapha of the Old Testament, and the like. If we seek to describe the talmudic rabbis, surely we cannot ask Philo to testify to their opinions. If we listen to Philo, surely we ought to hear – at least for the purpose of comparison and contrast – from books written by Palestinian Jews of various kinds. The Targumim are allowed no place at all because they are deemed "late." But documents which came to redaction much later than the several Targumim (by any estimate of the date of the latter) make rich and constant contributions to the discussion.

Within a given chapter, the portrayal of the sources will move rapidly from biblical to Tannaitic to Amoraic sources, as though the line of development were single, unitary, incremental, and harmonious, and as though there were no intervening developments which shaped later conceptions. The contrast between the results set forth here, documents viewed in groups, with attention to how ideas differ, document by document, when they do, or do not evolve from earlier to later writings, when they do not, and Urbach's rather simple-minded repertoire of this, that, and the other thing, is striking. Differentiation among the stages of Tannaitic and Amoraic sayings tends to be episodic. Commonly, slight sustained effort is made to treat them in their several sequences, let alone to differentiate among schools and circles within a given period.

The uniformities are not only temporal. There is no differentiation within or among the sayings Urbach adduces in evidence: all of them speak equally authoritatively for "the sages." Urbach takes with utmost seriousness his title, the sages, their concepts and beliefs, and his "history," topic by topic, reveals remarkably little variation, development, or even movement. Urbach does little more than just publish his card files. That is because his skill at organization and arrangement of materials tends to outrun his interest in differentiation and comparison within and among them, let alone in the larger, sequential history of major ideas and their growth and coherent development over the centuries. One looks in vain for Urbach's effort to justify treating "the sages" as essentially a coherent and timeless group.

Readers will hardly find surprising the judgment that Urbach's "history" is simply uncritical. He never deals with the question, how do we know that what is attributed in a given document, often redacted centuries after the events of which it speaks, to a named authority really was said by him? Yet we must ask, if a saying is assigned to an ancient authority, how do we know that he really said it? If a story is told, how do we know that the events the story purports to describe actually took place? And if not, just what are we to make of said story and saying for historical purposes? Further, if we have a saying attributed to a first-century authority in a document generally believed to have been redacted five hundred or a thousand years later, how do we know that the attribution of the saying is valid, and that the saying informs us of the state of opinion in the first century, not only in the sixth or eleventh in which it was written down and obviously believed true and authoritative? Do we still hold, as an axiom of historical scholarship, *ein muqdam umeuhar* ["temporal considerations do not apply"] – in the Talmud?! And again, do not the sayings assigned to a first-century authority, redacted in documents deriving from the early third century, possess greater credibility than those first appearing in documents redacted in the fifth, tenth, or even fifteenth centuries? Should we not, on the face of it, distinguish between more and less reliable materials? The well-known tendency of medieval writers to put their opinions into the mouths of the ancients, as in the case of the Zohar, surely warns us to be cautious about using documents redacted, even formulated, five hundred or a thousand or more years after the events of which they speak. Urbach ignores all of these questions and the work of those who ask them. The result is a reprise of Moore: not history but dogmatic theology.

Paul and Palestinian Judaism. A Comparison of Patterns of Religion. By E.P. Sanders (London: SCM Press, 1977).

So far as Sanders's earlier book has a polemical charge, it is to demonstrate (pp. 420-21) that "the fundamental nature of the covenant conception...largely accounts for the relative scarcity of appearances of the term 'covenant' in Rabbinic literature. The covenant was presupposed, and the Rabbinic discussions were largely directed toward the question of how to fulfill the covenantal obligations." This proposition is then meant to disprove the conviction ("all but universally held") that Judaism is a degeneration of the Old Testament view: "The once noble idea of covenant as offered by God's grace and obedience as the consequence of that gracious gift degenerated into the idea of petty legalism, according to which one had to earn the mercy of God by minute observance of irrelevant ordinances." Once more issues of Protestant theological concern govern the category formation for a book on Judaisms.

Still, what Sanders did wrong in his 1992 work, he did right in his 1977 book. That is, he differentiated carefully among the evidence for diverse Judaisms and described each in its own terms. Thus his "Palestinian Judaism" is described through three bodies of evidence, described, quite properly and intelligently, one by one: Tannaitic literature, the Dead Sea Scrolls, and Apocrypha and Pseudepigrapha, in that order. The excellence of Sanders's earlier work lies in its explicit recognition that we may describe "Judaisms," each Judaic system attested by its own canonical writings. Here is no single, unitary, incremental, harmonious, lowest common denominator "Judaism," such as Sanders in 1992 has given us.

But as we saw at the outset, the work in the model of Moore and Urbach still is organized around Protestant Christian theological categories. To each set of sources, Sanders addresses questions of systematic theology: election and covenant, obedience and disobedience, reward and punishment and the world to come, salvation by membership in the covenant and atonement, proper religious behavior (so for Tannaitic sources); covenant and the covenant people, election and predestination, the commandments, fulfillment and transgression, atonement (Dead Sea Scrolls); election and covenant, the fate of the individual Israelite, atonement, commandments, the basis of salvation, the gentiles, repentance and atonement, the righteousness of God (Apocrypha and Pseudepigrapha, meaning, specifically: Ben Sira, I Enoch, Jubilees, Psalms of Solomon, IV Ezra).

This is not to suggest Sanders's covenantal nomism is a fabrication of his own; to the contrary, the datum he proposes can certainly be shown to accord with sayings here and there. At issue is whether he has formed a judgment of proportion and consequences. Is this issue the generative concern, the governing consideration, in the Judaic systems the documents of which Sanders reads? Sanders's search for patterns yields a common pattern in "covenantal nomism," which, in general, emerges as follows (p. 422):

> The "pattern" or "structure" of covenantal nomism is this: (1) God has chosen Israel and (2) given the law. The law implies both (3) God's promise to maintain the election and (4) the requirement to obey. (5) God rewards obedience and punishes transgression. (6) The law provides for means of atonement, and atonement results in (7) maintenance or re-establishment of the covenantal relationship. (8) All those who are maintained in the covenant by obedience, atonement, and God's mercy belong to the group which will be saved. An important interpretation of the first and last points is that election and ultimately salvation are considered to be by God's mercy rather than human achievement.

Anyone familiar with Jewish liturgy will be at home in that statement. Even though the evidence on the character of Palestinian Judaism derives from diverse groups and reaches us through various means, Sanders argues that covenantal nomism was "the basic type of religion known by Jesus and presumably by Paul...." And again, "covenantal nomism must have been the general type of religion prevalent in Palestine before the destruction of the Temple." But whether the various Judaisms of the time and place will have found in these ideas the center of their statement, whether this common denominator really formed the paramount agenda of thought and of piety, is a different question.

My account of Rabbinic Judaism answers that question in the negative; Rabbinic Judaism had other concerns than those of Protestant Christianity; it solved other problems; its theology and law made a statement that attended to different issues altogether, even though, on the issue important to Sanders, the writers could have concurred, casually and tangentially, with what he thought they should think on the questions critical to his polemic. That is how Sanders imposes on his evidence a Liberal Protestant theological agendum, defending his particular Judaism from Protestant condemnation. Accordingly, he simply does not come to Rabbinic Judaism to uncover the issues of Rabbinic Judaism, about which he cares very little and knows less.

He brings to the Rabbinic sources the issues of Pauline scholarship and Paul. This blatant trait of his work, which begins, after all, with a long account of Christian anti-Judaism hardly requires amplification. In fact, Sanders does not really undertake the systemic description of earlier Rabbinic Judaism in terms of its critical tension. True, he isolates those documents he thinks may testify to the state of opinion in the late first and second centuries. But Sanders does not describe Rabbinic Judaism through the systemic categories yielded by its principal documents.

While I think he is wholly correct in maintaining the importance of the conceptions of covenant and of grace, the polemic in behalf of Rabbinic legalism as covenantal does not bring to the fore what Rabbinic sources themselves wish to take as their principal theme and generative problem. For them, as he says, covenantal nomism is a datum. So far as Sanders proposes to demonstrate the importance to all the kinds of ancient Judaism of covenantal nomism, election, atonement, and the like, his work must be pronounced a success but trivial. So far as he claims to effect systemic description of Rabbinic Judaism ("a comparison of patterns of religion"), we have to evaluate that claim in its own terms.

The Mishnah certainly is the first document of Rabbinic Judaism. Formally, it stands at the center of the system, since the principal subsequent Rabbinic documents, the Talmuds, lay themselves out as if they were exegeses of Mishnah (or, more accurately, of Mishnah Tosefta). It follows that an account of what Mishnah is about, of the system expressed by Mishnah and of the worldview created and sustained therein, should be required for systemic comparison such as Sanders proposes. Now if we come to Mishnah with questions of Pauline-Lutheran theology, important to Sanders and New Testament scholarship, we find ourselves on the peripheries of Mishnaic literature and its chief foci. True, the Mishnah contains a very few relevant, accessible sayings, for example, on election and covenant. But on our hands is a huge document which does not wish to tell us much about election and covenant and which does wish to speak about other things. Sanders's earlier work is profoundly flawed by the category formation that he imposes on his sources; that distorts and misrepresents the Judaic system of those sources. To show that Sanders's agendum has not been shaped out of the issues of Rabbinic theology, I shall now adduce negative evidence on whether Sanders with equal care analyzes the inner structure of a document of Rabbinic Judaism.

Throughout his "constructive" discussions of Rabbinic ideas about theology, Sanders quotes all documents equally with no effort at differentiation among them. He seems to have culled sayings from the diverse sources he has chosen and written them down on cards, which he proceeded to organize around his critical categories. Then he has constructed his paragraphs and sections by flipping through those cards and commenting on this and that. So there is no context in which a given saying is important in its own setting, in its own document. This is Billerbeck scholarship.

The diverse Rabbinic documents require study in their own terms. The systems of each – so far as there are systems – have now been thoroughly uncovered and described, as an examination of the companion volume to this one, *Introduction to Rabbinic Literature*, shows for more than a score of them. The way the several systems relate and the values common to all of them have now been spelled out. The work now completed simply closes off the notion that we may cite promiscuously everything in every document (within the defined canon of "permitted" documents) and then claim to have presented an account of "the Rabbis" and their opinions is not demonstrated and not even very well argued. We hardly need dwell on the still more telling fact that Sanders has not shown how systemic comparison is possible when, in point of fact, the issues of one document, or of one system of which a document is a part, are simply not the same as the issues of some other document or system; he is oblivious to all documentary variations and differences of viewpoint. That is, while he has succeeded in finding Rabbinic sayings on topics of central importance to Paul (or Pauline theology), he has ignored the context and authentic character of the setting in which he has found these sayings. He lacks all sense of proportion and coherence, because he has not even asked whether these sayings form the center and core of the Rabbinic system or even of a given Rabbinic document. To state matters simply, How do we know that "the Rabbis" and Paul are talking about the same thing, so that we may compare what they have to say? And if it should turn out that "the Rabbis" and Paul are not talking about the same thing, then what is it that we have to compare? I think, nothing at all.

IV. Historical: The Documentary Description of Rabbinic Judaism

Clearly, all prior descriptions of Rabbinic Judaism are characterized by one or more of these flaws:

1. Earlier scholars ignore the task of describing the sources, that is to say, the documents, their traits and perspectives. Documentary analysis is commonplace in Tanakh scholarship, J, E, P, and D rarely being invited to testify in common to a unitary account of the historical unity of the Torah, for example. No picture of Pentateuchal religion comprised of a harmony of the sources, or the lowest common denominator among the sources, or a sum of all sources, is apt to gain a solemn hearing in biblical studies. In New Testament scholarship it is routine to recognize that Matthew, Mark, Luke, and John formulate distinctive statements, and nobody incorporates sayings from this, that, and the other gospel into a harmonious account of what Jesus really said. I doubt that a "Christianity" written the way Sanders has written his two "Judaisms" will exercise much influence.

2. They take for granted the historicity of stories and sayings. The critical historical program of the nineteenth century has made no impact at all. I challenge Cohen and Sanders to point to a single work in ancient Israelite history that uses scriptural sources the way they use Rabbinic ones. In New Testament scholarship people routinely call into question the historicity of sayings and stories and devise methods for distinguishing the authentic from the fabricated.

3. But they all ignore the historical setting and context in which the ideas of a given "Judaism" took place. The social historical program of the twentieth-century humanities, with its interest in the relationship between text and context, idea and the circumstance of those who held that idea, has contributed nothing. So ideas exist disembodied, out of all relationship to the lives of those who held them or later on preserved the documents that present them.

4. And they all invoke for their category formations classifications alien to the sources, instead of allowing the documents to dictate their own generative and definitive categories of thought and inquiry. Categories, the sense of proportion and of structure and order, are lifted from one world and parachuted down upon the data of another. The recognition that one category formation cannot be imposed upon the data of a different culture – surely commonplace among historians of all periods, aware as they are of anachronism – has yet to register. The program of cultural

anthropology has not made a mark. That is why we can insist the rabbis of the Mishnah tell us their views concerning propositions important to Paul, even though they may have said nothing on the topics to which Paul accorded critical importance.

Now to turn to the approach worked out in my *The Doubleday Anchor Reference Library. Rabbinic Judaism. An Historical Introduction* (New York, 1995: Doubleday) and the many prior monographs summarized in that final statement of mine. The documentary approach provides a solution to these problems.

1. It asks about the circumstances, traits, and generative problematic of the several writings, from the Mishnah through the Talmud of Babylonia. In that way, each document is read in its own terms and setting.

2. The same method simply dismisses as not subject to falsification or verification attributions of sayings to named masters.

3. But, treating the document as irrefutable evidence of the viewpoint of those who compiled the document and how they saw matters, the documentary method asks about the context in which a given document's contents found consequence.

4. And the documentary method formulates issues as these are defined by the respective documents: their concerns, their problematic, their categorical structure and system. It further proceeds to the question of how several documents relate to one another, in the aspects of autonomy, connection, and continuity, as I shall explain.

In the picture of Rabbinic Judaism given there and in the monographs and books drawn together in that book, I will provide a history of ideas based on the sequence of documents and their intellectual relationships. I will examine a structure that rests upon the native categories of these same documents. And by paying attention to the (for Israel) world historical events prior to, and surrounding, the formulation of these documents, I will review the functioning of the system of Rabbinic Judaism in response to the circumstances and contexts of those who wrote the documents at hand. It goes without saying that I will rely for facts concerning a given time and its issues upon the character of the documents, not on the attributions of sayings or the narratives of stories alleged to have been said or to have taken place at a given time prior to the closure of the document itself. The result is a theory of the description of Rabbinic Judaism that pays close attention to the formulation of distinct sets of ideas at determinate times and in specific contexts, that is, in response to important events: the Mishnah read in response to the crisis of the later second century, in which it was written; the Yerushalmi read in response to the crisis of the later fourth and early fifth centuries, in which it was written; and so with the Midrash compilations.[2]

The documentary method followed there responds to the failures of the prior descriptions of "Judaism" as portrayed by Rabbinic, and other writings.

1. What if we recognize that documentary formulations play a role in the representation of compositions, so that the compositors' formulation of matters takes a critical place in the making of the documentary evidence?

2. And what if, further, we no longer assume the inerrancy of the Oral Torah's writings, so that attributions are no longer taken at face value, stories no longer believed unless there are grounds for disbelief (as the Jerusalem canard has it)?

Then the fundamental presuppositions of the received method of studying the history of Judaism prove null. And that fact bears in its wake the further problem: Since we cannot take their answers at face value, can we pursue their questions any more? In my judgment, the answer is negative. All work in the history of the formative age of the Judaism of the Dual Torah that treats documentary lines as null and attributions as invariably valid must be dismissed as a mere curiosity; a

---

[2]The one significant lacuna in this reading, of course, is formed by my sustained treatment of the Bavli as only an intellectual, not a social statement – a problem of hermeneutics and theology, not of social description. I have not set the Talmud of Babylonia into the context in the historical circumstance of those who produced it, but only in the setting of the intellectual problem addressed by them. My sense is that the solution to that problem will be found in the intellectual challenges of the earliest phases of Islam, that is, the seventh and eighth centuries. In that case, the Bavli will come to appear as parallel to the Yerushalmi. Just as the latter presented a religious doctrinal response to Christianity's triumph, the former will then emerge as a response to the advent of Islamic philosophy. The power of the Bavli to recapitulate religious beliefs in the rigorous disciplines of philosophy to produce a theological statement then will find its source in the eighth-century setting. No external evidence requires us to locate the Bavli prior to the eighth century. It remains for scholars of Judaism in earliest Islam to take up this possibility.

collection and arrangement of this and that, bearing no compelling argument or proposition to be dealt with by the new generation.

The question that demands a response before any historical issues can be formulated is this: How are we to determine the particular time and circumstance in which a writing took shape, and how shall we identify the generative problems, the urgent and critical questions, that informed the intellect of an authorship and framed the social world that nurtured that same authorship? Lacking answers to these questions, we find our work partial, and, if truth be told, stained by sterile academicism. Accordingly, the documentary method requires us to situate the contents of writings into particular circumstances, so that we may read the contents in the context of a real time and place. How to do so? I maintain that it is by reference to the time and circumstance of the closure of a document, that is to say, the conventional assignment of a piece of writing to a particular time and place, that we proceed outward from context to matrix.

I have defined the work as the movement from text to context to matrix. I have proposed that the relationships among documents run from autonomy through connection to continuity. That is, a text stands on its own; an author or set of writers have made decisions concerning the rhetoric, logic, topical and propositional program, that the document embodies. The context of one text is defined by the other texts to which, on demonstrable, formal bases, it clearly relates. A text also relates to other documents, being connected with them in some specific ways (the Talmuds to the Mishnah, the Midrash compilations to Scripture, for two self-evident examples). And, finally, all documents identified as authoritative or canonical in Rabbinic Judaism by definition form a continuity. A text thus finds its ultimate position within that larger matrix of a single religious system and structure that accounts for its preservation and imparts its ultimate significance. We have, then, a complex grid of three dimensions, the one to take the measure of documents and their ideas, the other to assess the historical unfolding of the Judaism – the unfolding Judaic religious system – to which those documents attest:

	LITERATURE	HISTORY	RELIGION
[1]	text and	autonomy	description
[2]	context	connection	analysis
[3]	matrix	continuity	interpretation

1. The work proceeds from document to system. Systemic description begins in the form analysis of documents: their rhetorical traits, principles of cogent discourse or logic, topical program and even (in most documents) propositional plan. The counterpart is systemic analysis of a document in its own terms. This work has been done for more than a score of documents and is spelled out and summarized in the companion volume to this one.

2. Systemic analysis proceeds to investigate the connection between and among groups of documents, for example, the Mishnah and its associated Midrash compilations, the Yerushalmi and its companions, and the like; it asks how these documents relate, and answers the question by an analysis of the category formation, and the system that formation adumbrates, such as is worked out in Part One of this book. The matter spills over, at the historical side, into an inquiry into the connection between and among documents, on the one side, and the circumstances in which an entire set of documents was produced, on the other. This work is fully summarized in Part Two of this book.

3. The problem of the matrix of writings, on the one side, and the continuity of all the documents viewed whole, carries us into the work of theological description, to which I now turn. Descriptions of how an entire corpus of literature holds together as a coherent, proportioned, and cogent statement – a theological system – and analyses of how the system viewed whole and complete (if open-ended to the history that would follow) require a different set of methods from those literary analytical and social historical inquiries that come to fruition in this book. The earliest exercises even now are underway, but I cannot yet see where they shall lead, for the entire labor on which this book rests, twenty years as a matter of fact, has required analysis, and I have now to turn to descriptive synthesis.

When we follow this procedure at its first two stages, as we have done in this book, we discover how, within the formation of the rabbinical canon of writings, the idea at hand came to literary expression and how it was then shaped to serve the larger purposes of the nascent canonical system as a whole. These purposes find their definition in the setting in which the documents took shape, group by group: the late second and third centuries, then the late fourth and fifth centuries. That is the basis of the picture of the formative history of Rabbinic Judaism set forth here. Since that history continued to unfold, and in our own day still presents surprises as the system of Rabbinic Judaism exhibits renewed vitality, it goes without saying that the picture given here is partial; but, so far as it goes, I should claim it also is definitive for the formative age of this, the normative Judaism.

Index

South Florida Studies in the History of Judaism